2 **Schematische Darstellung eines mehrschichtigen Netzwerks:**

In diesem Beispiel können die Knoten mehrere Zustände annehmen. Die erste Komponente ist durch Farben (Schwarz, Rot) gekennzeichnet, die zweite durch Formen (Kreise, Quadrate). Knoten interagieren durch drei Arten von Interaktionen, die durch volle, unterbrochene und gepunktete Linien dargestellt werden. Das System ist komplex, wenn sich Zustände als Funktion des Interaktionsnetzwerks ändern und sich gleichzeitig Interaktionen als Funktion der Zustände ändern. Es ist ein sich gemeinsam entwickelndes System, bei dem Zustände und Interaktionen einander aktualisieren, ähnlich wie bei einem Algorithmus.

Schematic representation of a multilayer network:

In this example, the nodes can have several states. The first component is given by colors (red, blue), the second by shapes (circles, squares). Nodes interact through three types of interaction that are represented by (full, broken, and dotted) lines. The system is complex if states change as a function of the interaction network and interactions change as a function of the states at the same time. It is a coevolving system, with states and interactions updating each other, similar to what an algorithm does.

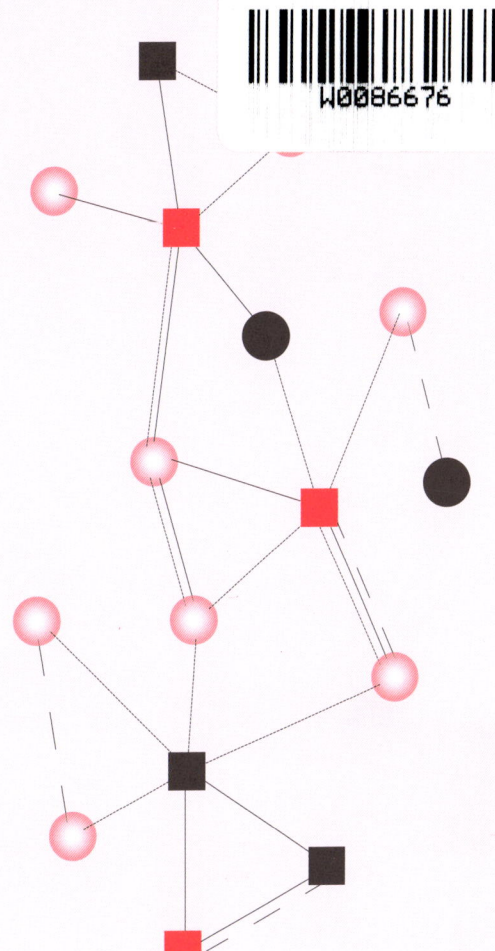

3

Beispiele für komplexe System sind:

jedes Ökosystem, jedes soziale System, jedes Finanzsystem, jede Zelle jedes Lebewesens, die komplizierte Abfolge von chemischen Reaktionen in der Photosynthese, ein Ameisenhaufen, das Gesundheitssystem, das Weltklima, das Internet usw.

Netzwerke sehen immer anders aus, sind niemals gleich: Sowohl die Art der Elemente (Menschen, Banken, Zellen etc.) als auch deren Beziehungen (Freundschaft, Geld, ausgetauschte Moleküle etc.) unterscheiden sich. Aber man kann alle komplexen Systeme mathematisch in einer einheitlichen Sprache beschreiben und ihre Eigenschaften analysieren.

Examples of complex systems are:

every ecosystem, every social system, every financial system, every cell of every living being, the complicated sequence of chemical reactions in photosynthesis, an anthill, the health system, the global climate, the Internet, etc.

Networks always look differently, they are never the same: both the types of their elements (people, banks, cells, etc.) and their relationships (friendship, money, exchange of molecules, etc.) differ from one another. But it is possible to describe all complex systems mathematically using a uniform language and to analyze their properties.

Quelle **Sources**   Stefan Thurner, Rudolf Hanel, Peter Klimek, *Introduction to the Theory of Complex Systems,* Oxford University Press, 2018

Technologie im Gespräch 2020
Discussing Technology 2020

Inhalt
Contents

Hannes Androsch / Martin Kugler

Für die globale Mehrfachkrise sind wir nur schlecht gerüstet

Zu den schon seit Längerem bestehenden großen Herausforderungen der Zukunft wie dem demografischen Wandel, Dekarbonisierung und Digitalisierung ist nun noch die Coronakrise hinzugekommen, die dauerhafte Spuren in der Welt hinterlassen wird. Alle diese Problemfelder sind systemischer Natur und eng mit der wachsenden Komplexität der Welt verknüpft. Wir brauchen neue Zugänge, um mit diesen Herausforderungen fertigwerden zu können. Und wir brauchen eine wesentlich stärkere Kooperation in der Welt.

Seit nunmehr 75 Jahren leben wir in Österreich in einer Periode des Friedens und der Freiheit, des wachsenden Wohlstands und steigender Lebensqualität. Dass das alles andere als selbstverständlich ist, wird uns derzeit deutlich vor Augen geführt. Mit der Coronapandemie hat gewissermaßen eine neue Zeitrechnung begonnen. Noch sind die Auswirkungen dieses viralen Flächenbrandes nicht in ihrer Gesamtheit abzusehen, doch eines ist jetzt schon klar: Weder im Alltagsleben noch in der Wirtschaft werden wir so bald zum bislang Gewohnten zurückkehren. Die Welt wird eine andere sein. Man steigt nie zweimal in denselben Fluss, wir müssen uns auf vielfach geänderte Umstände einstellen – auch deshalb, weil es nicht die letzte Pandemie gewesen sein wird, die über die Welt rollt.

Die zahlreichen Hilfspakete, die ad hoc geschnürt wurden, konnten zwar das Schlimmste verhindern, doch den wirtschaftlichen Rückgang vermochten sie nicht aufzuhalten. Die vor uns liegenden Jahre bedeuten langsameres Wachstum und deutlich mehr Arbeitslose. Dagegen muss mit einem entschlossenen, international abgestimmten Wiederhochfahrprogramm angekämpft werden. Ein Schwerpunkt der Investitionen müssen jene Bereiche sein, die schon vor der Coronakrise reformbedürftig oder vernachlässigt waren. Allen voran sollten Forschung, Technologie und Innovation (FTI) gestärkt werden. Das muss rasch geschehen: Wir haben es in den vergangenen Jahren nicht geschafft, aus dem Mittelbereich in die Gruppe der Innovation Leaders vorzustoßen, und zurzeit verlieren wir gerade weitere wertvolle Jahre. Wir brauchen dringend eine neue FTI-Strategie mit entsprechender Steigerung der Ressourcen.

Hannes Androsch / Martin Kugler

We Are Ill Prepared for the Multiple Global Crisis

The coronavirus crisis, which will leave a permanent mark on the world, has been added to those major challenges of the future we have been faced with for some time now, including demographic change, decarbonization, and digitization. All of these problem areas are systemic by nature and closely related to the world's growing complexity. New approaches are needed for us to be able to cope with these challenges. And we need much more closer cooperation in this world for it to hold out.

In Austria we have been living in an age of peace and freedom, of growing prosperity and an increasing quality of life for seventy-five years now. That this can by no means be taken for granted we are currently being forced to realize. In a way, the coronavirus pandemic has launched a new era. The impact of this viral conflagration is not yet foreseeable in its entirety, but one thing is clear already: neither in our everyday lives nor in the economy will we be able to return to old habits soon. This world will be a different one. You cannot step into the same river twice—we have to adjust ourselves to circumstances that have changed in many respects also because this will not have been the last pandemic to inundate the world.

The numerous ad-hoc rescue packages that have been put together could probably prevent the worst, but they were not able to stop economic decline in itself. The years lying before us will bring slower growth and distinctly higher unemployment rates. This must be fought against with a resolute and internationally concerted reboot. Investments must focus on those areas that wanted reform or were neglected even before the coronavirus crisis. First of all, research, technology and innovation (RTI) must be strengthened. This must happen rapidly: during the past years we have failed to catch up with the group of innovation leaders from a middle position and are currently about to lose more precious years. We urgently need a new RTI strategy with resources boosted accordingly.

Die Coronapandemie hat eine Reihe von Schwachstellen des heutigen Gesellschafts- und Wirtschaftssystems offengelegt und weiter verschärft. Man nehme die enge Vernetzung der Welt als Beispiel: Die Globalisierung und die Ausweitung der Liefer- und Wertschöpfungsketten auf die ganze Welt haben zwar in den vergangenen Jahrzehnten große Effizienzgewinne mit sich gebracht und geholfen, Millionen von Menschen aus der Armut zu befreien. Doch nun erweist sich, wie verletzlich dieses System ist: Sobald es an einer Stelle ein Problem gibt, kann sich diese Störung kaskadenartig im gesamten Netzwerk ausbreiten und die Produktion ganzer Wirtschaftszweige lahmlegen.

Deutlicher als jemals zuvor wird nun sichtbar, dass wir in einer tiefen systemischen Krise stecken, in der viele Krisenerscheinungen einander überlagern und beeinflussen. Das beginnt bei Umweltthemen wie dem Klimawandel, dem Biodiversitätsverlust und der Umweltverschmutzung und reicht über wirtschaftliche Probleme wie Stagnation, weit verbreitete Armut und Ungleichheit bis hin zu demografischen Ungleichgewichten, Migration und Anpassungsschwierigkeiten an die Digitalisierung. Zudem gerät die weltpolitische und -wirtschaftliche Lage wegen der feindseligen Rivalität zwischen den USA und China sowie anderer Brandherde wie etwa des Himalaya-Gebiets oder des östlichen Mittelmeers (Syrien, Libyen) aus den Fugen. Die angesichts der globalen Bedrohungen vernünftige und notwendige Zusammenarbeit wird dadurch immer stärker gefährdet bzw. verunmöglicht.

Nun wird diese Mehrfachkrise noch von der Coronapandemie und ihren Folgen überlagert. Dies macht es noch schwieriger, die langfristigen Herausforderungen der Zukunft zu meistern. Wenn wir ehrlich sind, sind wir für die Bewältigung zum Beispiel des demografischen Wandels (Überalterung unserer Gesellschaft), der Dekarbonisierung (Kampf gegen den Klimawandel) oder der Digitalisierung zurzeit schlecht oder gar nicht gerüstet.

Die demografische Bombe tickt

Eine ähnlich herausfordernde Epoche war die industrielle Revolution, die vor 200 Jahren die Welt grundlegend zu verändern begann. Die heutigen komplexen Anforderungen scheinen demgegenüber sogar noch größer zu sein, und das schon allein wegen der wachsenden Erdbevölkerung: Um 1800 gab es erstmals eine Milliarde Menschen auf der Erde, um 1900 waren es bereits zwei, 2010 schon mehr als acht und inzwischen bewegt sich die Zahl in Richtung zehn Milliarden. Daraus resultieren globale Bedrohungen wie Klimaerwärmung, Umweltverschmutzung und demografische Ungleichgewichte. Damit verbunden ist die zentrale Herausforderung der Migration, die in den meist wohlhabenderen Zielländern immer öfter zu xenophoben Abwehrhaltungen führt. Klar ist, dass Europa mit seinen 500 Millionen Einwohnern nicht 250 Millionen Wirtschaftsmigranten aufnehmen kann. Ebenso klar ist aber auch: Ohne Migration wird Europa immer mehr vergreisen. Davon deutlich abzugrenzen sind Flüchtlingsbewegungen: Menschen in Not müssen wir helfen – und es steht zu befürchten, dass die Flüchtlingsströme angesichts der Krisenerscheinungen weiter zunehmen werden. Mit einer Mentalität à la »my country first and alone« wird man das nicht lösen können.

The coronavirus pandemic has exposed and aggravated a number of weaknesses of today's social and economic systems. Let us take the world's connectivity as an example: globalization and the expansion of supply and value creation chains around the world may have led to enormous gains in efficiency and helped to relieve millions of people from poverty—but now this system has proven extremely vulnerable: as soon as a problem comes up in one place, the interference it causes may cascade throughout the entire network and paralyze the production of entire industries.

It has now become more distinctly visible than ever before that we are in the middle of a deep systemic crisis in which multiple critical phenomena overlap and influence one another. This ranges from such ecological issues as climate change, loss of biodiversity, and pollution to such economic problems as stagnation, widespread poverty and inequality, demographic imbalances, migration, and difficulties in adjusting to digitization. In addition, the global political and economic situation is getting out of hand because of the hostile rivalry between the United States and China and due to other trouble spots in the region of the Himalayas and the Eastern Mediterranean (Syria, Libya). Intensified cooperation, which would seem reasonable and necessary in the face of global dangers, is therefore increasingly jeopardized or made impossible.

On top of that, the coronavirus pandemic and its consequences have now superimposed themselves on this multiple crisis, which makes it even more difficult to cope with the long-term challenges posed by the future. Being honest to ourselves, we must admit that we are currently insufficiently or even not prepared at all to handle demographic change (population aging), decarbonization (the fight against climate change), or digitization, for example.

The demographic bomb is ticking

The Industrial Revolution, which began to turn the world upside down two hundred years ago, was a similarly challenging epoch. By comparison, today's complex demands appear to be even greater, simply due to the growing world population. By 1800, the population on earth had, for the first time, risen to more than a billion people; by 1900 their number had climbed to two billions; by 2010 it had already reached eight billions, and in the meantime we are moving toward ten billions. From this result such global threats as global warming, pollution, and demographic imbalances. This goes hand in hand with the central challenge of migration, which more and more often leads to xenophobic hostility in the (mostly wealthy) destination countries. It is evident that Europe, with its 500 million inhabitants, is not in a position to take in 250 million economic migrants. But it is equally obvious that, without migration, Europe will age disproportionately. This must clearly be differentiated from refugee movements: we are obliged to help people in need—and we must fear that the floods of refugees will continue to rise in the face of various crisis phenomena. We will certainly not be able to solve this with a mentality that goes "my country first and alone."

Klimawandel zwischen Apokalypse und Untätigkeit

Weiters sehen wir uns mit der enormen Herausforderung konfrontiert, den Klimawandel zu bekämpfen und seine negativen Auswirkungen zu begrenzen, um unsere Lebensgrundlagen zu sichern. Tatsache ist, dass der vom Menschen verursachte Klimawandel eine der größten Herausforderungen ist, vor der wir als Menschheit insgesamt stehen. Unser aller Wohlstand wurde lange Zeit auf Kosten der Umwelt und der Ausbeutung natürlicher Ressourcen erwirtschaftet. Nun aber, im Wissen und Bewusstsein um die negativen Auswirkungen, können wir diesen Weg nicht fortsetzen, wollen wir nicht unsere Zukunft und vor allem jene unserer Kinder und Enkel riskieren. Für den Kampf gegen den Klimawandel und die Anpassung an die geänderten Verhältnisse bedarf es rasch umfassender Maßnahmen, die sich nicht auf ein paar kosmetische Aktionen beschränken dürfen. Zum einen ist jeder und jede Einzelne gefragt und gefordert, doch es braucht zum anderen auch und vor allem die richtigen Rahmenbedingungen, die von der Politik gesetzt werden müssen. Dazu ist mehr Ehrlichkeit in der Diskussion erfordert: Ohne einschneidende Maßnahmen wird es nicht gehen, wenn Österreich bis 2040 wirklich CO_2-neutral werden will. Zurzeit ist Österreich mit einem fast doppelt so hohen Treibhausgasausstoß wie die Schweiz ein besonderer Klimasünder. Hoffnungen, dass die Coronakrise die Emissionen dauerhaft senken könnte, werden von Experten bezweifelt: Die Beschränkungen des Verkehrs und des Wirtschaftslebens werden höchstens eine Delle im langfristigen Trend hinterlassen. Umweltökonomen sehen indes jetzt die Chance, bei der notwendigen Wiederbelebung der Wirtschaft eine Richtung einzuschlagen, die zu einem nachhaltigeren und ressourcenschonenderen System führt. Der »Green Deal«, den die Europäische Kommission vorgeschlagen hat, kann dafür ein guter Ansatzpunkt sein.

Durchgreifende Digitalisierung aller Lebensbereiche

Eine mindestens genauso schwierig zu bewältigende Herausforderung ist die Digitalisierung. Die umfassende Vernetzung sowie der verstärkte Einsatz von künstlicher Intelligenz (KI), Algorithmen, Machine Learning, Big Data und Robotern haben bereits nahezu alle Bereiche von Wirtschaft und Gesellschaft erfasst: Landwirtschaft, Sicherheitsdienste und Bergbau genauso wie Industrie, Medizin, Mobilität, den Pflegebereich, Haushalte usw. Infolge der Coronakrise wird sich die digitale Transformation noch weiter beschleunigen. Millionen Menschen und praktisch alle Unternehmen haben in den Wochen von Lockdown und Homeoffice die Erfahrung gemacht, dass man viele Dinge genauso über digitale Plattformen erledigen kann. In vielen Sektoren wurden – auch aus der Not heraus – neue digitale Angebote und Services geschaffen. Wandeln werden sich nach der Unterbrechung der globalen Zulieferketten auch Produktion und Lagerhaltung, um die Verwundbarkeit zu reduzieren. Ein wesentliches Werkzeug dafür sind digitale Technologien – von vernetzten Kreislaufwirtschaftssystemen bis hin zu Robotern, die eine Produktion in Europa wieder wettbewerbsfähig machen könnten.

Climate change between apocalypse and inactivity

Furthermore, we find ourselves confronted with the huge challenge of fighting climate change and containing its negative impacts, so as to secure our basic means of livelihood. It cannot be denied that climate change, which is man-made, is one of the biggest challenges humankind as a whole is faced with. For a long time, the wealth of all of us has been accumulated at the cost of the environment and through the exploitation of natural resources. But now, knowing about and being aware of the negative effects, we cannot continue on this path if we do not wish to risk our own future and, above all, that of our children and grandchildren. The struggle against climate change and the adjustment to altered circumstances urgently require comprehensive action to be taken that must not be limited to a few nips and tucks. On the one hand, each individual matters and is requested to contribute, while, on the other hand, policymakers must first and foremost ensure to create a proper general framework. This process calls for more honesty when discussing the matter: without taking drastic measures, Austria will not succeed in becoming carbon-neutral by 2040. Presently, Austria is a particularly bad climate offender, its production of greenhouse gases being almost twice as high as that of Switzerland. Experts cast doubt upon hopes that the coronavirus crisis could possibly contribute to a lasting decrease of emissions: the limitations of traffic and industries will, at best, leave a minor dent in the long-term trend. Environmental economists, however, see a chance now to alter the direction toward a more sustainable and resource-saving system when taking the necessary measures to revive the economy. The Green Deal proposed by the European Commission could be a useful starting point in this regard.

Consistent digitization in all spheres of life

Another challenge that is at least just as difficult to tackle is digitization. All-encompassing networks and an intensified use of artificial intelligence (AI), algorithms, machine learning, big data, and robots have seized almost all spheres of society and the economy: agriculture, security services, mining, industries, medicine, mobility, nursing and healthcare, households, etc. As a consequence of the coronavirus crisis, digital transformation will accelerate even more. During the weeks of lockdown and telework, millions of people and practically all companies made the experience that many things can just as well be handled on digital platforms. New digital offers and services have been created in many sectors, some out of sheer necessity. Following the interruption of global supply chains, production and stockkeeping will also go through a process of transformation so as to reduce their vulnerability. A vital tool for this will be digital technologies—from networked circular economy systems to robots, which could be a chance to restore the competitiveness of production in Europe.

Die technologische Entwicklung ist mit großen Chancen, aber auch mit ebenso großen Risiken verbunden. Digitale Technologien haben das Potenzial, unser Leben zu erleichtern, das Wirtschaften effizienter zu machen, die Produktion in Europa zu sichern, die Führerschaft bei manchen Zukunftstechnologien zurückzuerobern und ein wichtiges Hilfsmittel zur Überwindung der vielfältigen Krisen in der Welt zu bieten. Um diese Chancen nutzen zu können, müssen wir gleichzeitig die Gefahren in den Griff bekommen. Das betrifft etwa Sicherheitsfragen, (steuer-)rechtliche, ethische und wirtschaftliche Problemfelder oder die Notwendigkeit, entsprechende Spielregeln zu schaffen. Das digitale Zeitalter bringt überdies die Gefahr mit sich, einen antidemokratischen Überwachungsstaat und/oder einen manipulierenden Überwachungskapitalismus zu organisieren. Die Fortschritte im Bereich der KI dürften zwar nicht so rasch vor sich gehen wie noch vor Kurzem angenommen; auch die Angst vor einer »Superintelligenz« und vor »Singularität« (davor, dass KI-Systeme die menschliche Intelligenz überflügeln) scheint auf absehbare Zeit reichlich übertrieben. Dennoch besteht die Sorge, dass technische Systeme in großem Stil menschliche Tätigkeiten übernehmen könnten und uns die Arbeit ausgeht. Das betrifft in erster Linie monotone bzw. leicht erlernbare Routinetätigkeiten sowie schwere oder gefährliche Arbeiten (»dull, dirty and dangerous tasks«). Gleichzeitig aber entstehen auch viele neue, bessere und höher qualifizierte Arbeitsplätze, die freilich andere, zum Teil wesentlich höhere Qualifikationen erfordern.

Bildung und soziale Abfederung

Um die neuen Möglichkeiten sinnvoll nutzen und Krisen wirksam begegnen zu können, braucht man auf allen Ebenen gut ausgebildete Menschen, die mit den digitalen Technologien richtig umzugehen wissen. In der neuen digitalen Welt geht es nicht mehr um rauchende Schornsteine, sondern um rauchende Köpfe. Unser Bildungssystem indes ist noch nicht einmal am Höhepunkt des Industriezeitalters angekommen und folglich hoffnungslos veraltet im Verhältnis dazu, was das digitale Zeitalter an Qualifikationen und Flexibilität erfordert. Soziale Durchlässigkeit und damit ein Stück weit mehr Gerechtigkeit wird es ohne Beseitigung der Bildungsarmut und Schaffung von Chancengleichheit im Bildungsbereich nicht geben.

Die digitale Transformation wird sich auch im Bildungswesen beschleunigen. Nicht zuletzt bei den Schulschließungen im Zuge der Coronakrise zeigte sich, welche Potenziale in diesen Technologien stecken, aber auch, welche Probleme dabei noch zu lösen sind und was bisher alles versäumt wurde – Österreich liegt auch in diesem Bereich weit hinten. Es ist höchst an der Zeit, sämtliche Bildungseinrichtungen aus der schulischen Kreidezeit raschest ins Digitalzeitalter zu bringen, indem jede Klasse ein Smartboard erhält, Schulclouds, WLAN-Netzwerke und entsprechende Server- und Druckerkapazitäten eingerichtet und Schülerinnen und Schüler mit Tablets oder Notebooks ausgestattet werden. Zudem müssen alle Lehrerinnen und Lehrer digital lehrfähig gemacht werden.

Eine wichtige Lehre aus der industriellen Revolution lautet, dass der Wandel nicht schmerzlos vor sich ging und der Fortschritt erst mit gehöriger Verzögerung in die Breite wirkte: Es dauerte einige Generationen, bis die von Innovationen gespeiste

Technological progress comes both with big opportunities and equally big risks. Digital technologies have the potential to make our lives easier and business more efficient, to secure production in Europe, to reconquer leadership in a number of future-oriented technologies, and to offer an important tool for overcoming the world's manifold crises. In order to seize these opportunities, we must simultaneously come to grips with the dangers. This includes, for example, matters of security, legal and tax issues, ethic and economic problems, and the necessity to establish appropriate rules of the game. Moreover, the digital age holds the danger of administrating an antidemocratic surveillance state and/or a manipulative surveillance capitalism. Progress in the field of AI may not happen as rapidly as was still assumed only recently; similarly, the fear of a form of "superintelligence" or "singularity" (of AI systems outperforming human intelligence) seems to be heavily exaggerated at least as far as the foreseeable future is concerned. It is nevertheless worried that technological systems will take over human activities on a larger scale and that we will run out of work. This concerns first and foremost monotonous and easily learnable routine jobs or dull, dirty, and dangerous tasks. At the same time, numerous new, better, and more highly qualified jobs will be created, which, however, will demand different and partly more superior skills.

Education and social cushioning

In order to be able to make use of the new possibilities in a meaningful way and confront crises effectively, we need well-trained people at all levels who know how to properly handle the digital technologies. What counts in the new digital world are buzzing brains instead of fuming funnels. Yet our educational system has not even arrived at the peak of the industrial age yet and is therefore hopelessly outdated given the qualifications and flexibility the digital age demands. Social permeability, which naturally comes with more fairness, cannot be achieved without remedying educational deprivation and offering equal chances in the area of education.

Digital transformation will also speed up within the education sector. It was not least the closure of schools during the coronavirus crisis that revealed both the potentials behind these technologies and the old problems and deficits that are still to be tackled—Austria lags far behind in this domain as well. It is high time to take all of our educational institutions from the academic Cretaceous to the digital age without the slightest delay by furnishing all classes with SMART Boards, school clouds, wireless LAN networks, and appropriate server and printer capacities and by providing all students with tablets or notebooks. What is more, it is absolutely vital to enable all teachers to conduct their lessons digitally.

An important lesson learned from the Industrial Revolution was that change had not happened painlessly and that progress only made itself more widely felt with considerable delay: it took several generations before innovation-fed prosperity arrived in broader strata of society. Those living in that

Prosperität in breiten Gesellschaftsschichten ankam. Die Menschen, die in dieser Umbruchzeit lebten, spürten vorerst kaum etwas von den langfristigen segensreichen Wirkungen des Wandels. Im Gegenteil: Sie litten massenhaft unter prekären sozialen Zuständen. Ignoriert man diese Konsequenzen technologischer Neuerungen, sind gigantische Ungleichgewichte, politische Umwälzungen und Unruhen die Folge. Klar beschrieben wurden diese Prozesse schon Mitte des 19. Jahrhunderts von Friedrich Engels und Karl Marx. Der Rest ist Geschichte.

Es gibt viele Hinweise, dass heute in der digitalen Revolution ähnliche soziale Prozesse ablaufen: Auf der einen Seite schafft die Plattformökonomie – ein auf Daten beruhender Kapitalismus ohne (Anlage-)Kapital – neue Unternehmensgiganten, welche die Wirtschaft dominieren und immer größeren gesellschaftlichen und politischen Einfluss erlangen; auf der anderen Seite entsteht aber auch ein digitales Proletariat und ein digitales Prekariat in Form einer »Gig-Ökonomie« mit schlecht bezahlten Tätigkeiten bei formeller Selbständigkeit (»Ich-AGs«) und hoher Abhängigkeit.

Wir müssen daher nicht nur Menschen für die digitale Welt fit machen, sondern den Wandel auch sozial abfedern und die Betroffenen auffangen, um zu verhindern, dass sich das Geschehen des 19. Jahrhunderts wiederholt. Soziale Abstiegsängste, allgemeine Sicherheitsängste, Verdrängungs- und Identitätsängste sind der Boden, auf dem Populismus und Opportunismus gedeihen.

Internationale Kooperation erforderlich

Alle krisenhaften Erscheinungen, denen wir uns derzeit gegenübersehen, haben zwei Dinge gemeinsam: Erstens treffen sie die gesamte Welt, und zweitens sind sie allesamt systemischer Natur. Demografische und klimatische Veränderungen sowie die Digitalisierung sind für alle Menschen, Gesellschafts- und Wirtschaftssysteme relevant; ebenso die Pandemie – das Virus schert sich nicht um Grenzen, es weiß gar nicht, dass es sie gibt. Nationalismus, Isolationismus und Protektionismus können daher keine langfristig erfolgreichen Rezepte sein. Man braucht neben nationalen Maßnahmen auch eine intensive internationale Zusammenarbeit. Dies gilt erst recht für die europäische Kooperation: Um im zunehmenden Spannungsverhältnis zwischen China und den USA nicht zwischen die Stühle zu fallen, muss Europa massive Zukunfts- und Modernisierungsprogramme in entsprechendem Umfang durchführen. Es wäre doppelt bitter, wenn die nationalstaatlichen Sonderwege, die manche EU-Mitgliedsländer in der Coronakrise eingeschlagen haben, sich nach deren Ende nicht wieder zu einem gemeinsamen Strom vereinigen würden. Ein Land wie Österreich, dessen Wohlstand und Wohlfahrt zu mehr als 50 Prozent von Export und Auslandstourismus abhängen, kann die Wirtschaft nicht mit nationaler Quarantäne und geschlossenen Grenzen wiederbeleben. Es bedarf des Räderwerks eines unbehinderten europäischen Binnenmarkts und einer freizügigen Weltwirtschaft sowie Reisefreiheit.

period of transition initially hardly benefited from the long-term positive effects of change. Quite the opposite was true: the masses suffered under precarious social conditions. If these consequences of technological innovation are ignored, gigantic social imbalances and political revolutions and unrests will follow. Friedrich Engels and Karl Marx distinctly described such processes as early as in the mid-nineteenth century.

There are many indicators that similar processes take place in today's digital revolution: on the one hand, the platform economy—a data-based form of capitalism without (invested) capital—creates new giant corporations dominating the economy and gaining increasing societal and political influence; on the other hand, this also leads to a digital proletariat and a digital precariat in the form of a "gig" economy, with poorly paid jobs in the formal guise of freelance work (self-employment of individuals to escape unemployment) and a high degree of dependence.

We must therefore not only prepare people for the digital world but must also cushion the changes brought about by digitization through social programs and by supporting those in need in order to prevent what happened in the nineteenth century from repeating itself. Fears of social decline, a general feeling of insecurity, repressed fears, and identity crises are a hotbed for populism and opportunism to thrive.

A call for international cooperation

All of the critical phenomena we are currently faced with have two things in common: first, they affect the whole world; and second, they are systemic by nature. Demographic and climatic changes and digitization concern all people, strata of society, and economic systems; this can also be said of the pandemic—the virus, too, ignores borders, it does not even know they exist. Therefore, nationalism, isolationism, and protectionism cannot be successful recipes in the long run. In addition to national measures, intensive international cooperation is called for. This applies even more to cooperation within Europe: so as to not be caught between two stools in the increasingly tense relationship between China and the United States, Europe needs to launch massive programs for the future and conduct modernization campaigns on a relevant scale. It would be twice as unfortunate if the separate national paths pursued by some EU member states during the coronavirus crisis did not, after it will have finally ended, converge again to form a single force. A country like Austria, more than fifty percent of whose wealth and welfare depend on export and international tourism, cannot revive its economy under national quarantine and with borders closed. It needs the wheelwork of an unrestricted European single market, a free global economy, and the freedom of travel.

Wegweiser durch die Komplexität der Krisen

Das dritte Gemeinsame aller aktuellen Krisen ist, dass sie eine gehörige Komplexität aufweisen. Unsere Gesellschaft und unser Wirtschaftssystem sind von einer hohen Konnektivität geprägt: Weltumspannende Netzwerke des Handels und der Kommunikation bis hin zu Social Media durchdringen alle Lebensbereiche und lassen neue Lebensstile und Verhaltensmuster entstehen. Darüber hinaus besteht eine hohe Interdependenz zwischen vielen verschiedenen Bereichen. So lässt sich beispielsweise Klimapolitik nicht ohne Digitalisierung denken, Migrationsfragen lassen sich nicht ohne grundlegende wirtschaftspolitische und ökologische Überlegungen lösen, usw.

Wegen der innigen Verknüpfung vieler Variablen, die einander auf vielen Ebenen beeinflussen, sind alle genannten Systeme komplex: Sie zeigen Reaktionen, mit denen man nicht rechnen würde. Komplexe Systeme weisen beispielsweise Kipppunkte auf, an denen sie ihre Eigenschaften sprunghaft verändern. Das ist etwa im Klimasystem der Fall: Wenn durch die Erwärmung Permafrostböden auftauen, werden große Mengen an Methan freigesetzt, die die Erwärmung weiter beschleunigen und eine unumkehrbare Entwicklung einleiten. Komplexe Systeme überraschen uns weiters mit Kaskadeneffekten, in denen sich eine Veränderung – wie ein Schneeball, der im Herabrollen von einem Berg immer größer wird – durch das gesamte System ausbreitet. Das ist etwa bei den eingangs erwähnten Lieferketten der Fall. Ein bekanntes Phänomen ist auch der sogenannte Schmetterlingseffekt, durch den sich eine kleine Ursache zu riesigen Konsequenzen in einem ganz anderen Bereich auswachsen kann.

Bei komplexen Systemen sind wir häufig auch mit nichtlinearen Veränderungen konfrontiert – etwa mit exponentiellem Wachstum, wie wir es jüngst bei der Ausbreitung des Coronavirus beobachten mussten. Mit solchen Eigenschaften komplexer Systeme können wir nur schwer umgehen. Denn sie überfordern in vielerlei Hinsicht unsere Auffassungsgabe: Wir tun uns sehr schwer, vielschichtige Beziehungsnetzwerke zu überblicken. Diese Unübersichtlichkeit führt zu Ungewissheit und Unsicherheit, sie erschwert auch die Steuerung von komplexen Systemen durch politische Entscheidungen.

Wir benötigen daher dringend neue Methoden, um komplexe Systeme erfassen und analysieren zu können. Damit befasst sich die Komplexitätsforschung, ein relativ junger Wissenschaftszweig, der in der Coronakrise durch Prognosemodelle zur Ausbreitung der Krankheit einige Publicity erlangte. In Österreich wurde vor einigen Jahren der Complexity Science Hub (CSH) Vienna ins Leben gerufen. Dessen Leiter, Stefan Thurner, war im Beraterstab des Gesundheitsministeriums vertreten und präsentierte dort wöchentlich Prognosen und Szenarien zum weiteren Verlauf der Pandemie.

Fahrplan durch dieses Jahrbuch

Dieses Jahrbuch zu den Alpbacher Technologiegesprächen 2020, die vom AIT Austrian Institute of Technology und dem ORF Radio Ö1 seit Jahren erfolgreich

A guide through the complexity of crises

A third aspect today's crises share is that all of them show a great deal of complexity. Both our society and our economic system are characterized by a high degree of connectivity: global networks of commerce and communication as well as social media permeate all spheres of life and encourage the emergence of new lifestyles and behavioral patterns. In addition, there is a high degree of interdependence among a multitude of diverse fields. Climate policy, for instance, is unthinkable without digitization, and migration issues cannot be solved without taking fundamental economic and ecological aspects into account, etc.

Because of the close interconnection of a bunch of variables influencing one another on multiple levels, all of the systems mentioned can be identified as complex: they respond in ways one would not expect. For example, complex systems have tipping points at which their properties change significantly und suddenly. This also holds true for the climate system: if permafrost thaws due to warming, large amounts of methane will be released, which will accelerate warming even further, thus introducing an irreversible development. Complex systems also take us by surprise through cascade effects, which means that a specific change will spread throughout the system—similar to a snowball becoming larger and larger while rolling down a slope. This applies to the supply chains mentioned earlier, for instance.

In complex systems, we are frequently also confronted with non-linear change—such as with exponential growth, as we were forced to observe only recently in the propagation of the coronavirus. It is extremely challenging for us to deal with the properties of complex systems, for they go beyond what we are capable of grasping in many respects: we find it very difficult to keep track of complex interrelated networks. This complexity leads to uncertainty and insecurity and also impedes the control of complex systems through political decision-making.

This is why we are in urgent need of new methods to grasp and analyze complex systems, which are the subject of complexity science, a relatively young scientific discipline that received quite some publicity during the coronavirus crisis by supplying forecast models on the spreading of the disease. In Austria, the Complexity Science Hub (CSH) Vienna was founded several years ago. Its president, Stefan Thurner, was a member of the advisory committee to the Federal Health Ministry, where he presented weekly prognoses and scenarios on the pandemic's progression.

A roadmap through this yearbook

This yearbook accompanying the Alpbach Technology Symposium 2020, which has been successfully organized by the AIT Austrian Institute of Technology and ORF Radio Ö1 for years, fully concentrates on the subject of complexity. The Alpbach Technology Symposium 2020 takes place in a digital hybrid format

veranstaltet werden, ist ganz dem Thema Komplexität gewidmet. Die Alpbacher Technologiegespräche finden coronabedingt in einem digitalen Hybridformat statt. Nach einer allgemeinen Einführung in das Wesen und die Eigenschaften komplexer Systeme und deren Erforschung sowie einem ausführlichen Interview mit dem Komplexitätsforscher Stefan Thurner werden eine Reihe konkreter Themen behandelt, die von hoher Komplexität gekennzeichnet sind. Den Anfang macht ein Überblick über komplexe Phänomene in den Bereichen Gesundheit und Biologie, inklusive erster Erkenntnisse aus der Coronapandemie. Sehr vielschichtig sind auch alle Themen rund um den Klimawandel – von Modellen, mit denen Zukunftsszenarien berechnet werden, bis hin zu den Herausforderungen, vor die uns die nötige »grüne Transformation« stellt. Auch in der Stadtplanung und der Gestaltung von Verkehrssystemen gilt es, unzählige Einflussfaktoren unter einen Hut zu bringen. Gleiches gilt für die Weiterentwicklung der Wirtschaftssysteme, die Erfindung neuer Technologien und die Ausbreitung von Innovationen. Dabei geht es unter anderem darum, die Systeme resilienter, also unempfindlicher gegenüber Störungen von außen, zu machen. Illustriert werden diese Themen durch aktuelle Forschungsarbeiten am AIT Austrian Institute of Technology und anderen Forschungseinrichtungen des Landes.

Ergänzend dazu finden Sie in diesem Jahrbuch auch einige aufschlussreiche Interviews, die das Thema in einen größeren Zusammenhang einbetten. Helga Nowotny, Grande Dame der österreichischen Wissenschaftsforschung, äußert ihre Überzeugung, dass wir lernen sollten, mit der Ungewissheit, die sich aus der immer komplexer werdenden Welt ergibt, zu leben und dafür die wissenschaftlich-technischen Möglichkeiten nutzen müssten. Gerald Bast, Rektor der Universität für angewandte Kunst Wien, argumentiert, dass künstlerische Methoden viel zur Lösung der komplexen Zukunftsprobleme beitragen könnten – und zwar dann, wenn man sie mit herkömmlichen wissenschaftlichen Methoden kombiniert. Denn Künstlerinnen und Künstler seien sehr geübt darin, mit dem Ungewissen umzugehen und aus eingefahrenen Denkstrukturen herauszutreten. Faszinierende Beispiele für ein künstlerisches Herangehen an das Thema liefern die Arbeiten der Wiener Künstlerin Judith Fegerl, derzeit Artist in Residence am AIT. ✖

Hannes Androsch, geboren 1938 in Wien, ist Aufsichtsratsvorsitzender des AIT Austrian Institute of Technology, Vorsitzender des RFTE Rats für Forschung und Technologieentwicklung und war bis Juni 2016 Aufsichtsratsvorsitzender der FIMBAG Finanzmarktbeteiligungsgesellschaft des Bundes. In seiner politischen Tätigkeit (SPÖ) war er u. a. Abgeordneter zum Nationalrat (1966–1970), Bundesminister für Finanzen (1970–1981) und Vizekanzler (1976–1981). Danach war er Generaldirektor des Creditanstalt-Bankvereins (1981–1988) und Vorsitzender der Oesterreichischen Kontrollbank AG (1985–1986).

1989 gründete er die AIC Androsch International Management Consulting GmbH und begann 1994 den Aufbau einer industriellen Beteiligungsgruppe (Austria Technologie & Systemtechnik AG, Österreichische Salinen AG u. a.). 2004 errichtete er die »Stiftung Hannes Androsch bei der Österreichischen Akademie der Wissenschaften« und ist dort seit 2005 Mitglied des Senats. Ehrendoktorate und Ehrensenator verschiedener österreichischer und internationaler Universitäten, u. a. der Montanuniversität Leoben und der Universität New Orleans, USA.

due to the coronavirus pandemic. Following a general introduction to the nature and properties of complex systems and their analysis and an extensive interview with complexity scientist Stefan Thurner, we will look into a number of specific themes marked by their high degree of complexity. We start with giving an overview of complex phenomena in the fields of health and biology, including first insights gained from our experiences with the coronavirus pandemic. Equally complex are all issues related to climate change—from models with the aid of which future scenarios can be computed to the challenges we are faced with because of the urgently needed Green Transformation. Similarly, city planning and the configuration of traffic and transport systems require the reconciliation of countless influencing factors. The same holds true for the further development of economic systems, the invention of new technologies, and the spread of innovations. A major criterion is to make our systems more resilient, i.e. less sensitive to interference from outside. These themes are illustrated by research projects currently conducted at the AIT Austrian Institute of Technology and other research institutions in the country.

In this yearbook you will also find some insightful interviews embedding the theme of complexity in a wider context. Helga Nowotny, the grande dame of science studies in Austria, expresses her convictions that we should learn how to live with an uncertainty that is the result of a world becoming increasingly complex, and that we must make use of the possibilities offered by science and technology. Gerald Bast, rector of the Vienna University of Applied Arts, argues that artistic methods could contribute a lot to the solution of the complex problems of the future—especially when combined with conventional scientific methods: after all, artists have a great deal of experience in dealing with uncertainties and step out of well-tried patterns of thought. Fascinating examples of an artistic approach to the subject are the works provided by the Viennese artist Judith Fegerl, currently artist-in-residence at the AIT.×

Hannes Androsch, born in Vienna in 1938, is Chairman of the Supervisory Board of AIT Austrian Institute of Technology and Chairman of RFTE Council for Research and Technological Development. Until June 2016, he was Chairman of the Supervisory Board of FIMBAG Finanzmarkt-beteiligungsgesellschaft des Bundes. During his political career (SPÖ), his positions included Member of the National Assembly (1966–1970), Federal Minister of Finance (1970–1981), and Vice Chancellor (1976–1981). After this, he served as Director General of Creditanstalt-Bankverein (1981–1988) and as Chairman of Österreichische Kontrollbank AG (1985–1986). In 1989, he founded AIC Androsch International Management Consulting GmbH, and in 1994 initiated the establishment of an industrial investment group (Austria Technologie & Systemtechnik AG, Österreichische Salinen AG, etc.). In 2004, he founded the "Hannes Androsch Foundation at the Austrian Academy of Sciences," where he has been a member of the senate since 2005. He has received honorary doctorates from and is an honorary senator of various Austrian and international universities, including the Montanuniversität Leoben and the University of New Orleans, USA.

Grundpfeiler der Komplexität

Cornerstones of Complexity

Martin Kugler und Stefan Thurner

Komplexe Systeme und ihre Erforschung

Viele Systeme in der Natur und in der Gesellschaft sind komplex. Ihre Eigenschaften lassen sich daher nicht so einfach vorhersagen und beeinflussen. Ein Crashkurs in Komplexitätsforschung – garantiert ohne mathematische Formeln.

Was ist ein komplexes System?

Komplexe Systeme bestehen aus einzelnen Elementen, die miteinander verknüpft sind und dadurch ein Netzwerk bilden. Die Eigenschaften der Elemente und die Verknüpfungen ändern sich dynamisch und beeinflussen einander: Der Zustand eines Elements hat Einfluss auf das Netzwerk, und das Netzwerk beeinflusst wiederum den Zustand der Elemente.

Solche Netzwerke sind etwa in der Biologie oder in sozialen Systemen allgegenwärtig. Sie haben mehrere interessante, oft unvermutete Eigenschaften: Zum einen bilden sie gemeinsam Eigenschaften und Zustände aus, die nicht einfach aus den Einzelteilen ableitbar sind (Emergenz). In diesem Sinn sind komplexe Systeme mehr als die Summe ihrer Teile; dieses Mehr ist das Netzwerk, der Zusammenhang der Einzelteile.

Zum anderen verändern sich Netzwerke und ihre Eigenschaften dynamisch: Früher oder später kommt ein Moment, an dem sie sich völlig anders verhalten, als man erwarten würde. Es gibt sogenannte Kipppunkte, an denen ein komplexes System plötzlich in einen anderen Zustand übergeht – es kommt beispielsweise zum Kollaps eines Systems.

Als interdisziplinäre Wissenschaft vereinigt die Komplexitätsforschung Beiträge aus vielen verschiedenen Bereichen wie etwa dem Studium der Selbstorganisation aus der Physik, der spontanen Ordnung aus den Sozialwissenschaften, der Chaostheorie aus der angewandten Mathematik oder der Theorie der Evolution aus der Biologie.

Worin liegt der Unterschied zwischen »komplex« und »kompliziert«?

Viele Phänomene bzw. Systeme sind kompliziert, aber deswegen noch lange nicht komplex. Komplexes Verhalten entsteht dann, wenn die unterschiedlichen Bauteile eines Systems und ihre Verbindungen einander

Martin Kugler und Stefan Thurner

Complex Systems and Their Analysis

Many systems found in both nature and society are complex. Their properties are therefore rather difficult to predict and influence. What follows is a crash course in complexity science—entirely devoid of mathematical formulae.

What is a complex system?

Complex systems consist of individual elements that are interrelated and thus form a network. The properties of these elements and their connections change dynamically and mutually influence one another: the state of a single element influences the network, and the network in turn influences the state of its elements.

Such networks are omnipresent in biology or social systems, for example. They exhibit a number of interesting and often unforeseen qualities. On the one hand, together they develop properties and states that cannot simply be deduced from individual elements (emergence). In this sense, complex systems are more than the sum of their individual parts; this added value is the network, the way in which the individual parts are connected.

On the other hand, networks and their properties change dynamically: sooner or later a moment arrives at which they will behave completely differently from what one would expect. There are so-called tipping points at which a complex system will suddenly switch to a different state in which the system will, for example, collapse.

An interdisciplinary science, complexity research combines contributions from a great diversity of fields, including the study of selforganization from physics, principles of spontaneous order from the social sciences, chaos theory from applied mathematics, or the theory of evolution from biology.

Wherein lies the difference between "complex" and "complicated"?

Although many phenomena or systems are complicated, they are far from being complex. Complex behavior develops when the individ-

beeinflussen und sich in Abhängigkeit voneinander über die Zeit verändern. Ein Beispiel aus der Physik: Elementarteilchenphysik ist zwar kompliziert, aber nicht komplex. Die Elementarteilchen wechselwirken zwar miteinander, aber sie wechselwirken alle gleich miteinander. Alle haben die gleichen Eigenschaften, keines ist gegenüber einem anderen ausgezeichnet. Ähnlich verhält es sich mit der Bewegung von Planeten: Diese und die Sonne ziehen einander durch die Gravitation an, die sich über die Zeit nicht verändert. Es ist unmöglich, dass einmal der Jupiter den Saturn stärker anzieht und dann vielleicht die Venus den Mars für drei Tage gar nicht. Die Bewegung der Planeten auszurechnen ist zwar ziemlich kompliziert, aber die Gravitation verändert sich nicht dynamisch mit der Bewegung.

Ganz anders ist das bei gesellschaftlichen Phänomenen. Ein extremes Beispiel: Wenn Person A Teil einer Mafia-Organisation ist und ein guter Freund, B, zum Boss des Syndikats aufsteigt, dann partizipiert A mit. Wenn B hingegen geächtet wird, hat das auch Auswirkungen auf das Leben von A. Das Netzwerk bewirkt also Veränderungen im Leben beider Personen. Diese Veränderungen führen wiederum zu einer Veränderung des Netzwerks: Wenn man wohlhabend ist, hat man viele Freunde. Wenn man plötzlich verarmt, verliert man Freunde. Im ersten Fall hat man viele Beziehungen zu anderen Menschen, die einem noch mehr Aktivitäten ermöglichen, durch die man vielleicht noch wohlhabender werden kann. Im zweiten Fall hat man vielleicht nur mehr die eigene Familie und keine anderen Beziehungen.

Das Beispiel zeigt, dass es bei komplexen Systemen ein Henne-Ei-Problem gibt: Man kann im Allgemeinen nicht einfach angeben, welche Veränderung die Ursache und welche die Wirkung ist. In einem Bankensystem z. B. sind die Verbindungen zwischen den Subjekten Kontrakte, etwa Kredite, die man einander gewährt. Diese bestimmen, wie in Zukunft Geld fließt. Abhängig davon verändert sich der Zustand der Wirtschaftssubjekte: Wenn jemand liquide ist, kann er weitere Kontrakte abschließen – das Netzwerk wird dadurch größer. Ist man finanziell eingeschränkt, kann man keine Deals mehr abschließen – dadurch reduziert sich das Netzwerk. Das wiederum hat Auswirkungen auf den künftigen Wohlstand der Subjekte.

Auch Freundschaften in der Schule sind komplexe Systeme: Kinder, die gute Noten haben, sind häufig enger mit anderen befreundet. Sie bewegen sich in anderen Netzwerken als Kinder mit schlechten schulischen Leistungen. Das hat wiederum Einfluss auf die künftigen Noten und die künftige Stellung in anderen Netzwerken. Die Gefahr dabei ist: Wenn nur gute Schülerinnen und Schüler einerseits und nur die schwächeren andererseits zusammen sind, führt das dazu, dass die schwächeren nicht mehr von den besseren mitgerissen werden. Die Folge ist eine immer stärkere Segregation.

Als Faustregel gilt: Wenn sich ein Netzwerk über die Zeit verändert und sich dadurch die Eigenschaften der Komponenten des Netzwerks verändern (was wiederum Rückwirkungen auf das Netzwerk hat), dann ist ein System meistens komplex. Die meisten komplexen Systeme sind ungemein

ual building blocks of a system and their conjunctions interrelate and mutually impact on one another, changing over time as they depend on one another. An example from physics: the physical theory of elementary particles is complicated but not complex. Elementary particles do interrelate, but always in the same way. All of them share the same properties, and none distinguishes itself from the others. This similarly applies to the movement of planets: they and the sun attract one another through gravitation, which remains unchanged over time. It is impossible for Jupiter to attract Saturn more strongly once in a while or for Venus to attract Mars not at all for a period of three days. Calculating the movement of the planets may be rather complicated, but gravitation does not change dynamically through movement.

This is entirely different with social phenomena. An extreme example: if person A belongs to a mafia organization, and a good friend, B, is promoted to the position of boss of the syndicate, A will benefit from B's promotion. Should B, however, be ostracized, this would also have an influence on A's life. The network consequently brings about changes to the lives of both. These changes in turn lead to changes in the network: if you are wealthy, you will have many friends; if you suddenly become poor, you will lose friends. In the first case, you have many relationships to other people, which will result in your being involved in even more activities, which will probably make you even wealthier. In the second case, probably only your family remains, and you have no other relationships.

This example shows that complex systems frequently come along with a chicken-and-egg problem: as a rule, it is difficult to say which change is the cause and which is the effect. In a bank system, for example, the connections between the subjects are contracts, such as mutually granted loans. These contracts will determine the future flow of money. The state of the economic subjects will change accordingly: if someone is liquid, they will be in a position to conclude further contracts—and the network will be growing; if your financial means are limited, you will not be able to close any more deals—and the network will decline. This in turn will impact on the subjects' future wealth.

Friendships at school are also complex systems: children whose grades are good will frequently be closer friends with others. Their networks will be different from those of children performing poorly at school. This in turn has an influence on their future grades and their future positions in other networks. The danger behind this is: when exclusively good pupils and exclusively weak pupils stay amongst themselves, the weaker ones will no longer be motivated by the better ones, which will result in increasing segregation.

kompliziert. Sehr viele Systeme auf dieser Welt sind komplex: jedes Ökosystem, jedes soziale System, jedes Finanzsystem, jede Zelle von Lebewesen, die komplizierte Abfolge von chemischen Reaktionen in der Photosynthese, ein Ameisenhaufen, das Gesundheitssystem, das Weltklima, das Internet usw.

Netzwerke sehen immer anders aus, sind niemals gleich: Sowohl die Art der Elemente (Menschen, Banken, Zellen etc.) als auch deren Beziehungen (Freundschaft, Geld, ausgetauschte Moleküle etc.) unterscheiden sich. Aber man kann alle komplexen Systeme mathematisch in einer einheitlichen Sprache beschreiben und ihre Eigenschaften analysieren. Die Entwicklung von entsprechenden Methoden und deren Anwendung ist der Kern der Komplexitätsforschung (Complexity Science).

Eigenschaften komplexer Systeme

Emergenz: Im Gegensatz zu lediglich komplizierten Systemen zeigen komplexe Systeme Emergenz. Das Wort stammt vom lateinischen »emergere« (»auftauchen«, »herauskommen«, »emporsteigen«) ab und bezeichnet die Herausbildung von neuen Eigenschaften oder Strukturen eines Systems infolge des Zusammenspiels seiner Elemente. Emergente Eigenschaften lassen sich nicht aus der isolierten Analyse des Verhaltens einzelner Systemkomponenten erklären oder ableiten. In der Philosophie des Geistes beispielsweise gehen viele Forscher davon aus, dass das Bewusstsein eine emergente Eigenschaft der Tätigkeit unzähliger Nervenzellen im Gehirn ist. Ein anderes Beispiel für Emergenz ist, wenn Menschenmengen etwa bei einer Großveranstaltung plötzlich in Panik ausbrechen. Allgemein nennt man solche Phänomene, die aus den Mikroeigenschaften der einzelnen Elemente und deren Wechselwirkung heraus emergieren, Makroeigenschaften. Emergenz wird manchmal als »Gegenteil« von Reduktionismus gesehen, bei dem versucht wird, das Ganze durch seine Elemente zu verstehen. Bei komplexen Systemen ist das nicht möglich.

Makroeigenschaften: Komplexe Systeme bilden häufig Makroeigenschaften aus. Sie können unterschiedliche Systemzustände einnehmen Ein einfaches, nicht komplexes Beispiel sind die Aggregatzustände von Wasser. Chemisch gesehen ist Wasser immer eine Ansammlung von Molekülen, die aus zwei Wasserstoff- und einem Sauerstoffatom bestehen. Je nach Temperatur bewegen sich die Moleküle unterschiedlich rasch und sind dadurch unterschiedlich stark aneinandergebunden: In der Kälte ist Wasser fest, bei Raumtemperatur flüssig, weiter erhitzt wird es dampfförmig. Ein anderes Beispiel für eine Makroeigenschaft ist der Zustand einer Volkswirtschaft: Es gibt die Situation, dass viele Menschen arbeitslos sind und wenig produziert wird; viele Menschen sind verarmt, niemand übernimmt mehr die Initiative. Dieselben Menschen mit denselben Fähigkeiten können aber auch in einem Zustand leben, in dem die Wirtschaft floriert, Vollbeschäfti-

The rule of thumb is: when a network changes over time, and the properties of its components change accordingly (which in turn causes the network to react), then a system mostly turns out to be a complex one. Most complex systems are highly complicated. A great many systems in this world are complex: every ecological system, every social system, every financial system, every single cell of an organism, the complicated succession of chemical reactions in photosynthesis, an anthill, the health system, the global climate, the Internet, etc.

Networks always look differently, they are never the same: both the types of their elements (people, banks, cells, etc.) and their relationships (friendship, money, exchange of molecules, etc.) differ from one another. But it is possible to describe all complex systems mathematically using a uniform language and to analyze their properties. The development of pertinent methods and their application are at the core of complexity science.

Properties of complex systems

Emergence: Contrary to systems that are merely complicated, complex systems are characterized by emergence. The term comes from Latin "emergere" ("appear," "come up," "come out," "arise") and describes the formation of new properties or structures within a system as a result of the interaction between its elements. Emergent properties cannot be explained or deduced from an isolated analysis of the behavior of a system's individual components. In the philosophy of mind, for instance, many scholars start out from understanding consciousness as an emergent property of the activity of innumerable nerve cells in the brain. Another example of emergence is when crowds suddenly get into a panic during a mass event. Such phenomena, emerging from microscopic properties of individual elements and their mutual relationships, are generally referred to as macroscopic properties. Emergence is sometimes regarded as the "opposite" of reductionism, where one seeks to comprehend the whole through its elements. This is not possible with complex systems.

Macroproperties: Complex systems frequently develop macroproperties. They can adopt various systemic states. A simple, noncomplex example would be the states of matter of water, for example. In chemical terms, water is an accumulation of molecules consisting of two atoms of hydrogen and one atom of oxygen. Depending on the temperature, the molecules move at different speeds and are therefore bound to each other more or less strongly: when it is cold, water is solid, at room temperature it is liquid, and when it is heated, it will become vapor. Another example for a macroproperty is the status quo of a national economy: there might be a situation in which many

gung herrscht und Überschüsse produziert werden, die umverteilt werden können. Zwischen diesen Zuständen gibt es häufig abrupte Übergänge, die sogenannten Kipppunkte.

Kipppunkte: In vielen komplexen Systemen gibt es kritische Punkte, an denen sich ein zuvor stabiler Zustand plötzlich verändert, an denen eine stetige Entwicklung abbricht, die Eigenschaften wechselt und die Makrozustände ändert. Erstmals verwendet wurde der Begriff Mitte der 1950er-Jahre bei Untersuchungen zur Rassentrennung. Dann machte er in der Ökonomie Karriere, heute wird er häufig im Zusammenhang mit Klimamodellen und dem Kippen von Ökosystemen verwendet. Als ein Kipppunkt im Klimasystem gilt z. B. das Auftauen von Permafrostböden; durch die Freisetzung von bis dahin im Boden gebundenem Methan würde sich die Erderwärmung massiv beschleunigen. Ein zentrales Problem bei der Erforschung von komplexen Systemen ist das Finden solcher Kipppunkte bzw. – noch grundlegender – jener Parameter, die zu abrupten Veränderungen des Gesamtsystems führen können. Bei vielen sozialen Systemen ist derzeit noch völlig unbekannt, welche Faktoren das sind. Als einer der wichtigsten Gründe für das Vorhandensein von Kipppunkten gilt, dass die Rückkoppelungen zwischen einem Netzwerk und seinen Elementen häufig nichtlinear sind.

Nichtlinearität: Komplexe Systeme weisen häufig nichtlineares Verhalten auf. Das bedeutet, dass die Änderung einer Inputgröße keinen proportionalen Effekt auf den Output hat. Vielmehr ist es möglich, dass sich der Output viel stärker oder sogar sprunghaft ändert – oder sich aber überhaupt nicht oder nur ganz geringfügig ändert. Ein höchst aktuelles Beispiel eines nichtlinearen Zusammenhangs ist die Ausbreitung des Coronavirus. Aus der Chaostheorie ist der sogenannte Schmetterlingseffekt bekannt: Er beschreibt, dass die minimale Änderung eines Parameters (im klassischen Beispiel das Flattern eines Schmetterlings) in einem System an ganz anderer Stelle riesige Auswirkungen haben kann (etwa einen Hurrikan). Ein Grund für solche großen Reaktionen kann in einem Kaskadeneffekt (auch Schneeballeffekt genannt) liegen: Wegen der starken Verbindungen zwischen den Komponenten kann z. B. ein Ausfall einer oder mehrerer Komponenten katastrophale Folgen für das Funktionieren eines Systems haben und zu einem Kollaps führen. Andere komplexe Systeme wiederum können sehr anpassungsfähig und resilient gegenüber Störungen sein, sodass selbst größere Veränderungen einzelner Parameter keine Reaktionen im Netzwerk hervorrufen; diese werden quasi vom Netzwerk »geschluckt«, indem es sich an die Veränderungen »anpasst« – es ist adaptiv.

Spontane Ordnung/Selbstorganisation: Viele komplexe Systeme bilden ohne äußeres Zutun von selbst einen stabilen Zustand aus. Dieses Phänomen ist in den Sozialwissenschaften als »spontane Ordnung«

people are jobless and little is produced; many people become impoverished, and no one will take the initiative any more. But the same people having the same abilities can also live in the state in which the economy flourishes, with full employment, overproduction, and the redistribution of surpluses. Between these states there are frequently abrupt transitions, so-called "tipping points."

Tipping points: In many complex systems there are critical stages at which a previously stable state suddenly changes—at which a steady development is interrupted, changing its properties and macrostates. The term was first used in the mid-1950s in studies on segregation. Then it carved out a career for itself in economics and today is frequently used in the context of climate models and ecological systems tipping over. For example, the thawing of permafrost ground is considered a tipping point in the climate system; through the release of methane, formerly bound to the ground, global warming would accelerate rapidly. A central problem in studying such complex systems is the identification of such tipping points or—even more fundamental—those parameters leading to abrupt changes in the overall system. In many social systems, these factors currently still lie completely in the dark. One of the most important reasons for the existence of tipping points is that the feedback loops between a network and its elements are frequently nonlinear.

Nonlinearity: Complex systems are frequently characterized by nonlinear behavior. This means that the alteration of an input variable has no proportional effect on the output. Rather, it is possible for the output to change much more substantially or even abruptly—or not at all or just very little. A highly topical example of a nonlinear context is the spread of the coronavirus. The so-called butterfly effect is known from chaos theory: it describes the fact that a minimal change of one parameter (in the classic example a butterfly flapping its wings) can have a huge impact (such as a hurricane) at an entire different location within a system. The reason for such a powerful reaction can be a cascade effect (also known as snowball effect): as components are closely connected to one another, the failure of one or several components can have catastrophic consequences for the functioning of a system and lead to its collapse. Other complex systems can, on the other hand, be extremely adjustable and resilient toward interference, so that even more substantial changes of individual parameters will not cause any reaction within the network; they are virtually "swallowed" by the network as it adjusts to the changes—is is adaptable.

bekannt, etwa im Fall von Herdenverhalten, bei dem eine Gruppe von Personen ihre Aktionen ohne zentrale Planung koordiniert. In den Naturwissenschaften spricht man etwa von Selbstorganisation, wenn sich Atome von selbst in einem Kristallgitter (z. B. Wasser in einer Schneeflocke) anordnen oder soziale Insekten einen Staat bilden (und gemeinsam z. B. einen Termitenbau errichten). Bestimmte Eigenschaften der Komponenten dieser Systeme sowie Interaktionsregeln sind die Voraussetzung für Selbstorganisation. Aus ihnen heraus lassen sich aber in den seltensten Fällen die Konsequenz oder das Ergebnis für das gesamte System vorhersagen. Das hängt auch damit zusammen, dass viele komplexe Systeme in starkem Austausch mit ihrer Umwelt stehen und sich nicht in einem stabilen Gleichgewichtszustand befinden, sondern etwa auf die Zufuhr von Energie von außen angewiesen sind.

Skalierung: Wenn komplexe Systeme größer werden, treten häufig Skaleneffekte auf. Wenn ein Tier doppelt so groß ist wie ein anderes, dann ist dessen Stoffwechsel nicht doppelt so groß, sondern etwas weniger. Ähnliches gilt für Städte, deren Energieverbrauch weniger stark steigt als die Größe; die Kriminalitäts- oder die AIDS-Rate wachsen hingegen überproportional oder superlinear. Solche Zusammenhänge können mit sogenannten Skalierungs- bzw. Potenzgesetzen formuliert werden. Dahinter verbirgt sich die Tatsache, dass mit dem Wachstum von Systemen nicht nur die Zahl der Komponenten größer wird, sondern sich auch die Wechselwirkungen zwischen diesen Elementen vermehren und verändern. Eine Folge davon ist, dass es kritische Größen geben kann, bei denen der Zustand eines komplexen Systems in einen anderen übergeht.

Pfadabhängigkeit: Komplexe Systeme sind typischerweise pfadabhängig. Das bedeutet, dass ihre Zukunft nicht nur von den derzeitigen Gegebenheiten abhängt, sondern auch von der Vorgeschichte des Systems bestimmt wird. Solche Systeme haben gewissermaßen ein Gedächtnis: Frühere Ereignisse in einem Netzwerk – auch rein zufällig aufgetrete Änderungen – hinterlassen Spuren, auf denen das aktuelle Verhalten eines Systems gründet. Die Evolution von solchen Systemen folgt daher einem Zeitpfeil und ist nicht umkehrbar.

Spontaneous order/selforganization: Many complex systems develop a stable condition from within, without outside interference. In the social sciences, this phenomenon is known as "spontaneous order," such as in the case of herd behavior, with a group of people coordinating their actions without central planning. In the natural sciences this is referred to as selforganization, such as in the case of atoms forming a crystal structure of their own accord (e.g., water in a snowflake) or of social insects forming a state (and collaborate, for example, in building a termite mound). Components of these systems having certain properties and functioning according to specific rules of interaction are preconditions for selforganization. However, it is very rarely possible for us to predict from them the consequence or result for the system as a whole. This has also to do with the fact that many complex systems intensely interact with their environment. They are not in a state of stable equilibrium but depend on being fed energy from outside.

Scaling: When complex systems become larger and larger, scale effects will frequently have to be taken into account. When an animal is twice as large as another, its metabolism will not be double but somewhat less. The same holds true for cities, whose energy consumption will not increase in proportion to their size; their crime or AIDS rates, on the other hand, will grow disproportionally high or in a superlinear fashion. Such relationships can be described by so-called scaling or power laws. This has to do with the fact that when a system grows, not only will the number of its components increase, but interactions between these elements will increase as well or change. As a result, a critical proportion may be reached at which the state of a complex system will pass over into another.

Path dependence: Complex systems are typically path-dependent. This means that their future existence depends not only on current conditions but is also determined by the system's previous history. Such systems have a memory, so to speak: earlier events within a network—including purely coincidental changes—leave their traces, on which the system's current behavior will be based. The evolution of such systems therefore follows an arrow of time and cannot be reversed.

Methoden der Komplexitätsforschung

In den vergangenen Jahrzehnten wurde eine ganze Reihe von Methoden entwickelt, mit denen die Eigenschaften komplexer Systeme untersucht werden können. Eine zentrale Annahme dahinter lautet, dass es relativ einfache Ursachen für komplexe Phänomene gibt und dass man diese Regeln finden kann. Dabei handelt es sich aber, ähnlich wie bei den Naturwissenschaften, um klare Interaktionsregeln. Oft wirken diese auf Netzwerke, wodurch es zu einer unglaublichen Anzahl von Rückkopplungsschleifen kommen kann. Oft sind die Zusammenhänge und Interaktionen nichtlinear und Lernalgorithmen unterworfen, usw. Über diese Regeln versucht man, das Verhalten von komplexen Systemen zu verstehen und die künftige Entwicklung von Makrozuständen vorherzusagen, um das System im Idealfall in eine gewünschte Richtung verändern zu können.

Im einfachsten Fall können Systeme mit statistischen Verfahren und Modellen analysiert werden, um in den Daten Interaktionsregeln, Zusammenhänge oder Muster festzustellen. Dazu gehören Ansätze wie Korrelationsanalysen oder Clusteringverfahren. Die Schwierigkeit dabei ist, sichere Aussagen darüber zu treffen, ob ein Zusammenhang bloß zufällig oder der Wirkung eines dritten, eventuell nicht beobachteten Faktors geschuldet ist oder auf einer kausalen Beziehung beruht. Für dieses Problem hat man entsprechende Methoden entwickelt, auch wenn der Nachweis von kausalen Zusammenhängen aufgrund der Henne-Ei-Problematik komplexer Systeme sowie der möglicherweise zahlreichen Rückkopplungsschleifen, die große Verwirrung zu stiften imstande sind, fast immer eine zentrale Herausforderung darstellt. Bei Zeitverläufen z. B. kann man künstliche Datensätze erzeugen, in denen die Zeitordnung verändert wird. Wenn diese Zeitreihe offensichtlich falsche Ergebnisse liefert, ist das ein Anzeichen für einen kausalen Zusammenhang. Das erlaubt zwar keine Aussage darüber, wie stark der Effekt ist, aber man kann sich dann auf die Suche nach den Mechanismen dahinter machen. Eine beliebte Methode ist das Bauen von Benchmark-Modellen, bei denen man genau weiß, wie die einzelnen Faktoren miteinander zusammenhängen. Wenn es in den realen Daten Abweichungen vom Verhalten solcher künstlichen Systeme gibt, lässt sich daraus schließen, dass es einen Effekt gibt, der im Idealfall kausal ist.

Ein beliebtes Verfahren der Komplexitätsforschung ist das computergestützte Nachbauen von Systemen. Eine seit den 1980er-Jahren gebräuchliche Methode sind sogenannte »agentenbasierte Simulationen«. Dabei werden unzählige Einheiten (Agenten) mit gewissen Entscheidungs- oder Handlungsmöglichkeiten sowie Interaktionsregeln programmiert. Aus dem Verhalten der einzelnen Agenten ergibt sich ein kollektives Systemverhalten, das aus den Eigenschaften der individuellen Bauteile nicht verstehbar ist (Emergenz). Auf diese Weise lassen sich z. B. das Entstehen von Verkehrsstaus oder kollektives soziales Verhalten sehr gut nachbilden.

Methods of complexity research

During the past decades, a number of methods have been developed by which the properties of complex systems can be analyzed. One of the central assumptions behind this is that the causes for complex phenomena are relatively simple, and that it is possible to find out about their rules. Similar to the natural sciences, the rules of interaction are clearly defined. They often impact on networks, which may result in a myriad of feedback loops. Conjunctions and interactions are frequently nonlinear and subject to learning algorithms, etc. Via those rules, researchers try to understand the behavior of complex systems and predict the future development of macrostates so as to ideally be able to steer the system into a desirable direction.

In the simplest of cases, systems can be analyzed with statistical methods and models in order to identify rules of interaction, correlations, or patterns within the data. They include such approaches as correlation analyses or clustering methods. The difficulty involved is to make definite statements as to whether a connection is merely the result of chance or due to the effect of a third factor that has probably not even been taken into consideration, or whether it depends on a causal relationship. Pertinent methods have been developed for this problem, although the proof of causal relationships poses almost always a major challenge due to the chicken-or-egg problem of complex systems and a multitude of possible feedback loops, which may create a lot of confusion. In the case of time sequences, for example, artificial datasets can be generated in which the order of time has been changed. Should it be evident that the results obtained from this time series are false, this will be a sign for a causal connection. Although this does not permit any conclusions as to the intensity of the effect, one can go in search of the mechanisms behind it. A popular method is the construction of benchmark models of which it is perfectly known in what ways the individual factors are interconnected. If the real data deviate from the behavior of such artificial systems, it can be concluded that the effect is ideally causal.

A favorite procedure in complexity research is the computer-assisted reconstruction of systems. A method that has been used since the 1980s is that of so-called "agent-based simulations." A myriad of units (agents) are programmed as having a certain degree of autonomy with regard to decision-making and acting while governed by specific rules of interaction. From the behavior of the individual agents results a collective behavior of the system that cannot be understood from the properties of the individual components (emergence). This is an excellent way of simulating traffic congestions or collective social behavior, for example.

Sobald man ein reales System in einem Simulator abzubilden vermag, kann man Szenarien durchspielen und ausprobieren, welche erwünschten und unerwünschten Folgen die Veränderung einer bestimmten Komponente mit sich bringt. Man kann unzählige mögliche Modelle bauen, in denen die Aktionen und Interaktionen zwischen den einzelnen Bauteilen unterschiedlich sind. Dann vergleicht man diese mit realen Daten und schließt diejenigen Modelle aus, die ein anderes Verhalten vorhersagen. In künstlichen Systemen kann man z. B. auch die Kipppunkte eruieren, an denen die Systeme ihre Eigenschaften radikal verändern.

Die Qualität solcher Modelle hängt davon ab, wie gut man die Wechselwirkungen zwischen den einzelnen Elementen kennt. Diese werden mit sogenannten »Interaktionsregeln« beschrieben. Wenn man z. B. den Straßenverkehr simulieren will, gibt es Regeln wie »Wenn ein Auto vor mir fährt, fahre ich nicht auf es auf« oder »Wenn ein Auto vor mir schneller fährt, fahre ich auch schneller«. Schwierig wird es, wenn die Interaktionsregeln nichtlinear sind – und das ist in der realen Welt häufig der Fall. Ein Beispiel: »Wenn das Auto vor mir langsamer wird, dann werde ich viel langsamer.«

Die Interaktionsregeln in agentenbasierten Simulationen beruhten in der Vergangenheit oft auf mehr oder weniger guten Annahmen. Das hat sich in jüngster Zeit durch Big Data und künstliche Intelligenz geändert. Mit diesen Verfahren können die Interaktionen zwischen einer großen Zahl von Elementen in einem System direkt, simultan und genau beobachtet werden. Diese »Parametrisierung« von Modellen anhand realer Daten hat die Qualität von Simulationsmodellen stark verbessert.

Es gibt bisher noch keine umfassende Theorie von komplexen Systemen. Als Flaschenhals gilt die Tatsache, dass es noch nicht für alle Phänomene und Aspekte adäquate mathematische Konzepte und Formulierungen gibt. Die höhere Rechenleistung von Computern und die immer bessere Verfügbarkeit von großen Datensätzen können das nicht kompensieren. Denn ohne durchdachte Modelle bringen Big Data und künstliche Intelligenz wenig Fortschritt beim Verständnis komplexer Systeme. Neue Erkenntnisse sind immer davon abhängig, dass die richtigen Fragen gestellt und gute Theorien formuliert werden. Unter Komplexitätsforschern kursiert der Satz: »Big data without big theory is big bullshit.«

Umgang mit komplexen Systemen

Der Mensch kann mit komplexen Systemen nicht gut umgehen, weil sie seine mentalen Kapazitäten übersteigen. Er kann die riesigen Netzwerke von Abhängigkeiten, wechselseitigen Einflüssen und dadurch hervorgerufenen Veränderungen sowohl der Teile als auch der gesamten Systeme nicht handhaben und schon gar nicht bis zur letzten Konsequenz durchdenken, um daraus Schlüsse zu ziehen. Daher können wir bis heute komplexe Systeme meist nicht oder nur minimal kontrollieren oder managen.

As soon as a real system can be reflected in a simulator, it will be possible to reenact and try out scenarios to find out what desirable and unwanted implications the alteration of a certain component will entail. Once can build countless possible models featuring diverse actions of and interactions between individual components. Subsequently, they will be compared to real data so that those models predicting a different behavior can be excluded. In artificial systems it is also possible to determine the tipping points at which the systems will radically change their properties.

The quality of such models depends on how well the interdependencies between the individual elements are known. These are defined by so-called "rules of interaction." If, for example, road traffic is to be simulated, there will be such rules as "If there is a car in front of me, I will not run into it from behind," or "If the car in front of me drives faster, I will also drive faster." This will be more difficult when interaction rules are nonlinear—which is frequently the case in the real world. For example: "If the car in front of me slows down, I will drive much more slowly."

In the past, the rules of interaction in agent-based simulations were founded on more or less accurate assumptions. This has changed in recent times due to big data and artificial intelligence. Thanks to these methods, interactions amongst a multitude of elements within a system can be observed directly, simultaneously, and accurately. This "parameterization" of models by means of real data has considerably improved the quality of simulation models.

So far, there is no comprehensive theory on complex systems. The fact that there are no adequate mathematical concepts and formulations yet for all phenomena and aspects is considered a bottleneck. This cannot be compensated by increased computer capacities and the improved availability of large datasets. For without sophisticated models, big data and artificial intelligence will mean only little progress when it comes to understanding complex systems. New insights always depend on the right questions being asked and on smart theories being formulated. There is a phrase circulating among complexity scientists: "Big data without big theory is big bullshit."

How to handle complex systems
Humans cannot deal with complex systems so well because such systems surpass their mental capacities. Humans are incapable of grasping the huge networks of interdependencies, mutual impacts, and resulting changes in systems as a whole and in their individual parts, not to mention thinking them through down to the last consequence, in order to draw the right conclusions. This is why they mostly

Unsere Vorfahren haben sich so einiges ausgedacht, um dennoch mit einer komplexen und vernetzen Welt umzugehen, die sie nicht beherrschen konnten: übernatürliche Kräfte, Geister, das Schicksal, die Sterne usw. Mit der Erfindung wissenschaftlicher Methoden erkannte man, dass man viele Phänomene verstehen und großen Nutzen aus diesen Erkenntnissen ziehen kann – darauf beruht jegliche Technologie. Das funktioniert, indem man Systeme in immer kleinere Einzelteile zerlegt und diese immer besser versteht: Reduktionismus. Bei einfachen Systemen kann man durch die Kenntnis der Einzelteile auch das große Ganze verstehen; das gilt etwa für weite Teile der Physik, Chemie oder Molekularbiologie. Doch bei komplexen Systemen kommt man mit dieser reduktionistischen Vorgangsweise nicht weiter, weil man die Interaktionsnetzwerke nicht außer Acht lassen darf, will man das System nicht zerstören.

Beim Umgang mit komplexen Systemen war die Entwicklung leistungsfähiger und leistbarer Informationstechnologie bahnbrechend. Computer und Sensoren erlauben uns heute nicht nur, Daten zu sammeln und zu verarbeiten. Es ist vielmehr erstmals möglich geworden, sämtliche Interaktionen zwischen allen Elementen eines komplexen Systems zu erfassen und über die Zeit zu verfolgen. Damit lässt sich etwa das Risiko eines Zusammenbruchs von Medizin-, Finanz- oder Wirtschaftsnetzwerken berechnen.

Erst wenn man gute Methoden hat, um die Mechanismen hinter dem Verhalten komplexer Systeme zu verstehen, kann man dieses Wissen anwenden, um Systeme so umzubauen, dass sie besser funktionieren, kostengünstiger, widerstandsfähiger usw. werden.

Ein Beispiel dafür, was diese Methoden zu leisten imstande sind, ist die Beurteilung eines Wirtschaftsstandortes. Traditionellerweise wird die Wirtschaftsleistung über Einzelparameter wie etwa die Arbeitslosenquote, das Wirtschaftswachstum, das Bruttoinlandprodukt oder Export- und Importquoten definiert. Diese sagen aber wenig über Einzelbereiche der Wirtschaft aus. Jedes Unternehmen ist mit anderen Betrieben und Branchen verwoben, alle sind Teile nationaler und internationaler Produktions-, Handels- und Liefernetzwerke. Diese kann man mit Methoden der Komplexitätsforschung gesamtheitlich untersuchen. In Modellen lässt sich die systemische Bedeutung einzelner Unternehmen für den Wirtschaftsstandort, quasi der Wert eines einzelnen Unternehmens für das Wirtschaftsökosystem einer Region oder eines Landes, erkennen. Man kann z. B. Fragen beantworten wie: Wie wichtig ist ein spezieller Betrieb für das Funktionieren der lokalen Wertschöpfungsketten? Was passiert, wenn eine Akteurin, ein Akteur ausfällt? Welche Schockwellen löst das für andere Akteur*innen oder Partner*innen aus – oder passiert gar nichts? Umgekehrt kann man auch den Einfluss des Umfeldes – von Zulieferern, Kundinnen und Kunden, strategischen Partnern usw. – auf ein Unternehmen beziffern.

fail to control or manage complex systems to this day or are able to do so only to a minimum extent.

Our ancestors contrived many a thing in order to be able to cope with a complex, networked world out of their control nevertheless: supernatural powers, spirits, destiny, the stars, etc. When scientific methods were invented, man recognized that it was possible to understand many phenomena and benefit greatly from these insights— which provides the basis for any form of technology. It functions by breaking systems down into smaller and smaller fragments and by understanding them better and better: reductionism. When systems are simple, one can understand the great whole by knowing its individual parts; this holds true for wide fields of physics, chemistry, or molecular biology. But in the case of complex systems this reductionist approach will not take us any further because we must not ignore interaction networks unless we wish to destroy the system.

When it comes to dealing with complex systems, the development of efficient and affordable information technology proved a game changer. Today, computers and sensors allow us to not only collect and process data. It has also become possible for the first time to trace the entire number of interactions between all of the elements of a complex system and keep track of them over time. In this way, the risk of a breakdown of medical, financial, or economic networks can be calculated.

Only if one has the appropriate methods at hand to understand the mechanisms behind the behavior of complex systems, can this knowledge be applied in order to rebuild systems in such a way that they will function more efficiently and become more inexpensive, resilient, etc.

An example of what these methods are capable of achieving is the evaluation of business locations. Traditionally, economic performance is defined through individual parameters, such as unemployment rate, economic growth, gross domestic product, or export and import quotas. However, these parameters reveal little about individual economic sectors. Each enterprise is connected to other enterprises and branches, all of which are part of national and international production, commerce, and supply networks. These can only be analyzed holistically with the methods of complexity research. Models make it possible to identify the systemic relevance of individual businesses for a location, i.e. the "value" of an individual enterprise for a region's or a country's economic ecosystem. In this way it is possible to answer questions like "How important is a specific company for the functioning of local value creation chains?," "What happens if a player drops out?," or "What shock waves will this trigger for other players or partners—or will nothing happen at all?" On the other hand, it is also

Eine kurze Geschichte der Komplexitätsforschung

Die Komplexitätsforschung ist eine relativ junge Wissenschaft. Aber sie hat eine längere Vorgeschichte. Zu Beginn des 20. Jahrhunderts wurde mit der Relativitätstheorie und der Quantenphysik deutlich, dass die bis zu diesem Zeitpunkt gängigen wissenschaftlichen Methoden nicht mehr unbedingt zum Ziel führen. Spätestens seit Isaac Newton werden Phänomene der Natur meistens als lineare Beziehungen von Ursache und Wirkung zwischen isolierten Objekten aufgefasst, die sich durch einfache mathematische Gesetze beschreiben lassen. Bei der klassischen reduktionistischen Vorgangsweise werden komplizierte Phänomene in einfachere zerlegt, die man verstehen kann. Am Ende wird daraus wieder auf das gesamte System rückgeschlossen, das man so letztlich auch begreifen kann. Diese Methode war ungemein erfolgreich und dominiert die Wissenschaft bis heute.

Man bemerkte jedoch, dass es viele Phänomene gibt, bei denen dies nicht oder nur ungenügend funktioniert – nicht nur in der Physik, sondern auch in der Evolutions- oder der Chaostheorie. Zudem ergaben sich durch Globalisierung, Informationstechnologie oder Nachhaltigkeit völlig neue Herausforderungen, für die zunehmend wissenschaftliche Antworten notwendig wurden. Es zeigte sich, dass man neue Methoden zur Analyse und Handhabung der zugrundeliegenden komplexen Systeme braucht. Im Gegensatz zur traditionellen Wissenschaft, die versucht, Komplexität zu reduzieren, indem sie die einzelnen Komponenten eines Systems in einer isolierten Umgebung untersucht, rückten ab Mitte des 20. Jahrhunderts die dynamischen Wechselwirkungen und Zusammenhänge zwischen einzelnen Elementen ins Zentrum wissenschaftlicher Aufmerksamkeit.

Historisch gesehen hat die Komplexitätsforschung zwei Wurzeln. Eine findet sich vor allem in den 1970er-Jahren in mehreren Bereichen: In der Ökonomie machte sich eine Gruppe um Friedrich Hayek, aufbauend auf den klassischen Theorien der österreichischen Schule der Nationalökonomie, Gedanken darüber, wie sich Märkte selbst organisieren. In den Kulturwissenschaften fragte etwa der Anthropologe und Kybernetiker Gregory Bateson, wie Menschen kommunizieren, ihr Handeln koordinieren und sich z. B. Religionen entwickelt haben. In den Gesellschaftswissenschaften gelangte beispielsweise der Ökonom Thomas Schelling zu wichtigen Einsichten in die Funktionsweise sozialer Segregation. Viele Methoden, die heute in der Netzwerktheorie verwendet werden, wurden ursprünglich in der Soziologie entwickelt.

Die andere Wurzel entspringt in den Naturwissenschaften, zuerst vornehmlich in der Physik. Enrico Fermi etwa hatte schon in den 1950er-Jahren begonnen, das Phänomen von Phasenübergängen im Magnetismus – also kritischen Änderungen von Makrozuständen zwischen magnetisch und nichtmagnetisch – mit den ersten Simulationsmodellen simpler Atomeigenschaften zu erklären. In der Biologie bemühte man sich um ein fundamentales Verständnis nichtlinearer Phänomene wie der Evolution. In der Chemie suchte man nach Erklärungen für »dissipative Strukturen«,

possible to quantify the impact of an environment—of suppliers, clients, strategic partners, etc.—on a company.

A brief history of complexity research

Complexity research is a relatively young science, which nevertheless has a longer history. At the beginning of the twentieth century, relativity theory and quantum physics made it clear that the conventional scientific methods employed at the time had stopped being successful solutions in all of the cases. At least since Isaac Newton, natural phenomena have mostly been understood as linear relationships of cause and effect between isolated objects that can be described by simple mathematical laws. According to the classic reductionist approach, complicated phenomena are divided up into simpler ones that are easy to understand. In the end, conclusions are drawn about the system as a whole, which can eventually be grasped in this way. This method was immensely successful and has dominated science to this very day.

However, it was realized that there are many phenomena for which this approach did not function at all or worked only insufficiently—not only in physics, but also in evolution or chaos theory. In addition, globalization, information technology, or sustainability entailed entirely new challenges that increasingly required answers from science. It turned out that the analysis and handling of the complex systems at the core of this required new methods. Instead of traditional science, which seeks to reduce complexity by analyzing individual components of a system in an isolated environment, dynamic interrelationships and connections between individual systems shifted into the focus of scientists' attention from the mid-twentieth century onward.

Historically, complexity science has two different roots. One can be found in a number of disciplines particularly in the 1970s: in economics, a group around Friedrich Hayek gave some thought to the ways in which markets organize themselves, building on the classic theories of the Austrian School of National Economics. In the cultural sciences, the anthropologist and cyberneticist Gregory Bateson investigated into how people communicate and coordinate their actions and into how religions, among other things, developed. In the social sciences, the economist Thomas Schelling arrived at important insights into the mechanisms of segregation. Many methods applied in today's network theory were originally developed in sociology.

The other root lies in the natural sciences, first of all in physics. Enrico Fermi had begun as early as in the 1950s to explain the phenomenon of phase transition in magnetism—i.e., critical changes of macrostates from magnetic to nonmagnetic—with the earliest simulation

vor allem in der Biologie relevante unumkehrbare Prozesse. In den Neurowissenschaften begann man durch die Beschäftigung mit der kollektiven
Aktivität von Neuronen kognitive Fähigkeiten zu verstehen. In der aufstre-
benden Wissenschaft der Ökologie ging es von Anfang an um Beziehungen
zwischen Organismen und Umwelt, um ökologische Netzwerke und Rückkopplungsschleifen. Ein frühes Ergebnis dieser Art des Denkens war sicher
der Bericht *Die Grenzen des Wachstums* an den Club of Rome 1972, in
dem Dennis und Donella Meadows die Dynamik globaler Entwicklungen
computergestützt simulierten. Die Voraussagen dieses Werkes waren
bekanntermaßen katastrophal falsch, müssen aber aus damaliger Sicht
als ernsthafter Versuch gewertet werden. Im Nachhinein ist klar, dass
dieses Unterfangen scheitern musste, da zu diesem Zeitpunkt weder
Chaostheorie, Netzwerktheorie noch die heutigen Methoden für komplexe
Systeme existierten.

In der Mathematik tauchten neue Ansätze wie das Konzept der
fraktalen Geometrie und die Chaostheorie auf. Auch die Computerwissen-
schaften brachten die Entwicklung neuer Konzepte mit sich: Aus den
Anfängen der Spieltheorie, der Informationstheorie und der künstlichen
Intelligenz entstanden Methoden zur mathematischen Erfassung komplexer Phänomene. Ab den 1980er-Jahren wurden die ersten agentenbasierten
Simulationsmodelle gebaut.

Einige diese Strömungen fanden im Jahr 1984 zusammen, als einige
visionäre Köpfe im us-Bundesstaat New Mexico das Santa Fe Institute
(sfi) gründeten. In unmittelbarer Nähe zum Los Alamos National Laboratory
(wo in den 1940er-Jahren das Manhattan-Projekt zum Bau von Atombomben
lief und später bahnbrechende Entwicklungen in der Computertechnik und
anderen Bereichen gelangen) richteten namhafte Forscher wie die Nobel-
preisträger Philip Anderson, Kenneth Arrow und Murray Gell-Mann ein
Grundlagenforschungsinstitut ein, das sich interdisziplinär mit grundlegenden Fragen der Wissenschaft beschäftigen sollte. Mit flachen Hierarchien,
ohne fixe Fächereinteilungen und für unkonventionelle Forscher aus aller
Welt offen etablierte sich das sfi als Ort der engen Zusammenarbeit
zwischen Physikern, Biologen, Ökonomen, Paläontologen, Meteorologen,
Mathematikern, Archäologen, Medizinern, Ökologen, Historikern, Computer-
wissenschafter, Statistikern usw. Das Ziel war und ist es, befruchtet durch
andere Wissenschaftsdisziplinen mithilfe neuer Methoden und Konzepte
anderer Disziplinen die eigene Fachrichtung besser zu verstehen. Als
Schmelztiegel unterschiedlichster Denkrichtungen wurde das Santa Fe
Institute der »Geburtsort der interdisziplinären Erforschung komplexer
Systeme«, wie es der ehemalige Präsident Geoffrey West einmal beschrieb.

Von Santa Fe aus strahlte die Komplexitätsforschung, die nach und
nach an Konturen gewann und bald erste reale Probleme etwa bei der
Bekämpfung von Grippeepidemien, der Entwicklung des Konzepts geneti-
scher Netzwerke oder der ersten agentenbasierten Modelle von Aktien-
märkten lösen konnte, in alle Welt aus. Es entstanden mehrere einschlägige

models of simple atomic properties. In biology, scientists sought to develop a fundamental understanding of such nonlinear phenomena as evolution. In chemistry, researchers went in search of explanations for "dissipative structures," irreversible processes mainly relevant in biology. Neuroscientists began looking into cognitive abilities by dealing with the collective activities of neurons. The emerging science of ecology dealt with the relationships between organisms and the environment, ecological networks, and feedback loops from the very start. An early result of this way of thinking was certainly the report *The Limits of Growth* to the Club of Rome in 1972, in which Dennis and Donella Meadows simulated the dynamics of global developments with computer-aided methods. The forecasts made in this work are known to have been disastrously wrong, but they must be seen as a serious attempt from the perspective of that time. In retrospect it is clear that the endeavor was forced to fail, since neither chaos and network theories nor today's methods for complex systems existed then.

Such new concepts as fractal geometry and chaos theory made their appearance in mathematics. Similarly, computer science went hand in hand with the development of new concepts: methods for the mathematical identification of complex phenomena began developing in the early days of game theory, information theory, and artificial intelligence. The first agent-based simulation models were built from the 1980s onward.

Some of these movements converged in 1984, when several great visionary minds founded the Santa Fe Institute (SFI) in the US state of New Mexico. In the immediate vicinity of the Los Alamos National Laboratory (where the Manhattan Project for the construction of nuclear bombs was conducted in the 1940s and where pioneering accomplishments in computer technology and other fields were achieved later on), such renowned scientists as Nobel laureates Philip Anderson, Kenneth Arrow, and Murray Gell-Mann established an institute for basic research that was to deal with fundamental scientific issues in an interdisciplinary fashion. Characterized by flat hierarchies and renouncing the categorization of disciplines, the SFI established itself as an institution that was open to all unconventional researchers around the globe—a place where physicists, biologists, economists, paleontologists, meteorologists, mathematicians, archeologists, medical scientists, ecologists, historians, computer scientists, statisticians, etc. collaborated closely. The goal was, and still is, to improve the knowledge of one's own scientific discipline through cross-fertilization and with the aid of new methods and concepts of other fields of studies. A melting pot of most diverse schools of thought, the Santa Fe Institute became the "birthplace of the interdisciplinary analysis of complex systems," as its former president Geoffrey West put it once.

Institute wie etwa das CABDyN Complexity Centre der Universität Oxford, das Institute for Cross-Disciplinary Physics and Complex Systems (IFISC) in Spanien, das Centre for Complex Systems Studies (CCSS) an der Universität Utrecht, das Institute for Complex Systems (ISC) des National Research Council in Rom, das Max-Planck-Institut für Physik komplexer Systeme, die Complexity Research Group an der London School of Economics and Political Science, das Center for Social Dynamics and Complexity (CSDC) an der Arizona State University oder der Complexity Science Hub (CSH) in Wien. Der 2015 gegründete Hub ist eine Initiative von AIT Austrian Institute of Technology, Central European University, Donau-Universität Krems, Technische Universität Graz, Internationales Institut für Angewandte Systemanalyse (IIASA), Medizinische Universität Wien, Technische Universität Wien, Wirtschaftsuniversität Wien, Institut für Molekulare Biotechnologie (IMBA), Veterinärmedizinische Universität Wien und Wirtschaftskammer Österreich (WKO), um gemeinsam Expertise für Komplexitätsforschung aufzubauen. ✕

Starting out from Santa Fe, complexity research, which gradually took shape and soon proved able to solve the first real problems—such as in the fight against influenza epidemics, the conception of genetic networks, or the first agent-based models of stock markets—made its way around the world. Relevant institutes were founded, such as the University of Oxford's CABDyN Complexity Centre, the Institute for Cross-Disciplinary Physics and Complex Systems (IFISC) in Spain, the University of Utrecht's Centre for Complex Systems Studies (CCSS), the Institute for Complex Systems (ISC) at the National Research Council in Rome, the Max Planck Institute for the Physics of Complex Systems, the Complexity Research Group at the London School of Economics and Political Science, the Arizona State University's Center for Social Dynamics and Complexity (CSDC), and the Complexity Science Hub (CSH) in Vienna. The Hub created in 2015 is an initiative of the AIT Austrian Institute of Technology, the Central European University, the Danube University Krems, the Graz University of Technology, the International Institute for Applied Systems Analysis (IIASA), the Medical University of Vienna, the Vienna University of Technology, the Vienna University of Economics & Business, the Institute of Molecular Biotechnology (IMBA), the University of Veterinary Medicine Vienna, and WKO to collaboratively generate expertise on complexity science. ✕

Beiträge zur Diskussion

Contributions to the Discussion

Stefan Thurner im Gespräch

»Big data without big theory
is big bullshit«

Stefan Thurner, Leiter des Complexity Science Hub Vienna, über die bisherigen Erfolge und die Probleme seines Wissenschaftszweiges

Wo steht die Komplexitätsforschung heute? Haben sich die hohen Erwartungen in manchen Bereichen bereits erfüllt?

Stefan Thurner ist Physiker und Komplexitätsforscher. Seit 2009 ist er Professor für die Wissenschaft komplexer Systeme an der Medizinischen Universität Wien. Er ist externer Professor am Santa Fe Institute und seit 2015 Präsident des Complexity Science Hub Vienna. Vom Klub der Bildungs- und Wissenschaftsjournalisten wurde er als österreichischer Wissenschafter des Jahres 2017 ausgezeichnet.

Stefan Thurner: Ja, ein gutes Beispiel für eine konkrete Anwendung von Ergebnissen der Komplexitätsforschung ist die Epidemiologie, etwa die Bekämpfung neuartiger Epidemien. Ende der 1990er-Jahre haben Forscher am Santa Fe Institute erkannt, wie zentral die Rolle von Netzwerken bei der Seuchenausbreitung sein kann, haben sich im Detail mit dem Infektionszyklus zwischen Vögeln, Schweinen und Menschen befasst und verstanden, dass man die Infektionskette unterbrechen muss – und das am einfachsten bei Hühnern. Öffentlich bekannt wurde das Schlachten zahlreicher Hühner in Hongkong, was wahrscheinlich die Ausbreitung einer neuen Vogelgrippewelle stark eingedämmt hat. Forscher wie der britische Biologe und Physiker Bob May haben mit ihren Beiträgen zur Epidemiologie auf Grundlage der Komplexitätsforschung vielleicht Millionen von Menschenleben gerettet.

Wichtig sind auch Durchbrüche in der Virologie: Noch vor 20 Jahren gab es unter den meisten Epidemiologen die Gewissheit, dass es so etwas wie eine kritische Impfrate gibt: Wenn man genügend Menschen impft, erreicht man irgendwann einen kritischen Punkt, an dem es zu keiner bevölkerungsweiten Ausbreitung einer Seuche mehr kommen kann. Das stimmt, wenn man annimmt, dass Menschen durch ein Zufallsnetzwerk miteinander verbunden sind. In der Praxis stellt sich das jedoch ganz anders dar: Selbst wenn man viele Menschen impft, besteht dennoch eine beträchtliche Wahrscheinlichkeit, dass eine große Welle kommen kann. Das hängt von den Strukturen der sozialen Netzwerke in einer Gesellschaft

Stefan Thurner is a physicist and complexity researcher. He holds a full professorship for the Science of Complex Systems at the Medical University of Vienna since 2009. He is external professor at the Santa Fe Institute and, since 2015, president of the Complexity Science Hub Vienna. He was awarded the title Austrian "Scientist of the Year 2017" by the Club of Education and Science Journalists.

An interview with Stefan Thurner

"Big data without big theory is big bullshit"

Stefan Thurner, president of the Complexity Science Hub Vienna, about the previous successes and problems of his scientific discipline

What is the status quo of complexity research? Have the high expectations been met in some of the fields?

Stefan Thurner: Yes, an excellent example of a concrete application of the findings of complexity research is epidemiology, such as the fight against new epidemics. In the late 1990s, researchers of the Santa Fe Institute recognized the central role of networks when it comes to the spread of epidemic plagues. They studied the cycle of infection amongst birds, pigs, and humans and understood that it was important to interrupt the chain of infection—which works most easily in the case of chickens. The slaughter of numerous chickens in Hong Kong, which is believed to have successfully contained a new wave of bird flue, became publicly known. Thanks to their contributions to epidemiology based on complexity research, such scientists as the British biologist and physician Bob May have probably saved the lives of millions of people.

The breakthroughs achieved in virology are equally vital. Only twenty years ago most epidemiologists were absolutely convinced that there was something like a critical vaccination rate: with a sufficient number of people vaccinated, a critical point would be reached one day at which the epidemic will be unable to continue spreading across the population. This is true if it is assumed that people interact with each other within a random network. In practice, this has turned out to be completely different: even if many people are vaccinated, there is still a considerable probability that a major wave is released. It depends

und von den Bewegungsmustern ab. Kennt man diese, lassen sich klare Kriterien ableiten, wann auf gesellschaftlicher Ebene ein Impfschutz erreicht ist und wann nicht. Solche Erkenntnisse können ebenfalls Millionen Menschenleben retten.

Ein anderes Beispiel sind Verkehrsmodelle, die von Forschern wie dem deutschen Soziologen und Physiker Dirk Helbing seit den 1990er-Jahren entwickelt werden. Solche Ansätze verändern die Welt ebenfalls unmittelbar: Man kann keine selbstfahrenden Autos bauen, ohne zu verstehen, wie Verkehrsteilnehmer agieren und interagieren. Hinter solchen Entwicklungen steckt jahrelange Arbeit. Da klebt natürlich nicht überall das Schild »Complexity Science« drauf, aber in Wirklichkeit ist es nichts anderes.

Eine weitere wichtige Errungenschaft der Komplexitätsforschung ist die Erkenntnis der Relevanz der sogenannten »Skalierungsgesetze«. Wird ein komplexes System größer, gibt es oft typische Veränderungen der Eigenschaften, etwa wenn man die Zahl der Einwohner einer Stadt und das Einkommen der Menschen vergleicht: Je größer eine Stadt, umso höher im Schnitt das Pro-Kopf-Einkommen – höher, als ein linearer Zusammenhang nahelegen würde. Umgekehrt verhält es sich beim Energieverbrauch: Wird eine Stadt doppelt so groß, braucht man nicht doppelt so viel Energie für ihre Versorgung, sondern deutlich weniger. Diese Einsicht erlaubt einen völlig neuen Umgang mit Städtebau und Urbanisierung, die global gesehen zu den zentralen Herausforderungen des 21. Jahrhunderts zählen. Die innovativen Erkenntnisse im Bereich Urbanisierung der letzten Jahre kommen aus der Komplexitätsforschung.

In vielen anderen Bereichen ist die Komplexitätsforschung aber noch nicht so weit ...

Thurner: Noch nicht so ein Triumph sind etwa Mosaikimpfstoffe. Das AIDS-Virus zum Beispiel verändert sich sehr schnell; auf herkömmlichem Weg produzierte Impfstoffe wirken daher schon bald nicht mehr. Mit unseren Methoden hoffen wir, dem Virus ein Schnippchen schlagen zu können. Man nimmt, vereinfacht gesprochen, eine Blutprobe eines Patienten und analysiert, welche Oberflächenformen eines Virus darin vorkommen. Dann bringt man diese Strukturen in einen Simulator ein und berech-

on the social structures of a society's networks and on its patterns of movement. Provided they are known, definite criteria can be deduced as to when immunization protection will be reached at a societal level and when not. Such insights can also save millions of human lives.

Another case in point are traffic models, which have been developed by researches like the German sociologist and physicist Dirk Helbing since the 1990s. Such approaches directly impact on the world as well: one cannot build self-driving cars without understanding how road users act and interact. There are years of work behind these developments. True, not all of them have been labeled "complexity science," but in reality this is where they come from.

Another important achievement of complexity science is the recognition of the relevance of so-called "scaling laws." When a complex system grows larger, its properties frequently change in a typical fashion, such as when you compare the number of a city's inhabitants and their income: the larger a town, the higher the per capita income will, on average, be— higher than a linear correlation would suggest. The reverse applies when it comes to energy consumption: when a town has become twice as large, it will not consume the twofold amount of energy to survive, but significantly less. This insight permits an entirely new approach to town planning and urbanization, which, from a global perspective, rank among the central challenges of the twenty-first century. Innovative knowledge in the field of urbanization gained in recent years derives from complexity research.

In many other areas, however, complexity research has not made that much progress ...

Thurner: Mosaic vaccines, for instance, have not been such a great triumph yet. The AIDS virus mutates extremely rapidly; conventionally produced vaccines therefore stop being effective extremely soon. We hope to be able to outsmart the virus with our methods. Simply put, one takes a blood sample from a patient and analyzes it to find out about the surface forms of a virus occurring in it. Then this structure is fed into a simulator to calculate what these surfaces will probably be looking like after two weeks, having

net, wie die Oberflächen durch ständige Mutationen nach zwei Wochen wahrscheinlich aussehen werden. Gelingt das in kürzerer Zeit, kann man künstlich Antikörper gegen die zu erwartenden Formen produzieren. Man führt die Evolution quasi im Computer durch und ist damit schneller als die echte Evolution. Bei Affen funktioniert das schon gut, beim Menschen laufen klinische Studien. Das ist eine sehr vielversprechende und richtungsweisende Strategie für die Pharmakologie der Zukunft. Es geht gleichsam um ein Wettrennen zwischen Computer und Evolution.

Die Komplexitätsforschung war und ist auch in der derzeitigen Corona-pandemie sehr gefragt. Sie und Ihr Team am Complexity Science Hub (CSH) Vienna beraten die österreichische Bundesregierung bei der Festlegung der Maßnahmen zur Eindämmung der Krankheit. Was machen Sie da genau?

Thurner: Wir waren Teil des Prognosekonsortiums des Gesundheitsministeriums. Seit Anfang März erstellen wir mit einem epidemiologischen Modell – das erweitert wurde, um die Möglichkeit der Quarantäne einbeziehen zu können – Kurzfristprognosen für die Anzahl der COVID-19-Fälle sowie die zu erwartende Betten- und Intensivbettenbelegung. Diese Voraussagen reichen eine Woche, maximal zehn Tage in die Zukunft. Obwohl das verwendete Modell, wie wir erst jetzt erkennen, die Veränderungen der sozialen Netzwerke durch den Lockdown nicht ganz optimal abbildet, kann man den Verlauf der Infektionskurven für den genannten Zeitraum doch sehr gut prognostizieren. Wir haben weiters ein Best-Case- und ein Worst-Case-Szenario erarbeitet, um jeden Tag bewerten zu können, in welche Richtung sich die Dinge entwickeln. Wir haben uns auch mit Bewegungsmustern der Bevölkerung beschäftigt, um festzustellen, wie die Maßnahmen wirken. Am CSH Vienna haben wir einen »Economic Shock Explorer« implementiert, der bei Annahme eines gewissen wirtschaftlichen Szenarios – etwa wo und in welchen Sektoren (z. B. im Tourismus oder in Schlachthöfen) welche Arbeitskräfte ausfallen – darüber Auskunft gibt, wie sich die Wirtschaftsleistung ändert.

Wir haben eine Reihe von Landkarten erstellt, auf denen man auf einen Blick erkennen kann, wo es wie viele gefährdete Personen gibt, z. B. über 65-Jährige, die auch Diabetiker sind. Außerdem haben wir eine Corona-Ampel entwickelt, mit deren Hilfe die Zahl der COVID-19-Fälle pro 10.000 Einwohner in den letzten 14 Tagen dargestellt wird.

undergone constant mutation. If we succeed in finding out about this in a shorter period of time, antibodies fighting the predicted forms can be produced artificially. This is evolution carried out in the computer to overtake real evolution. It already functions well with monkeys, and clinical tests on humans are being conducted at the moment. This is a highly promising and groundbreaking strategy for the pharmacology of the future. It is practically a race between computer and evolution.

Complexity research has been and continues to be in great demand during the current coronavirus pandemic. You and your team at the Complexity Science Hub (CSH) Vienna have been advising the federal government of Austria in what measures should be taken to contain the disease. What exactly have you been doing?

Thurner: We have been part of the Federal Health Ministry's prognosis pool. Since March, we have provided short-term prognoses for the number of COVID-19 cases and the bed and intensive care occupancies in hospitals using an epidemiological model, which was expanded at one point so as to be able to take into account the possibility of quarantine. Our forecasts look ahead for a period of a week or a maximum of ten days. Only now have we found out that the model we have been using has not ideally reflected the changes in social networks brought about by the lockdown, but in spite of this it is possible to predict the course of infection curves for the period mentioned really well. We have worked out a best-case and a worst-case scenario so as to be able to evaluate every single day in which direction things are evolving. We have been studying the population's movement patterns to find out about the impact of the measures taken. At the CSH Vienna we have implemented an Economic Shock Explorer, which, based on the assumption of a certain economic scenario—such as where and in what sectors (e.g., tourism or slaughterhouses) workforce will become redundant to what extent—provides information as to how the economic performance will change.

We have drawn up a number of maps indicating at a glance where there live how many persons at risk, such as persons over sixty-five suffering from diabetes. What is more, we have developed a Corona Traffic

Hätte man so ein Mittel europaweit zur Verfügung, könnte man Grenzen zwischen Regionen im grünen Bereich problemlos öffnen. Wo Zonen hingegen gelb oder rot sind, ist Vorsicht geboten. Von dort sollte man niemanden in grüne Zonen einreisen lassen.

Jetzt arbeiten wir an der Nachbereitung der ersten Welle der Coronapandemie. Wir fragen beispielsweise: Was wäre, wenn gar keine Maßnahmen gesetzt worden wären? Was, wenn der Lockdown eine Woche später durchgesetzt worden wäre? Was, wenn es den Ärztefunkdienst nicht gegeben hätte? Und so weiter. Wir haben eine fast 100 Länder umfassende Datenbank aller Maßnahmen und der Zeitpunkte ihrer Durchsetzung erstellt, die jetzt auch von der WHO verwendet wird. Durch den Vergleich von Infektionskurven wollen wir herausfinden, welche Maßnahme wie gut wirkt. Das kann für die zweite Welle hilfreich sein. Wir wollen damit auch die Konsequenzen der Rücknahme von Maßnahmen verstehen. Weiter verstärkt haben wir unsere Arbeit auch im Bereich der Erstellung von Lieferketten, um mögliche lawinenartige Folgen von Ausfällen besser verstehen und simulieren zu können, die glücklicherweise in Österreich nicht aufgetreten sind. Entwickelt wurde beispielsweise ein Frühwarnsystem, das uns hilft, die Nahrungsmittelversorgung eines Landes besser abzubilden. Vieles davon ist allerdings schwierig umzusetzen, weil uns viele Daten nicht in ausreichendem Maß zur Verfügung stehen.

Sie und ihre Forscherkollegen forderten immer wieder den Zugang zu bestimmten Daten ein. Warum ist das so wichtig?

Thurner: Wir können viele Systeme im Computer modellieren, simulieren und so manche komplexe Phänomene sehr gut beschreiben. Mit diesen Computermodellen kann man untersuchen, wie sich einzelne Parameter auf das Verhalten von Gesamtsystemen auswirken. Man kann etwa die Punkte berechnen, an denen ein System in einen anderen Zustand kippt. Wendet man diese Modelle auf die Realität an, kommt man allerdings schnell an eine Reihe von Grenzen. Wir wissen etwa über soziale Netzwerke und das Verhalten von Individuen nicht genug. Uns fehlen Werte, um unsere theoretischen Modelle richtig zu parametrisieren. Hier kommen Big Data ins Spiel: Aus der Analyse einer großen Zahl realer Daten können wir die richtigen Parameter für Modelle bestimmen. Das lässt sich unter Einhaltung aller Normen für Datenschutz und

Light that allows to show the number of COVID-19 cases per 10,000 inhabitants for the past two weeks. If such a tool were available throughout Europe, borders between green-light regions could be opened without qualms. However, where the zones are yellow or red, caution is called for. No one living in such a zone should be allowed to enter a green one.

Currently, we are post-processing the first wave of the coronavirus pandemic. We wish to find out what would have happened if no measures at all had been taken, if the lockdown had been implemented a week later, or if there had been no emergency medical radio service, etc. We have compiled a database of all measures taken in almost 100 countries and of the dates of their implementation, which is now also used by WHO. By comparing infection curves we seek to find out the effectiveness of the individual measures, which can be helpful for a second wave. This should also help us understand the consequences of the withdrawal of measures. We have also intensified our work in studying the set-up of supply chains to better comprehend and simulate possible snowballing implications of non-performance, which fortunately did not occur in Austria. We have, for example, developed an early warning system that helps visualize a country's food supply more distinctly. However, many of these things are difficult to implement because data are not made available to us in sufficient amounts in the relevant fields.

You and your fellow researchers have demanded access to specific data time and again. Why is this so important?

Thurner: We are able to model or simulate many systems in the computer and illustrate many a complex phenomenon very well. These computer models help us analyze in what ways individual parameters influence the behavior of overall systems. For example, it is possible to calculate those points at which a system will tip over into another state. If these models are applied to reality, however, you will soon be confronted with their limits. We are not sufficiently informed about social networks and the behavior of individuals, for instance. We lack the necessary values to parameterize our theoretical

Privacy durchführen, denn es geht nicht darum, wer persönlich hinter Daten steckt. Damit werden Modelle direkt für die Praxis anwendbar. Idealerweise ergibt sich am Ende eine konkrete Handlungsanleitung, die vielleicht sogar policy-relevant ist. Wichtig ist auch, dass Modelle helfen können, unbeabsichtigte Folgen von Lösungsvorschlägen rechtzeitig zu erkennen.

In der Vergangenheit lagen aber viele solche auf Datenanalysen beruhenden Vorhersagen ziemlich weit daneben ...

Thurner: Alle Daten dieser Welt reichen nicht aus, um ein gutes Modell zu erstellen. Was meine ich damit? Ein Modell ist dann gut, wenn es die richtigen Vereinfachungen vornimmt. Das ist theoriegetrieben: Nur eine gute Theorie bringt ein tieferes Verständnis und das Vertrauen, sich auf die Resultate verlassen zu können. Um eine gute Theorie zu entwickeln, muss man erst einmal die richtigen Fragen stellen und dann die Zusammenhänge verstehen. Es stimmt einfach nicht, dass man nur mehr Daten nehmen muss und die künstliche Intelligenz darin Muster finden kann, die sich selbst erklären. Wir sind meilenweit von einem »Ende der Theorie« entfernt, wie es von manchen postuliert wird. Ein Kollege am Santa Fe Institute meinte dazu treffend: »Big data without big theory is big bullshit.« Das heißt nicht, dass das nicht eines Tages möglich sein wird; es heißt nur, dass wir weit davon entfernt sind.

Dieser Fehler wird in geradezu spektakulärem Ausmaß etwa bei der unkritischen Verwendung künstlicher Intelligenz gemacht: Man kommt irgendwie zu irgendwelchen Daten, meist viel zu wenigen, spielt damit ohne Verständnis herum, bastelt zusammengestoppelte Algorithmen mit im Netz gefundenen Programmteilen und kann dann das ausgespuckte Ergebnis nicht interpretieren. Dennoch wird das Ergebnis dann publiziert und verwirrt letztlich alle – und morgen funktioniert es nicht mehr. Dieser Zugang, der leider immer häufiger zu beobachten ist, ist eher ein »Ende der Wissenschaft« denn ein »Ende der Theorie«. So viel zur Kehrseite dieser Methoden.

Ein gutes Simulationsmodell zu konstruieren setzt voraus, dass man entsprechend ausgebildete Menschen zur Verfügung hat, die einerseits gut mit Daten umgehen können und andererseits über Fachwissen in Bereichen

models properly. This is where big data comes into play: by analyzing large amounts of real data, we are able to define the pertinent parameters for our models. This can be done entirely without violating the provisions of data protection and privacy, for who is behind these data personally does not interest us at all. In this way, models will become applicable in practice. Ideally, the outcome will be concrete recommendations for action that may even become relevant for the implementation of a specific strategy. It is also important that models permit us to recognize unintended consequences of proposed solutions in time.

But in the past many predictions based on such data analyses have been wide off the mark…

Thurner: All data in the world would not suffice to build a good model. What do I mean by this? A model is only good when it makes the right simplifications. This is theory-driven: only a good theory will lead to a deeper understanding of things and to the confidence that the results can be trusted. In order to develop a good theory you have to ask the right questions and then understand in what way things are connected. It is simply not true that you only have to obtain more data, in which artificial intelligence will then be able to detect patterns that are self-explanatory. We are miles away from an "end of theory," as is postulated by some. A colleague of mine at the Santa Fe Institute remarked on this problem aptly: "Big data without big theory is big bullshit." That does not mean that this will not be possible one day; it only means that we are still far away from it at the moment.

This mistake is made to a spectacular extent when it comes to the uncritical use of artificial intelligence, for example: people get hold of some data somehow, which is mostly far from being sufficient, and play around with them ignorantly, constructing some makeshift algorithms with software fragments found online and subsequently failing to interpret the result that has been coughed up. The result is published nevertheless, and in the end everyone will be confused—and on the next day, the whole thing will break down. Unfortunately, such an approach can be observed more and more often. It is the "end of

wie Ökonomie, Epidemiologie, Molekularbiologie oder Neurowissenschaften verfügen sowie theoretische Konzepte verstehen und quantitativ denken können. Diese Qualifikationen sollten idealerweise in einer Person verbunden sein. Denn man muss an jedem Punkt wissen, welche Schwierigkeiten sich in anderen Bereichen ergeben. Personen, die diese Qualifikationen in sich vereinen, sind relativ rar, werden doch nach wie vor Menschen meist nur in einer Fachrichtung ausgebildet. Universitäten bereiten uns wunderbar auf die Gegebenheiten des späten 20. Jahrhunderts, nicht aber für die großen Probleme der Zukunft vor. Ich bin überzeugt, dass man einen neuen Ausbildungsmix anbieten muss. Complexity Science bietet hier eine Möglichkeit.

Manchmal hört man, dass Modelle und Simulationen neben Theorie und Empirie eine neue, dritte Art sind, die Welt zu betrachten und etwas über sie herauszufinden. Ist das auch Ihre Ansicht?

Thurner: Ich weiß nicht, ob das so neu ist: Schon Johannes Kepler hat ein Modell entwickelt und mit dessen Hilfe darüber nachgedacht, warum die Planeten so zueinander angeordnet sind, wie sie das sind. Simulation ist zunächst einmal nichts anderes: Ich entwickle ein Modell von etwas, baue es mit Vereinfachungen nach und kann dann damit spielen. Als Kind spielt man mit Spielzeugautos und lernt dabei, dass sie kaputtgehen, wenn man damit gegen die Wand fährt. Eine Simulation ist oft nichts anderes als eine Art von Modell.

Simulation kann allerdings noch etwas anderes sein: In vielen Disziplinen ist es im Unterschied zu den Naturwissenschaften nicht möglich, einen Versuch so oft zu wiederholen, wie man will. Als Historiker sieht man, wie die Geschichte verlaufen ist – und das war es. Man kann die Geschichte nicht wiederholen. Damit ist aber insofern Schluss mit Wissenschaft, als man in der Wissenschaft etwas reproduzieren können sollte. Man kann den Zweiten Weltkrieg zu beschreiben versuchen, aber man hat keine Möglichkeit zu sagen, was sich zugetragen hätte, wenn z. B. das Wetter anders gewesen wäre. In einer Simulation könnte man im Prinzip Tausende Varianten eines geschichtlichen Ereignisses mit vielen kleinen Variationen ablaufen lassen. Dann schaut man, ob etwas anderes herauskommt, wenn man Parameter wie das Wetter ändert. Ich meine das jetzt nur als Beispiel – es gibt natürlich kein vernünftiges Modell des Weltkriegs mit dem

science" rather than the "end of theory." So much for the downside of these methods.

Constructing a good simulation model requires people with professional skills who know how to handle data, who are experts in fields like economics, epidemiology, molecular biology, or neuroscience, and capable of comprehending theoretical concepts and thinking quantitatively. These qualifications should ideally be combined within a single person. It is necessary to be aware at each step of the difficulties that may arise in other fields. Personalities uniting all of these qualifications within themselves are relatively rare, as people are still mostly trained in only a single discipline. University education prepares us for the situation that was prevalent in the late twentieth century but not for the big problems of the future. I am convinced that a new educational mixture has to be offered. Complexity science is one possibility.

It is sometimes heard that models and simulations, alongside theory and empiricism, represent a third way of looking at the world and finding out about it. Would you agree?

Thurner: I am not sure if this is really that new. Even Johannes Kepler developed a model and used it as a tool to find out why the planets are configured in the way they are. In the first place, simulation means nothing else than developing a model of something, reconstructing it in a simplified way, and playing around with it. Children play with toy cars and learn that they will break when you crash them into a wall. Simulation is frequently nothing other than a kind of model.

But simulation can also be something else. Different from the natural sciences, it is not possible in many disciplines to repeat an experiment as often as you like. As a historian you can look back at the course of history—and that's it then. History cannot be repeated. In this respect, this puts an end to it as a science because in science you should be able to reproduce things. You can try to describe World War II, but there is no possibility so find out what it would have been like if, for example, the weather had been different. Basically, in a simulation you could play out thousands of variants of a historical event with a

Wetter als Parameter. Man kann auf diese Weise heraus-finden, welche Faktoren wesentlich sind, jedoch nur dann, wenn man die Regeln in dem Modell richtig formuliert hat. Wenn die Interaktionsregeln falsch sind, ist oft alles falsch. In den vergangenen 20 Jahren hat man viele Modelle mit schlechten und oberflächlichen Interaktionsregeln erstellt und dementsprechend einigen fundamentalen Unsinn produziert. Wenn man die Interaktionsregeln nicht gut genug kennt, ist das Modell sehr oft die Bits nicht wert, in denen es programmiert ist. Das ändert sich jetzt, wie bereits erwähnt, mit Big Data drastisch: Immer öfter kann man die Interaktionsregeln direkt beobachten. Werden die Interaktionsregeln im Idealfall so in ein Modell einge-füttert, wie sie in der Realität vorkommen, können die Simulationen wirklich gut werden. Das ist eine Wende, die uns eine neue Ära der Simulationsmodelle eröffnet.

Wenn es mittlerweile so gute Simulationsmodelle gibt, warum werden diese in der Praxis zur Fundierung von Entscheidungen so selten einge-setzt? Etwa von der Politik?

Thurner: Aus einem einfachen und verständlichen Grund: Viele Menschen, egal ob Wissenschafterinnen und Wissenschafter, Politikerinnen und Politiker oder Mana-gerinnen und Manager, verstehen heute Simulationen nicht und sind von den Parametern und Zusammenhän-gen überfordert. Und man trifft keine wichtigen Entschei-dungen auf Basis von etwas, was man nicht versteht. Dann bedient man sich lieber traditioneller Mittel auf einer Grundlage, die zwar ungenügend ist, die man aber versteht. Ich bin jedoch optimistisch: Wenn die Modelle so gut sind, dass sie Bauchentscheidungen erklären, und man intuitiv sichtbar machen kann, wie die Modelle funktionieren, dann findet ein Vertrauensbildungsprozess statt. Das wird Simulationen früher oder später auch in die Politik bringen. Die Entscheidungsträger und Entschei-dungsträgerinnen müssen sich auf die neuen Technolo-gien einlassen und bereit sein, mitzumachen und ein Feedback zu geben. Wissenschafterinnen und Wissen-schafter werden sich darauf einlassen müssen, die Simulationen, Annahmen usw. intuitiver zu kommunizie-ren. Dazu wird es neuer Formen der Zusammenarbeit von Politik und Wissenschaft bedürfen. Nichts wäre schlim-mer als unkritisches Vertrauen in Simulationen, die wie gesagt nur Modelle sind und falsch sein können.

myriad of minor variations. Then you would be able to see whether the result is different when you have changed such parameters as the weather. This is only an example—of course there is no reasonable model of the World War with the weather as a parameter. You can find out what factors are essential, but only if the rules in the model have been formulated properly. When the rules of interaction are false, frequently everything else will be false. In the past twenty years, many models working with bad or superficial rules of interaction were developed and, accordingly, the outcome was some profound nonsense. When you are not sufficiently familiar with the rules of interaction, the model will frequently not even be worth the bits that have been used to program it. This is about to change drastically now, as mentioned, thanks to big data: more and more often, the rules of interaction can be directly observed. When the rules of interaction are ideally fed into a model as they occur in reality, simulations can indeed turn out very well. This is a game changer that opens up a new era of simulation models for us.

If simulation models are really that good by now, why are they used so rarely in practice to back up decisions? In politics, for instance?

Thurner: Because of a simple and understandable reason: simulations are still beyond many people, be it scientists, politicians, or managers, who do not understand them and are overwhelmed by all the parameters and correlations. You do not base crucial decisions on something you do not understand, but rather employ traditional means on a basis that may be inadequate but is well understood. But I am an optimist: if models are that good that they are able to explain gut decisions and it is possible to show intuitively how these models function, a process of confidence building will take place. Sooner or later, this will also lead to simulations being used in politics. Decision-makers must be ready to engage with the new technologies and be willing to take part and give feedback. Scientists will have to do their best to communicate simulations, assumptions, etc. more intuitively. For this, new forms of collaboration between politics and science will be necessary.

Sobald man Phänomene in Simulatoren abzubilden imstande ist, kann man Szenarien durchspielen, die digitale Kopie der Welt leicht verändern und beobachten, ob das Ergebnis im Hinblick auf die Zielfunktion besser wird oder sich unerwünschte Folgen ergeben. Das ist oft sehr erhellend. Hat man etwa vor, ein neues Verkehrssystem einzuführen, und verfügt über ein System, in dem jeder Bürger virtuell Ampeln platzieren kann, um Verbesserungen durchzuprobieren, könnte man Menschen die Möglichkeit geben, sehr schnell zu erkennen, wie kompliziert scheinbar offensichtliche Dinge manchmal sind und wie viele unbedachte Nebenwirkungen eine Entscheidung oft nach sich zieht.

Verändert sich durch solche neuen Methoden unsere Sicht auf die Welt?

Thurner: Die Wissenschaft ist das beste Tool, um uns die Welt neu sehen zu lassen. Wissenschaft ist mehr als ein Modell. Modelle muss man als falsch verwerfen können. Modelle, für die das nicht gilt, haben eher poetischen Charakter. Die verschiedenen in den vergangenen 5000 Jahren zur Erklärung der Welt entwickelten Modelle sind Beispiele dafür. Einmal geht man von einer flachen Welt aus, dann wieder von einer runden, einmal von einer Kugel im Zentrum des Kosmos, dann wieder von einer Kugel an dessen Rand. Oder nehmen wir die Frage, wo der Mensch herkommt: Einmal ist er durch ein Wesen geschaffen, einmal entstammt er der Evolution. Mit Simulationen funktioniert das auf weit weniger abstrakte Weise.

In der Wissenschaft erstellt man nicht nur Modelle, sondern muss diese auch gegenüber anderen Expertinnen und Experten verteidigen, die sie zu falsifizieren versuchen. Wenn einem das öfter gelingt, lässt das darauf schließen, dass das Modell besser ist als andere, weil es stimmigere Antworten gibt. Auf Dauer verandert sich dadurch kollektiv die grundsätzliche Sicht auf die Welt. Wenn Menschen die Welt anders wahrnehmen, handeln sie auch anders und stellen z. B. neue Produkte her. Der neue Blick verändert also die Welt tatsächlich. Wenn man etwa auf einmal versteht, wie Viren funktionieren, verwandelt das die Welt. Menschen sterben nicht mehr massenhaft an Seuchen, wie sie das Millionen Jahre lang getan haben. Das ist eine drastische Änderung.

Nothing would be worse than uncritical confidence in simulations that are, as has been pointed out, merely models and could be false.

As soon as we are capable of visualizing phenomena in simulators, it will be possible to play through certain scenarios, slightly modify the digital copy of the world, and observe if the result will improve with regard to the target function or if undesirable consequences will be brought about. Sometimes this can be extremely enlightening. If you wish to introduce a new traffic system and have a tool at hand by which every citizen can place virtual traffic lights in order to try out improvements, people will be able to realize very quickly how complicated seemingly obvious things can sometimes be and how many unthought-of side effects a decision might frequently entail.

Will these new methods change our view of the world?

Thurner: Science is the best tool to introduce us to a new view of the world. Science is more than a model. It must be possible to reject models when they are wrong. Models of which this cannot be said are poetic in character more than anything else. The diverse models developed in the past 5000 years in order to explain the world are cases in point. One time it was assumed that the world was flat, another time we believed it was round, one time it was thought to be a sphere at the center of the universe, another time, a sphere on its fringes. Or let us consider the problem of the origins of humankind: one time humans are believed to have been shaped by a creator, another time they are seen as having sprung from evolution. Using simulation, this will work in a much less abstract way.

Science does not only build models—the models also have to be defended against other experts who try to falsify them. When you succeed in doing so more and more often, it can be assumed that the model is better than others because the answers it supplies are more coherent. Over time, the way in which we basically view the world will thus change collectively. When people perceive the world differently, they will also act differently and produce new products. A new way of looking at it will therefore indeed change the world. When you suddenly compre-

An welchen Themen arbeiten Sie am Complexity Science Hub Vienna, wenn nicht gerade das Coronathema alles dominiert?

Thurner: Für mich und meine Gruppe sind systemisches Risiko, Resilienz und Kollaps große Themen. Wie kann man Resilienz messen? Worin unterscheidet sich die Resilienz eines Bankensystems von der eines Ökosystems, eines Gesundheitssystems oder einer Zulieferkette? Wir haben bereits einige schöne Erfolge erzielt. Wir können heute beispielsweise das systemische Risiko in einem Bankensystem messen und quantifizieren, was vor 15 Jahren noch völlig unmöglich war – das hefte ich mir an die Fahnen. Man kann abschätzen, was ein Bankencrash kosten wird und unter welchen Umständen welches Bailout-Szenario optimal ist. Und man kann das Risiko, dass es zu Bankencrashs kommen wird, durch eine minimalinvasive Regulierung drastisch senken.

Medizin und Big Data – das ist ein extrem spannendes Thema. Bei einer Krankheit ist oft ein molekulares Netzwerk gestört. Durch einen Gendefekt etwa fällt nicht nur die Produktion eines Proteins aus, sondern ganze Kaskaden chemischer Reaktionen funktionieren nicht so, wie sie sollten. Daher kommt es oft nicht nur zu einer Krankheit, sondern gleichzeitig zu mehreren; man spricht von Multimorbidität. Aus großen, bevölkerungsweiten anonymisierten Datensätzen können wir solche Multimorbiditäten identifizieren und zu Clustern zusammenfassen. Kennt man den Cluster, kann man individuelle Krankheitsverläufe viel besser prognostizieren, als das heute der Fall ist. Ein großes Ziel ist es auch, Algorithmen zu formulieren, mit denen man Nebenwirkungen von Medikamenten und Therapien entdecken und nachweisen kann. Ein weiteres wichtiges Ziel ist es, die Effizienz und Qualität von Gesundheitssystemen abzubilden und in Simulatoren aufzuzeigen, wie man diese mit teils relativ einfachen Maßnahmen umfassend verbessern kann. Kennt man die Schwachstellen, kann man diese – ebenfalls minimalinvasiv – korrigieren und muss nicht warten, bis es zum Kollaps kommt, der bekanntlich oft sehr teuer ausfällt. Mich interessiert auch sehr, wie kollektive Meinungen entstehen und ob und – wenn ja – weshalb eine Fragmentierung der Gesellschaft droht. In der Ökonomie fasziniert mich vor allem die Frage der »Green Transition«. ✕

hend, for example, how viruses work, this will change the world. People will stop dying through mass extinction in epidemics as they have for millions of years. This is a drastic change.

What are you currently concerned with at the Complexity Science Hub Vienna when COVID-19 is not the all-dominant theme?

Thurner: For my team and me, the big issues are systemic risk, resilience, and collapse. How can resilience be measured? In what way does the resilience of a banking system differ from that of an ecosystem, a health system, or a supply chain? We have already had several very impressive successes. Today we are able to measure and quantify the systemic risk of a banking system, for example, which was still entirely impossible fifteen years ago—and for which I credit myself. You can estimate what a bank crash will cost and which bailout scenario will be ideal under which circumstances. And the risk of a possible bank crash can be drastically lowered through minimally invasive regulations.

Medicine and big data—this is an extremely exciting subject. Disease often involves the disorder of a molecular network. For example, a genetic defect will not only stop the production of a single protein, but entire cascades of chemical reactions will not function the way they should. As a rule, this entails multiple health conditions rather than merely one; we speak of multimorbidity. It is possible for us to identify such multimorbidities from large amounts of anonymized datasets collected throughout the population and then assign them to clusters. As soon as the cluster is known, it will be possible for us to predict the progress of individual health conditions much more precisely than this is the case today. It is also a primary goal of ours to formulate algorithms that will allow us to discover and prove adverse effects of drugs and therapies. I am also very much interested in the formation of collective opinions, and whether and—if yes—why they threaten to fragment society. What fascinates me particularly in economics is the problem of "green transition." ×

Helga Nowotny im Gespräch

»Man muss mit der Ungewissheit leben lernen«

Die Wissenschaftsforscherin Helga Nowotny plädiert dafür, die neuen Methoden der Komplexitätsforschung verstärkt dafür zu nutzen, Fragen bezüglich der Zukunft zu stellen und sich dadurch besser auf die Ungewissheit vorbereiten zu können – auch wenn die Zukunft klarerweise ungewiss bleibt.

Helga Nowotny ist eine international anerkannte Wissenschaftsforscherin und Professorin emerita der ETH Zürich. Sie war Gründungsmitglied und Vizepräsidentin des 2007 etablierten Europäischen Forschungsrats und von 2010 bis 2013 dessen Präsidentin. Sie ist Vorsitzende des ERA Council Forum Austria und Mitglied des Rates für Forschung und Technologieentwicklung.

Es heißt immer, dass die Welt heute so komplex und unübersichtlich geworden ist. Stimmt das wirklich? War die Welt im Mittelalter oder im 19. Jahrhundert wirklich so viel einfacher?

Helga Nowotny: Sicher nicht aus der Sicht derjenigen, die damals lebten. Als sich im 14. Jahrhundert die Pest über Europa ausbreitete, starb fast die Hälfte der Bevölkerung. Im 19. Jahrhundert erlebten die Menschen die Turbulenzen der Industrialisierung und rapiden Urbanisierung mit allen positiven und negativen Folgeerscheinungen. Wenn wir die Frage jedoch aus einer Makrosicht beantworten, sehen wir die enorme Zunahme an Vernetzung einer globalisierten Welt und somit eindeutig eine Zunahme an Komplexität durch die sich daraus ergebenden Verbindungen. Diese werden noch durch die Digitalisierung intensiviert. Zum geografischen Raum gesellt sich der virtuelle. Wir erleben gerade den Beginn einer Koevolution von Menschen und digitalen Technologien.

Wie kann und soll die Gesellschaft mit der zunehmenden Komplexität und der damit verbundenen wachsenden Unsicherheit umgehen?

Nowotny: Eine Folgeerscheinung der Coronakrise, die uns noch lange beschäftigen wird, ist das Leben mit größerer Ungewissheit. Es beginnt mit der bangen Frage, ob uns eine zweite Welle bevorsteht und ob und wann sich die Wirtschaft wieder erholen wird. Doch das ist nur der Anfang: SARS-COV-2 ist Teil einer Virusfamilie, die erstmals mit SARS 1 in Erscheinung getreten ist; daneben tauchen auch ständig andere Viren dieser Art wie das Ebola- oder das Schweinegrippevirus auf. Weitere Epidemien sind zu

Helga Nowotny is an internationally recognized theorist of science and professor emerita of the ETH Zurich. She was a founding member and Vice-President of the European Research Council and its President from 2010 to 2013. She is chair of the ERA Council Forum Austria and member of the Council for Research and Technology Development.

An interview with Helga Nowotny

"We have to learn to live with uncertainty"

Science researcher Helga Nowotny pleads for making greater use of the new methods of complexity research to ask questions about the future and thus be better prepared for uncertainty—even if the future will definitely remain uncertain.

One often hears that today's world has become so complex and confusing. Is that really true? Was the world really so much simpler in the Middle Ages or in the nineteenth century?

Helga Nowotny: Certainly not from the perspective of those who lived back then. When the plague spread across Europe in the fourteenth century, it killed almost half the population. In the nineteenth century, people found themselves confronted with the upheavals of industrialization and rapid urbanization and all the positive and negative consequences they entailed. If we answer the question from a macroperspective, however, we see the enormous increase in the interconnectedness of a globalized world and thus clearly a growth of complexity due to the resulting connections. These are further intensified by digitization. Virtual space joins the geographical space. We are witnessing the beginning of a coevolution of people and digital technologies.

How can and should society deal with this increasing complexity and the growing uncertainty associated with it?

Nowotny: A consequence of the coronavirus crisis, which will occupy us for a long time to come, is living with greater uncertainty. It starts with the anxious question of whether a second wave is imminent and whether and when the economy will recover. But this is only the beginning: SARS-COV-2 is part of a family of viruses that emerged with SARS 1; we have also seen the outbreak of Ebola and the swine flu caused by other viruses of this kind. Further epidemics are to be

erwarten, und deren Frequenz nimmt zu. Die Frage ist, ob der Ausbruch lokal begrenzt bleibt oder sich zu einer Pandemie auswächst. Verstärkt wird das Auftreten von Epidemien durch den Klimawandel, da die Pathogene sich neue Wirte suchen müssen. Dazu kommen die vielen anderen mit dem Klimawandel verbundenen Herausforderungen.

Wie sollen wir mit mehr Ungewissheit umgehen? Eine Krise legt immer Strukturmängel offen. Es hat sich gezeigt, dass wir nicht alles so unter Kontrolle haben, wie wir dachten. Weder waren die Regierungen vorbereitet, noch waren die Gesundheitssysteme in vielen Ländern finanziell, personell und organisatorisch gerüstet. Wenn 80 Prozent der Produktion aller in Europa benötigten Medikamente nach China ausgelagert wurden, stimmt etwas nicht. Die Antwort auf den Umgang mit mehr Ungewissheit lautet: Man muss mit der Ungewissheit leben lernen. Das schließt ein, dass wir die wissenschaftlich-technischen Möglichkeiten nutzen, um zu besseren Vorhersagen zu gelangen. Simulationsmodelle, wie sie in der Komplexitätsforschung verwendet werden, machen es möglich, viele Fragen bezüglich der Zukunft zu stellen – was geschieht, wenn …? Sie erlauben es uns, weiter in die Zukunft zu blicken und uns besser darauf vorzubereiten. Doch die Zukunft bleibt ungewiss.

Vorbereitet zu sein ist keine Frage der Anzahl von Spitalsbetten oder der anzulegenden Vorräte von Schutzanzügen. Es ist eine Frage der Denkweise, des Bewusstseins, dass Unerwartetes nicht nur passieren kann, sondern wird, und wie wir uns darauf vorbereiten können.

Wie kann die Wissenschaft darauf reagieren? Müssen sich auch Universitäten umstellen?

Nowotny: Die Universitäten stehen vor großen Herausforderungen. Sie spüren den Digitalisierungsschub unmittelbar, der freilich auch ein neues Experimentierfeld für die Ausbildung und Forschung eröffnet. Es wird aber auch zu einem Umdenken im Hinblick auf andere Formen von Internationalisierung kommen. Das us-amerikanische und britische Modell, das stark auf internationale Studierende setzt, ist in große Bedrängnis geraten, doch auch in Österreich wird man sich fragen müssen, wie trotz zukünftiger Einschränkung der weltweiten Mobilität Internationalisierung zu gewährleisten ist.

expected, and their frequency is increasing. The question is whether such outbreaks will remain local or explode into pandemics. The occurrence of epidemics is intensified by climate change, as the pathogens have to find new hosts. The many other challenges associated with climate change are also to be taken into consideration.

How are we to deal with more uncertainty? A crisis always reveals structural deficiencies. It turns out that we are not in control of everything as we liked to think. Governments were as badly prepared as many countries' health systems in terms of funds, personnel, and organization. The fact that eighty percent of the production of all medicines needed in Europe have been outsourced to China leaves no doubt that something is wrong. The answer to dealing with more uncertainty is that we have to learn to live with uncertainty. That includes using the scientific and technological opportunities to make better predictions. Simulation models, such as those used in complexity research, make it possible to ask many questions about the future—what happens if? They allow us to look further into the future and to prepare ourselves better for it. But the future will remain uncertain.

Being prepared is not a question of the number of hospital beds or of protective suits to have in reserve. It is a question of people's mindset, of being aware that the unexpected cannot only happen but will happen, and of how we can prepare for it.

How can science respond to this? Do universities also have to adapt?

Nowotny: Universities are facing great challenges. They are directly feeling the digitization push, which of course also opens up a new experimental field for education and research. Other forms of internationalization will also have to reconsidered. The US and British model, which relies heavily on international students, has come under great pressure, but in Austria too the question will have to be asked how internationalization can be guaranteed despite future restrictions on global mobility.

Die Coronapandemie hat einmal mehr gezeigt, wie eng die Welt heute verflochten und vernetzt ist und welch unliebsame Folgen das haben kann – von der raschen Ausbreitung einer Seuche bis hin zu den Lieferketten, die bei geringen Störungen zusammenbrechen. Daraus erwächst die Forderung nach einem resilienteren Weltsystem. Ist das auch ihre Meinung? Und wie macht man das?

Nowotny: Eine der Lehren, die wohl aus den letzten Monaten gezogen werden muss, hängt mit der Neustrukturierung der Globalisierung zusammen. Die Globalisierung hat viele Vorteile gebracht, wenngleich diese sehr ungleich verteilt waren und wesentlich zu einer Vertiefung bestehender Ungleichheiten beigetragen haben. Resilienz wird nur zu erreichen sein, wenn es gelingt, ein Denken und Formen von Organisation auf mehreren Ebenen zu praktizieren. Komplexität zu verstehen, besteht ja auch in einer dynamischen Mehrebenenanalyse. Eine simple Rückkehr zu regionalen Produkten oder heimischem Tourismus ist keine Option. Die Verbindung zwischen lokaler, nationaler, europäischer und globaler Ebene muss überdacht und neu gestaltet werden. Das erfordert neue rechtliche und politische Rahmenbedingungen, aber vor allem Mut zum Umdenken.

Kann der Mensch lernen, mit der zunehmenden Komplexität besser umzugehen – oder sind wir in den linearen Denkstrukturen, die wir aus unserer Evolution geerbt haben, gefangen?

Nowotny: Ich glaube nicht, dass uns die Evolution mit linearem Denken ausgestattet hat, im Gegenteil. Anthropologen sind voll des Staunens und der Bewunderung für die Komplexität, die sie bei Menschen angetroffen haben, die in Kleingruppen in entlegenen Gegenden ihr Überleben zu sichern verstanden. Ein Beispiel ist die unglaubliche Komplexität von Verwandtschaftssystemen oder die Fähigkeit, ohne Kompass im Ozean zu navigieren oder sich ohne Hilfsmittel im Dschungel zurechtzufinden. Lineares Denken ist das Erbe der Moderne. Sie hat lineare Planung und eine Ordnung im Denken mit sich gebracht, die weitgehend auf Dichotomien beruht. Diese Art des Denkens hat sich ebenso totgelaufen wie der lineare Fortschrittsglaube. Wir müssen lernen, wieder mehr in Prozessen zu denken, Feedback-Loops zu berücksichtigen und statt Dichotomien nicht linear strukturierte Relationen zu entdecken.

The coronavirus pandemic showed once again how closely inter-twined and interconnected the world is today and what unpleasant consequences this may have—from the rapid spread of a disease to supply chains that collapse with minor disturbances. This leads to the demand for a more resilient world system. What do you think about this? And how do we go about it?

Nowotny: One of the lessons to be learned from recent months clearly concerns the restructuring of globalization. Globalization has brought many benefits. However, these benefits have been very unevenly distributed and contributed significantly to deepening existing inequalities. Resilience can only be achieved if it will be possible to think and shape organization on several levels. After all, understanding complexity also involves a dynamic multilevel analysis. A simple return to regional products or domestic tourism is not an option. We must reconsider and redesign the connections between local, national, European and global levels. This requires a new legal and political framework but above all the courage to rethink things.

Can humans learn how to better cope with increasing complexity—or are they trapped in the linear thought structures they have inherited from their evolution?

Nowotny: I do not believe that evolution has furnished us with linear thinking—quite the contrary. Anthropologists are full of admiration for the complexity they have found in people who have managed to survive in small groups in remote areas. One example is the incredible complexity of kinship systems, another the ability to navigate the ocean without a compass or to find one's way through the jungle without any aids. Linear thinking is the heritage of modernity. It was modernity that established forms of linear planning and an order in thinking based largely on dichotomies. This way of thinking has played itself out as has the linear belief in progress. We must learn to think more in processes again, to take feedback loops into account, and to discover nonlinearly structured relations instead of dichotomies.

Eine Folge der wachsenden Unsicherheit ist das Wiedererstarken des Populismus, der einfache Lösungen für komplexe Probleme verspricht. Verbunden damit ist oft Skepsis bzw. Feindschaft gegenüber der Wissenschaft. Wie könnte man diesen gefährlichen Cocktail entschärfen?

> **Nowotny:** Bertrand Russell sagte einmal sinngemäß: »Zweifel sind etwas für intelligente Menschen, nur die Dummen glauben bereits die Antworten zu kennen.« Eine unerwartete Folge der Krise war, dass das Vertrauen in die Wissenschaft wieder zurückgekehrt ist. In der Not wissen Menschen wohl zu unterscheiden. Die Krise bot auch für die Öffentlichkeit Gelegenheit, zuzusehen, wie Wissenschaft funktioniert. Man konnte beobachten, dass Modelle je nach Annahme und unterschiedlicher Datenlage zu anderen Ergebnissen kommen – aber auch, dass Wissenschafterinnen und Wissenschafter unterschiedlicher Ansicht sein, sich aber schließlich doch einigen können. Deutlich wurde auch, wie das Verhältnis zwischen Wissenschaft und Politik im Idealfall funktionieren sollte. Entscheidungen werden letzten Endes von der Politik getroffen, die auf die Wissenschaft hören soll, sich aber nicht hinter einer globalen Aussage wie etwa »we follow the science« verstecken und im Fall, dass etwas schief geht, der Wissenschaft die Schuld geben kann.

Sie sagten eben, dass das Vertrauen in die Wissenschaft in der Coronakrise wieder zugenommen hat. Ist dieser Umschwung dauerhaft?

> **Nowotny:** Das gestiegene Vertrauen ist nichts, was Bestand haben muss. Die Wissenschaft ist gefordert, zu beweisen, dass sie es ist, die auch in Zukunft gut mit Ungewissheit umzugehen vermag. Sie dringt in den Bereich des noch Unbekannten und Ungewissen vor. Sie hat Methoden entwickelt, wie sie gewonnene Erkenntnisse und Ergebnisse der Forschung ständig überprüft. Alles wissenschaftliche Wissen ist immer nur vorläufig. Es wird durch besseres Wissen ergänzt oder ersetzt, und neue und bessere Fragestellungen werden zu mehr und besseren Erkenntnissen und Ergebnissen führen. Das ist die wichtigste Botschaft der Wissenschaft an die Gesellschaft und an die Politik: Wissenschaft ist ein Vorantasten in eine ungewisse Zukunft. Doch es gelingt immer wieder, robustes Wissen zu gewinnen, das uns weiter voranbringen wird.

One consequence of the growing uncertainty is the resurgence of populism, which promises simple solutions to complex problems. This is often accompanied by skepticism or hostility toward science. How could this dangerous cocktail be defused?

> **Nowotny:** Bertrand Russell once said that "in the modern world the stupid are cocksure while the intelligent are full of doubt." An unexpected consequence of the crisis was that confidence in science has returned. In times of need, people know to distinguish. The crisis also provided the public with an opportunity to watch how science works. It could be observed that models arrive at different results depending on assumptions and different data—but also that scientists with different views finally come to an agreement. It also became clear how the relationship between science and politics ought to function ideally. Decisions are ultimately made by politicians, who should listen to science but not hide behind a global statement like "we follow science" and, in case something goes wrong, blame science.

You just said that trust in science has increased again during the coronavirus crisis. Would you consider this a lasting turnaround?

> **Nowotny:** The grown confidence is not something that has to last. It is up to science to prove that it will be able to deal well with uncertainty in the future, too. Science advances into the sphere of the still unknown and uncertain. It has developed methods for constantly reviewing research findings and results. All scientific knowledge is always merely temporary. It is supplemented or replaced by better knowledge, and new and better questions will lead to more and better knowledge and results. This is science's most important message to society and policy-makers: science is a way of feeling its way into an uncertain future. But time and again robust knowledge can be acquired that will help us move forward.

Viele Experten meinen, dass wir zur Bewältigung der komplexen Zukunftsfragen viel mehr interdisziplinäres und systemisches Denken benötigen. Wie kann man z. B. an Universitäten eine höhere Interdisziplinarität erreichen? Versucht wird das ja schon seit Längerem. Wie die Erfahrung aber zeigt, ist das in der Praxis nicht so einfach.

Nowotny: Ja, gerade die Pandemie hat uns wieder einmal vor Augen geführt, wie wichtig es wäre, mit mehr Interdisziplinarität auf die Herausforderungen zu reagieren. An den Universitäten müsste sich vieles verändern, und die nun wohl einsetzende Digitalisierungswelle könnte wesentlich dazu beitragen. Konkret geht es um zwei, aus meiner Sicht dringend notwendige Änderungen, die mit dem Mindset beginnen müssen und entsprechend organisatorisch zu begleiten sind.

Zum einen müssen die Lehrenden erkennen, dass es bereits etliche hervorragende digitale Lehrangebote gibt, die sie in ihr Programm aufnehmen bzw. dazu nutzen sollten, gemeinsam mit den Studierenden einen höheren Grad an Verständnis zu erarbeiten. Zum anderen – und damit komme ich zum Thema Interdisziplinarität – müssten sich einige Lehrende zusammenschließen, um die Studierenden zu motivieren, gemeinsam und über disziplinäre Grenzen hinweg gut ausgearbeitete Problemstellungen in Angriff zu nehmen. Das erfordert neben kluger Vorbereitung organisatorische Flexibilität und volle Unterstützung vonseiten der Universitätsleitung. Zum Teil wurde das bereits während der Coronakrise etwa am Complexity Science Hub Vienna und an der MedUni vorgelebt. Es bleibt natürlich nicht bei einem Virus und den Folgen: Die Anzahl der Herausforderungen, die nur mithilfe der Wissenschaft zu bewältigen sind und nach einem wahren Interdisziplinaritätsschub verlangen, ist in der Postcoronazeit enorm groß. ✖

Many experts believe that we need much more interdisciplinary and systemic thinking to deal with the complex issues of the future. How can a higher level of interdisciplinarity be achieved at universities, for example? This has been attempted for quite some time. But experience shows that this is anything but easy in practice.

Nowotny: Yes, the pandemic in particular has once again left no doubt how important it would be to respond to the challenges with more interdisciplinarity. Many things would have to change at universities, and the wave of digitization that will now be probably setting in could make a significant contribution to this. Specifically, there are two changes that are, in my view, urgently called for—changes that must begin with the mindset and be accompanied by appropriate organizational measures.

On the one hand, teachers need to recognize that there are already a number of excellent digital offers that they should include in their programs or use to develop a higher level of understanding together with their students. On the other hand—which brings me to the subject of interdisciplinarity—some teachers would have to join forces in order to motivate students to tackle well-designed problems together and across disciplinary boundaries. In addition to clever preparation, this requires organizational flexibility and full support from the university management. Parts of such a strategy could already be observed during the coronavirus crisis at the Complexity Science Hub Vienna and at MedUni. This does not stop at a virus and its consequences, of course: the number of challenges that can only be mastered with the help of science and that require a true surge of interdisciplinarity will be enormous in the postcoronavirus era. **×**

Ausgewählte Themenbereiche

Selected Subject Areas

Das Netz des Lebens

Moleküle, Zellen, Organismen, Populationen und Ökosysteme bilden höchst komplexe Strukturen und haben vielschichtige Eigenschaften, die wir erst nach und nach zu verstehen lernen. Wie komplex alle Prozesse des Lebens einschließlich der unsere Gesundheit ausmachenden sind, zeigt sich derzeit auch im Zusammenhang mit der Coronapandemie.

Man schätzt, dass der Körper des Menschen aus rund 30 Billionen Zellen besteht. Dazu kommen noch einmal mindestens so viele Mikroorganismen, die auf und in ihm leben. Sie alle haben ihre spezifischen Funktionen innerhalb des großen Ganzen, das wir Organismus nennen. Sie arbeiten in diesem Rahmen eng zusammen, sind voneinander abhängig. Die rund 86 Milliarden Nervenzellen im menschlichen Gehirn beispielsweise sind mit je mindestens 1000 anderen Neuronen verknüpft. Gemeinsam bilden sie ein äußerst komplexes Netzwerk, das zum einen höhere kognitive Leistungen und Bewusstsein ermöglicht und zum anderen sehr dynamisch ist.

Von diesen Prinzipien ist die gesamte belebte Natur geprägt: Allerorts herrscht eine hochgradige Vernetzung – von molekularen Stoffwechselvorgängen über Organismen und Populationen bis hin zu Ökosystemen. Aus diesen vielschichtigen Beziehungsnetzwerken erwachsen neue Eigenschaften – man spricht von »Emergenz«. Zudem sind die Netze des Lebens niemals statisch, sondern verändern sich ständig. Ökosysteme beispielsweise erscheinen uns stabil, sind jedoch auf längere Sicht gesehen in stetigem Wandel: Neue Arten treten auf und verändern die Lebensbedingungen in ihrer Umgebung, was wiederum andere Arten betrifft.

Die vielen Wunder des Lebens haben uns Menschen schon immer fasziniert. Doch erst in jüngster Vergangenheit gelingt es uns zu verstehen, wie Leben funktioniert. Denn dazu ist es notwendig, nicht nur einzelne Vorgänge zu analysieren, sondern die Zusammenhänge zu sehen. Möglich wurde das durch neue Konzepte der Systembiologie und der Komplexitätsforschung. So bemerkte man etwa vor knapp zwei Jahrzehnten, als man immer mehr Genome sequenziert hatte, dass uns die Kenntnis der einzelnen Gene und der entsprechenden Proteine nicht wirklich voranbringt. Vielmehr müssen wir verstehen, wie diese mit anderen Molekülen zusammenhängen und wie sie reguliert werden. Das wurde erst durch die Entwicklung leistungsfähiger Computer möglich, in denen die gigantischen Datenmengen

The Web of Life

Molecules, cells, organisms, populations, and ecosystems form highly intricate structures and feature complex properties we only learn to understand little by little. The complexity of all processes related to life and health has recently also been revealed in the context of the coronavirus pandemic.

It is estimated that the human body consists of some 30 trillion cells. To these we have to add about the same number of microorganisms living on and inside it. All of them have their specific functions within the greater whole we refer to as organism. They closely work together within this framework, relying on one another. Each of the approximately 86 billion nerve cells of the human brain is connected to at least 1,000 further neurons, for example. Together, they make up an immensely complex network that enables a higher cognitive performance and form of consciousness on the one hand and is extremely dynamic on the other.

Living nature as a whole relies on these principles: everything is networked to a high degree—from molecular metabolic processes and organisms to populations and ecosystems. From these networked relationships arise new properties—a process referred to as "emergence." Moreover, webs of life are never static but adjust incessantly. To us, ecosystems, for example, appear to be stable, but in the long-run they are subject to constant change: new species appear, altering the living conditions of their environment, which in turn affects other species.

Humankind has always been fascinated by the miracles of life. But only since the more recent past have we been able to understand how life works. For to do so it is necessary to not only analyze individual processes but to also see the ways in which they are interconnected. This became possible through new concepts supplied by systems biology and complexity science. About two decades ago, when researchers succeeded in sequencing more and more genomes, it was realized that knowledge of the individual genes and their respective proteins would not take us any further. Rather, we need to understand how they relate to other molecules and how they are regulated. This only

aus Genetik, Proteomik oder Metabolomik verarbeitet und Modelle konstruiert und durchgespielt werden können.

Eine Krankheit kommt selten allein

Krankheiten treten häufig nicht unabhängig voneinander auf. Wenn es in einem molekularen Netzwerk an einer Stelle zu einer Störung kommt, etwa ein Gen mutiert oder ein Protein in zu geringer Menge produziert wird, kommt es oft zu Kaskadeneffekten und Störungen größerer Teile des Netzwerks. Dann hat man es nicht mit einem isolierten Gesundheitsproblem, sondern gleichzeitig mit mehreren Krankheiten zu tun. Die klinische Erfahrung zeigt, dass es in vielen Fällen typische Muster von sogenannten Komorbiditäten oder Multimorbiditäten gibt. So tritt Diabetes beispielsweise oft in Kombination mit Bluthochdruck auf.

Forscher am Complexity Science Hub (CSH) Vienna haben sich dieses Phänomen genauer angesehen und ein Computermodell von 131 Blöcken der »Internationalen statistischen Klassifikation der Krankheiten und verwandter Gesundheitsprobleme« ICD-10 konstruiert. In das Modell eingespeist wurden die – vollständig anonymisierten – Daten aller Krankenhausaufenthalte in Österreich aus den Jahren 1997 bis 2014; die Daten stammen aus dem österreichischen Abrechnungssystem und decken einen großen Teil der Bevölkerung ab. Durch eine Clusterung der Daten ist es dank dieses Modells möglich, nicht nur statistische Korrelationen zwischen verschiedenen Krankheitsbildern, sondern auch deren zeitliche Abläufe oder »Trajektorien« zu ermitteln. Das erlaubt es nun, mit einer gewissen Wahrscheinlichkeit vorherzusagen, wie sich der Gesundheitszustand eines bestimmten Patienten in den nächsten Jahren entwickeln könnte – was wiederum eine gezielte Prävention ermöglicht. Auch für die Planung eines Gesundheitssystems sind solche Informationen wertvoll, weil sich so ausmachen lässt, wie häufig gewisse Krankheiten in Zukunft auftreten könnten. Auch die Grundlagenforschung kann profitieren: Das Wissen um Ko- und Multimorbiditäten allein hilft zwar noch nicht, die dahinterliegenden molekularen Mechanismen zu verstehen, aber es kann durchaus Anhaltspunkte für die weitere medizinische Forschung liefern.

Komplexe Abläufe von Infektionen

Auch Infektionskrankheiten sind extrem komplex. Das beginnt schon beim Funktionieren des Immunsystems, mit dem sich Lebewesen unliebsame Krankheitserreger vom Leib halten. Im Laufe der Evolution haben sich mehrere Abwehrketten gebildet, die in Gang gesetzt werden, sobald ein potenzieller Krankheitserreger im Körper registriert wird. Sehr rasch kommt es zur Reaktion des sogenannten unspezifischen zellulären Immunsystems. Wenig später tritt eine spezifische Immunantwort durch Antikörper der

became possible thanks to the development of high-performance computers by which we can process gigantic amounts of genetic, proteomic, and metabolomic data, construct models, and run simulations.

Disease is rarely an isolated phenomenon

Pathologic conditions rarely occur independently of one another. When a disorder manifests itself at one point of a molecular network, such as when a gene mutates or a protein is only produced in insufficient quantities, this frequently sets off cascade effects and disorders in larger parts of the system. Then we are not faced with an isolated health problem but with several diseases simultaneously. Clinical experience shows that in many cases there are typical patterns of so-called comorbidities or multimorbidities. Diabetes, for example, commonly occurs in combination with high blood pressure.

Researchers at the Complexity Science Hub (CSH) Vienna have looked into this phenomenon more closely and constructed a computer model consisting of 131 blocks of the "International Statistical Classification of Diseases and Related Health Problems," ICD-10. Completely anonymized data from hospitalizations in Austria from 1997 to 2014 were fed into the model; the data were derived from the official Austrian accounting system and cover large parts of the population. Thanks to this model and by using the method of data clustering it is now possible to determine not only statistical correlations between various disease patterns but also their progression over time or along "trajectories." This permits us to predict with a certain degree of probability how the state of health of a particular patient might develop over the coming years—which again allows for systematic prevention. Information of this kind is also useful for planning a health system because it can be foreseen at what frequency particular diseases might occur in the future. Fundamental research could benefit from this approach as well: although knowledge about co- and multimorbidities by itself does not contribute to understanding the molecular mechanisms behind them, it may well supply reference points for further medical research.

Complex progression of infections

Infections, too, are extremely complex. This starts with the way the immune system, by which living creatures ward off unwanted pathogens, works. In the course of evolution, several defense mechanisms have developed, which are activated as soon as a potentially pathogenic germ is registered inside the body. A so-called non-specific,

unterschiedlichsten Klassen (IgA, IgG, IgM usw.) auf: Diese Moleküle erkennen eine bestimmte Viren- oder Bakterienart, binden sich an diese und signalisieren dadurch bestimmten Immunzellen, dass sie den Eindringling unschädlich machen sollen.

Im Körper ist ständig eine Unzahl von Abwehrmolekülen und -zellen präsent, die u. a. dafür sorgen, dass man gegen gewisse Krankheitserreger immun ist. In diesem komplexen Geschehen treten bisweilen aber auch Probleme auf, etwa wenn das Immunsystem auf an sich harmlose Eindringlinge überschießend reagiert. Das äußert sich beispielsweise in Heuschnupfen, kann aber auch zu einem lebensgefährlichen anaphylaktischen Schock führen. Die Diagnostik von Allergien ist ein gutes Beispiel dafür, wie schwierig es ist, diese komplexen Netzwerke zu verstehen und durch eine passende Therapie günstig zu beeinflussen. Der Wiener Allergieforscher Rudolf Valenta hat einen Chip entwickelt, mit dem anhand eines einzigen Blutstropfens mehr als 120 verschiedene Allergene simultan getestet werden können. Mithilfe solcher individueller Allergen-Reaktionsprofile können relativ einfach Kreuzallergien und Veränderungen im Lauf der Zeit diagnostiziert werden.

Ähnlich verhält es sich im Fall der aktuellen Coronapandemie: Es gibt unzählige Einflussfaktoren und Reaktionswege, wie eine Infektion mit SARS-COV-2 abläuft. Detailwissen dazu ist derzeit noch Mangelware. Um Licht in das Dunkel zu bringen, werden derzeit – zusätzlich zu spezifischen PCR-Tests, die eine akute Infektion nachweisen, und Antikörpertests, die eine bereits überstandene Infektion belegen – weitere Testverfahren entwickelt, die tiefere Einblicke in das Geschehen ermöglichen. Valenta beispielsweise arbeitet an einem Testchip, mit dem die Körperreaktionen auf rund 150 Bausteine des Coronavirus überprüft werden können: Welcher Teil des Virus ruft welche Art von Immunreaktion hervor? Am AIT Austrian Institute of Technology wurde gemeinsam mit Partnern (Vetmeduni Vienna, MedUni Wien, Universität für Bodenkultur) ein hochgenauer Multiplextest etabliert, der mehrere Teile des Virus und mehrere Arten von Antikörpern im Visier hat. Das soll Details zu den molekularen Abläufen im Zuge der Immunabwehr sichtbar machen.

Epidemiologie: Wie sich Krankheiten ausbreiten

Extrem komplex ist auch die Ausbreitung von Krankheitserregern. Wenn diese ungebremst verläuft, wächst die Zahl der Infizierten exponentiell. Es gibt zahlreiche Einflussfaktoren, die mitbestimmen, wie ein Krankheitserreger von einer Population Besitz ergreift. Diese Mechanismen werden in der Wissenschaft der Epidemiologie systematisch erforscht – in der Hoffnung, daraus Hinweise abzuleiten, wie man die Ausbreitung einer Krankheit bremsen oder sogar stoppen könnte. Wie schwierig das ist, dafür liefert die aktuelle Coronapandemie ein beredtes Beispiel. Da man COVID-19-Erkrankungen erst nach der Entwicklung eines Impfstoffes wird stoppen

cell-mediated immune response sets in very fast. This is followed by a specific, antibody-mediated immune response, involving antibodies of various classes (IgA, IgG, IgM, etc.): these molecules recognize a specific type of virus or bacterium, bind to it, and thus signalize to specific immune cells that they are to disarm the invader.

A myriad of defense molecules and cells are constantly present in the human body, seeing to its immunity to certain pathogens, among other things. Occasionally, problems may arise in the course of these complex processes, for example when the immune system responds to harmless intruders in an exaggerated fashion. This may manifest itself in hay fever but can also lead to life-threatening anaphylactic shock reactions. Diagnosing allergies perfectly illustrates how difficult it is to understand these complex networks and influence them favorably through some suitable therapy. The Viennese allergy researcher Rudolf Valenta has developed a chip that lends itself to testing 120 different allergens simultaneously by means of a single blood drop. Thanks to such individual allergen response profiles it is possible to diagnose cross-reactivities and mutations over time relatively easily.

The case of the current coronavirus pandemic is similarly complex: there are innumerable factors of influence and ways of response in the progression of a SARS-COV-2 infection. Presently, detailed knowledge is still scarce. In addition to specific PCR tests detecting acute infection and antibody tests attesting recovery from infection, further test methods are currently being developed to gain more in-depth knowledge. For example, Valenta is working on a test chip by which bodily reactions to some 150 components of the coronavirus can be examined: which part of the virus leads to which type of immune response? The AIT Austrian Institute of Technology and its partners (Vetmeduni Vienna, Medical University of Vienna, Vienna University of Natural Resources and Life Sciences) have established a highly accurate multiplex test that has its sights on a number of components of the virus and on several types of antibodies. This is to supply detailed information about molecular processes in the context of immune defense.

Epidemiology: how disease proliferates

The proliferation of pathogens is extremely complex as well. If not contained, the number of infected persons will rise exponentially. There are numerous influencing factors that play a role in codetermining in what ways a pathogenic organism takes hold of a population. Epidemiology systematically explores these mechanisms—hoping to arrive at conclusions as to how the spreading of a disease could be decelerated or even stopped. The current coronavirus pandemic is a telling example of how demanding this is. As it will only be possible to

können, galt als Ziel aller Maßnahmen, die Gesundheitssysteme, vor allem die Kapazität zur Verfügung stehender Intensivbetten, nicht zu überfordern.

Zur Abschätzung der Zahl der in nächster Zeit Infizierten wurden epidemiologische Simulationsmodelle herangezogen. In Österreich kamen im Wesentlichen zwei Verfahren zum Einsatz. Die Forschergruppen waren als Berater des Gesundheitsministeriums tätig und lieferten allwöchentlich Prognosen für die nächste Zukunft. Die Datengrundlage stammte aus dem elektronischen Epidemiologischen Meldesystem des Bundes, in das Bezirks-verwaltungsbehörden manche Daten einspeisen.

- SIR-Modelle beschreiben mithilfe von Differenzialgleichungen, wie sich drei Gruppen von Menschen zeitlich entwickeln: die für eine Infektion Anfälligen (S, susceptible), die Infizierten (I) und die Gesun-deten bzw. Verstorbenen (R, removed). Dieses Grundmodell, das vor rund 100 Jahren entwickelt wurde, hat eine Schwache: Es ignoriert, dass Menschen in unterschiedlichem Ausmaß Kontakt miteinander haben. Dieses Ausmaß hängt von den sozialen Netzwerken ab, in denen Menschen leben. Am CSH Vienna wurde von Forschern um Stefan Thurner und Peter Klimek vor einigen Jahren ein Modell entwickelt, das den unterschiedlichen Kontakt bzw. die soziale Distanz zwischen Menschen explizit berücksichtigt (SIRX-Modell). Dieses Modell erwies sich als perfekt geeignet, die Quarantäne von Erkrankten und ein eigenverantwortliches »Social Distancing« in die Berechnungen einzubeziehen. In der Praxis sind damit Prognosen von ein bis zwei Wochen möglich.
- Einen anderen Weg gehen sogenannte »agentenbasierte Systeme« wie jenes, das von einem Konsortium um Niki Popper (TU Wien und DWH GmbH) entwickelt wurde: Bei diesem Verfahren werden im Computer sehr viele Individuen, deren Eigenschaften und Verhaltens-weisen nachgebildet. Dadurch lassen sich im Prinzip die Kontakte zwischen Menschen und möglichen Übertragungswege ziemlich realitätsnah nachbilden. Das Problem bei diesem Ansatz ist allerdings, dass man sehr genau wissen müsste, wie groß die jeweiligen Kontakt- und Transmissionswahrscheinlichkeiten sind, was man etwa anhand von Verkehrs- oder Handydaten mehr oder weniger gut schätzen kann. Wobei der Grundsatz gilt: Die Modelle sind nur so genau wie die Parameter, die man einführt. Da sich falsche Annahmen sehr stark auf die Dynamik des Modells auswirken, sind agentenbasierte Systeme in der Praxis nur für kurzfristige Prognosen (bis zu einer Woche) tauglich.

Ergänzt wurden diese beiden Verfahren – die, so berichten Insider, im Wesentlichen zu ähnlichen Ergebnissen kamen – durch ein Analogiemodell, das Mathematiker um Norbert Mauser (Wolfgang-Pauli-Institut) entwickelt haben. Dieses verzichtete größtenteils auf Annahmen, sondern bildete das Geschehen in Österreich mithilfe von Daten der vorangegangenen Entwick-

stop COVID-19 after a vaccine has been developed, all measures were aimed at avoiding overtaxing the capacity of available intensive care units.

Epidemiological simulation models were relied on to estimate the number of people who would become infected in the foreseeable future. In Austria, basically two methods were used, with teams of researchers advising the Federal Ministry of Health and supplying weekly prognoses. The basic data used derived from the Federal Government's electronic epidemiological reporting system, into which district authorities feed certain data information.

- Running with differential equations, SIR models describe the development over time within three compartments of individuals: those susceptible to contracting an infection (S), those infected (I), and those removed (R), i.e. immune or deceased individuals. This basic model, which was developed about 100 years ago, has one particular weakness: it ignores that the rate of contacts between people varies, depending on the social networks to which they belong. Several years ago, the team of researchers led by Stefan Thurner and Peter Klimek at the CSH Vienna therefore conceived a model that explicitly takes into account varying contact rates and the social distance between people (SIRX model). This model has proven perfectly capable of considering the quarantine of those infected and self-imposed social distancing in its computations. In practice it is possible to establish prognoses looking one to two weeks ahead.

- So-called "agent-based models" like the one developed by a pool of scientists headed by Niki Popper (Vienna University of Technology and dwh GmbH) employ a different method: a large number of individuals and their properties and behaviors are simulated in the computer, which essentially permits a quite realistic visualization of the contacts between people and possible transmission trajectories. However, the problem with this approach is that it requires a fairly precise knowledge of the respective probabilities of contact and transmission, which can be estimated more or less reliably from traffic or mobile data. The following principle applies: the models are only as accurate as the parameters that have been introduced. As false assumptions considerably influence the model's dynamics, in practice agent-based systems only lend themselves to short-term prognoses (up to one week).

These two methods, which according to reports from insiders basically supplied similar results, were complemented by an analogical modeling approach developed by mathematicians around Norbert Mauser

lung in China nach – mit (zumindest am Anfang der Ausbreitung der Pandemie) erstaunlich genauen Ergebnissen.

Welche Maßnahmen wirken wie gut?

Das Hauptproblem aller Modelle ist, dass – wie erwähnt – zu ihrer Kalibrierung möglichst genaue Daten zur Verfügung stehen müssen. Da das SARS-COV-2-Virus erst Ende 2019 erstmals registriert wurde, ist das Wissen um seine Eigenschaften und sein Verhalten noch spärlich. Doch mit den Wochen und Monaten, in denen die Pandemie über die Erde rollte, klärten sich manche Fakten, sodass mittlerweile einige fundiertere Aussagen getroffen werden können. Etwa über Gedankenspielereien der Sorte »Was wäre, wenn ...«. Nach Angaben der TU Wien wäre der Gipfel der Zahl der gleichzeitig Erkrankten viermal so hoch gewesen, wenn der Lockdown in Österreich eine Woche später erfolgt wäre. Ein anderes interessantes Ergebnis: Das Schließen von Schulen und Geschäften (zusätzlich zu den Abstands- und Hygieneregeln) allein hätte nicht ausgereicht, um die Ausbreitung der Krankheit in ausreichendem Ausmaß zu bremsen; erst die gleichzeitig erfolgte starke Reduktion der Freizeitkontakte führte zum gewünschten Ergebnis.

Mittlerweile kann man auch schon genauere Aussagen darüber treffen, welche Maßnahmen bei der Eindämmung der Virusausbreitung tatsächlich geholfen haben. Auch dieses Wissen könnte bei einer zweiten Coronawelle lebensrettend sein. An vielen Forschungsinstituten der Welt wurde unmittelbar nach Beginn der Pandemie begonnen, detaillierte Daten über getroffene Maßnahmen zu sammeln und dem Infektionsgeschehen gegenüberzustellen. Am CSH Vienna wurde beispielsweise eine Datenbank mit mehr als 170 verschiedenen Maßnahmen in mehr als 40 Staaten erstellt. Der Ländervergleich ist wichtig, um die Wirkung verschiedener Maßnahmen auseinanderrechnen zu können, wurden diese doch meist nicht einzeln, sondern bündelweise eingeführt – allerdings nicht überall zu den gleichen Bündeln geschnürt. Organisationen wie die Weltgesundheitsorganisation WHO fassen diese Datenbanken zusammen und nehmen Auswertungen vor. Erste Ergebnisse wurden Anfang Juni im Fachblatt The Lancet veröffentlicht. Demnach stellte sich – bei allerdings noch bescheidener Beweiskraft – als wichtigste Maßnahme das Einhalten von mindestens einem Meter Abstand heraus, gefolgt vom Tragen von Gesichtsmasken und dem Einsatz von Visieren, Schutzbrillen und Brillen. Die Studienautoren betonen, dass auch diese Vorkehrungen zusammengenommen keinen 100-prozentigen Schutz garantieren, sondern immer durch andere Maßnahmen wie regelmäßiges und gründliches Händewaschen ergänzt werden müssen.

Resilienz von Gesundheitssystemen

Eines der Hauptziele der gegen die Coronapandemie ergriffenen Maßnahmen war es, das Gesundheitssystem nicht zu überfordern. Es stellt

(Wolfgang Pauli Institute). It largely did without assumptions but visualized what was going on in Austria with the aid of data deriving from previous developments in China—with surprisingly accurate results (at least during the early phase of pandemic spreading).

The effectiveness of measures

As has been pointed out, the chief problem of all models is that data with as much accuracy as possible have to be made available. As the virus referred to as SARS-COV-2 was first registered toward the end of the year 2019, knowledge about its properties and behavior is still scarce. But during the weeks and months in which the pandemic has swept over Earth, several facts have cleared up so that it has meanwhile become possible to draw a number of well-founded conclusions—in the context of such mind games as "What if..." According to information supplied by the Vienna University of Technology, the peak of infections contracted simultaneously would have been four times as high if Austria had locked down the country a week later. Another interesting result: closing schools and stores (in addition to social distancing and hygiene rules) would not have been enough to sufficiently curb the dissemination of the disease; only taking the parallel measure of substantially reducing leisure contacts brought the desired result.

In the meantime, it is also possible to make more precise statements as to what measures actually helped contain the proliferation of the virus. This knowledge might save lives, should a second wave of COVID-19 occur. Immediately after the pandemic had begun, numerous research institutes started collecting detailed data about measures taken and relating them to the way the infection was spreading. At the CSH Vienna, for example, a database containing more than 170 different measures taken in more than 40 countries was set up. Drawing comparisons between countries is crucial to be able to tell the effects of individual measures apart, for in most cases they were not implemented one by one but in sets, which, however, differed from country to country. Organizations like the World Health Organization (WHO) consolidate these databases, on the basis of which evaluations are conducted. First results were published in early June in the medical journal *The Lancet*. According to these findings, which, however, are still based on modest evidence, maintaining a safe distance has turned out to be the most important measure, followed by wearing face masks and using visors, protective goggles, and spectacles. The authors of the study emphasize that these precautions, even if combined, do not guarantee 100 percent protection but should always be complemented by further measures, such as regular and careful handwashing.

sich die Frage, wie resilient das System zur Behandlung von Erkrankten überhaupt ist. Auch auf diese Frage haben Forscher des CSH Vienna kürzlich eine Antwort gefunden. Dazu wurde ein umfassendes Simulationsmodell des nationalen Gesundheitssystems entwickelt, in dem alle Patientinnen und Patienten sowie Ärztinnen und Ärzte als anonymisierte Avatare vertreten waren. Kalibriert wurde dieses Modell, das alle 121 Bezirke des Landes abdeckt, mit – vollständig anonymisierten – realen Daten. Dann wurde ein Stresstest durchgeführt, indem ein Gesundheitsdienstleister nach dem anderen aus dem System entfernt wurde und die Veränderungen der Patient*innenströme registriert wurden. Unterhalb einer kritischen Zahl von Anbietern traten schließlich kaskadenartige große Patient*innen-verschiebungen auf, sodass in bestimmten Regionen keine Anbieter mit freien Kapazitäten mehr zu finden waren. Die auf diese Weise gemessene regionale Resilienz unterscheidet sich von Bezirk zu Bezirk. Bemerkens-wert ist, dass sich diese Ergebnisse nicht mit simplen Pro-Kopf-Vergleichen von Ärzt*innen- und Bevölkerungsdichten, sondern nur ermitteln lassen, wenn man in Betracht zieht, wie sich das Netzwerk durch eine Störung restrukturiert. Nur so kann man systemrelevante Gesundheitsdienstleister identifizieren. Wenn man weiß, wo die Schwachstellen liegen, lassen sich diese auf relativ günstige Weise beheben, ohne dass es erst zu einem Engpass oder gar einem Kollaps kommen muss, die auf jeden Fall wesentlich teurer kommen würden.

Mit Simulationsmodellen kann auch zu einem gewissen Grad in die Zukunft geblickt und ermittelt werden, ob etwa auch in einigen Jahren genügend qualifiziertes Personal zur Verfügung stehen wird, oder ob in bestimmten Regionen durch kommende Pensionierungswellen oder Nichtnachbesetzung offener Stellen ernsthafte Engpässe auftreten werden. Dabei werden demografische Verschiebungen und eine Vermehrung von chronischen Krankheiten (durch die Alterung der Bevölkerung) genauso berücksichtigt wie etwa neu geschaffene medizinische Fakultäten. Das Ergebnis einer Studie des CSH Vienna für 21 europäische Länder ist sehr aufschlussreich: Praktisch überall werde es zwar möglich sein, in Ruhestand tretende Ärzt*innen durch nachrückende Jungmediziner*innen zu ersetzen. Doch es gibt einen starken Trend weg von der Allgemeinmedizin hin zur Spezialisierung. Im Fall von Österreich ergab sich zusätzlich eine anhaltende Verschiebung aus dem niedergelassenen Bereich zu angestellten Spitals-ärzt*innen. Die Forscherinnen und Forscher regen daher gezielte Anreize an, um diesen Trends gegenzusteuern.

Borkenkäfer & Co

Die Methoden der Komplexitätsforschung und besonders epidemio-logische Modelle können mit großem Gewinn auch in vielen anderen Bereichen Anwendung finden. Ein höchst aktuelles Beispiel ist die Ausbrei-tung von Schädlingen wie etwa von Borkenkäfern in Fichtenwäldern. Unter

The resilience of healthcare systems

One of the main goals of the measures taken to fight the coronavirus pandemic was to prevent an overload of the healthcare system. The basic question arises as to how resilient the system actually is with regard to the treatment of infected patients. Scientists of the CSH Vienna have recently come up with an answer. A comprehensive computer simulation of the national healthcare system was developed in which all patients and physicians were represented as anonymized avatars. The model, which comprised all of the country's 121 districts, was calibrated with—fully anonymized—real data. Then a stress test was conducted in the process of which health service providers were removed from the system one by one while changes in the influx of patients were registered. Below a critical number of providers, shifts in patient flows began cascading so that in certain regions it was no longer possible to spot providers offering free capacities. The degree of regional resilience thus measured differs from district to district. It is remarkable that one will not arrive at these results through simple per capita comparisons between physicians and population densities but only when considering how the network restructures in the case of interference. Only in this way can health service providers that are relevant for the system be identified. When the weak points are known they can be repaired at relatively reasonable costs without leading to a bottleneck or even collapse in the first place, which in any case would be considerably more expensive.

To a certain degree, computer simulation can also be used to look into the future and find out whether enough qualified staff will be available in a few years' time or whether serious bottlenecks will occur in certain regions due to waves of retirement or the non-replacement of vacancies. The method not only takes into account demographic shifts and a rise of chronic diseases (due to population aging) but also newly established medical university units. The findings of a study conducted at the CSH Vienna for 21 European countries are highly informative: It will be possible to replace retiring physicians by junior doctors practically everywhere. However, a strong tendency can be observed away from general practitioners toward medical specialists. In addition, a lasting shift from physicians running their own practice to employed hospital physicians has been found in the case of Austria. Researchers therefore suggest offering incentives to systematically counteract such adverse trends.

Bark beetles and the like

The methods of complexity science in general and epidemiological models in particular are also applicable in many other fields—and very profitably at that. A most recent example is the proliferation of

Federführung von Forschern der Wiener Universität für Bodenkultur und des Internationalen Instituts für angewandte Systemanalyse (IIASA) in Laxenburg wurde ein SIR-Modell für mehrere Waldschädlinge erstellt – konkret für den Buchdrucker, der derzeit den Fichtenbeständen vor allem im Waldviertel den Garaus macht, und den Birken-Moorwald-Herbstspanner, der in Skandinavien wütet. Das Modell wurde mit Daten der vergangenen Jahrzehnte gespeist. Das Ergebnis: Zum einen ist der lokale Schädlingsdruck entscheidend, zum anderen aber auch die Landschaftsstruktur – also die Verbindungen zwischen verschiedenen Forstrevieren. Das Modell, das in Zukunft noch verfeinert werden soll, erlaubt nun Vorhersagen, wie sich die Borkenkäfer weiter ausbreiten werden. Das ermöglicht eine zielgerichtete Bekämpfung durch genaues Monitoring am kritischen Stellen und umgehende Entfernung befallener Bäume aus dem Wald.

Krankes Milchvieh frühzeitig erkennen

Komplexitätsforscher sind derzeit auch in einem anderen Bereich der Landwirtschaft begehrte Kooperationspartner: Der CSH Vienna ist an dem österreichischen Kompetenzzentrum D4Dairy beteiligt, in dem 31 Wirtschafts- und 13 Forschungsinstitutionen einen Innovationssprung in der Milchwirtschaft erreichen wollen. Das D4 im Projektnamen steht für Digitalisierung, Datenintegration, Detection (Entdeckung bzw. Erkennung von Problemen) und Decision Support (Unterstützung bei Entscheidungsfindungen). Ein wesentlicher Projektteil befasst sich mit der Erhebung von Gesundheits- und Vitaldaten von Kühen durch innovative Sensoren und der Auswertung dieser Daten, um Krankheiten möglichst frühzeitig erkennen zu können. Dafür werden Methoden zur Datenmodellierung eingesetzt, die ursprünglich für die Humanmedizin entwickelt wurden.

Bienenschwärme und künstliche Austern

Auch in der biologischen Grundlagenforschung rücken die Erfassung und Beherrschung der komplexen Lebensvorgänge immer mehr ins Zentrum. An der Universität Graz wurde 2019 die interfakultäre Initiative »Complexity of Life in Basic Research and Innovation« (COLIBRI) gegründet. Forscherinnen und Forscher der naturwissenschaftlichen, der sozial- und wirtschaftswissenschaftlichen sowie der umwelt-, regional- und bildungswissenschaftlichen Fakultät bündeln ihr Fachwissen aus den jeweiligen Bereichen. Zum Einsatz kommen etwa analytische sowie computergestützte Methoden der Theorie strategischer Interaktion (Spieltheorie), der Netzwerkanalyse, der Optimierungstheorie und der Theorie der Entscheidungsfindung unter Unsicherheit. Zu den Schwerpunkten der Forschung gehört beispielsweise die Dynamik kollaborativer, synergistischer und symbiotischer Systeme wie etwa natürlicher oder technischer Schwarmintelligenzsysteme.

pests such as that of bark beetles in spruce forests. Under the supervision of researchers of the University of Natural Resources and Life Sciences in Vienna and the International Institute of Applied System Analysis (IIASA) in Laxenburg, a SIR model has been developed for a number of forest pests—to be concrete, for the European spruce bark beetle, which is currently annihilating spruce populations in the Waldviertel region in Lower Austria, as well as the autumnal moth, which is raging in Scandinavia. The model was fed with data of past decades. The result: what is crucial is the local infestation pressure on the one hand and the landscape structure—the ways in which the various forest districts are connected—on the other. The model, which is to be improved in the future, permits forecasts as to how the bark beetle will continue to spread. This allows for systematic control through accurate monitoring of critical areas and a prompt removal of infested trees from forests.

Identifying sick dairy cattle at an early stage

Complexity scientists are currently also much in demand as collaborating partners in agriculture: the CSH Vienna cooperates with the Austrian competence center D4Dairy, where 31 business partners and 13 research institutions aim to bring about a major innovation leap in dairy farming. The D4 in the name of the project refers to digitization, data integration, detection, and decision support. A major part of the project is concerned with the collection of health data and vital signs of cows through innovative sensors and with the analysis of the collected data so as to recognize diseases at an early stage. Methods of data modeling are employed that were originally developed for human medicine.

Swarms of bees and artificial oysters

In fundamental biological research, too, the acquisition and control of complex vital processes are increasingly shifting into focus. The initiative "Complexity of Life in Basic Research and Innovation" (COLIBRI) was launched at the University of Graz in 2019. Experts of three departments (the Department of Natural Sciences, the Department of Social and Economic Sciences, and the Department of Life, Regional, and Educational Sciences) pool knowledge from their respective fields. Analytical and computer-aided methods related to the theory of strategic interaction (game theory), network analysis, mathematical optimization, and theory of choice under uncertainty are employed. Research concentrates, among other things, on the dynamics of collaborative, synergistic, and symbiotic systems, including natural or computational collective intelligence systems.

In diesem Bereich betreten Forscher der Uni Graz seit Jahren völliges Neuland: Aus der Art, wie sich etwa Bienenschwärme organisieren, wurden Algorithmen abgeleitet, die man in kleine schwarmbildende Roboter – etwa in künstliche Muscheln, Insekten oder Fische – implementiert hat. Nun wird untersucht, wie diese »Modellorganismen« mit »echten« Tieren interagieren, welche Rückkopplungsschleifen sich dabei ergeben und wie sich evolutionäre Algorithmen an dieses »Zusammenleben« anpassen. Diese Biohybrid-IKT-Systeme sollen Wissen darüber generieren, wie die komplexen Netze der Natur funktionieren und reguliert werden. Die Forscher erwarten, dass ihre Arbeit Auswirkungen auf Landwirtschaft, Tierhaltung und Umweltschutz haben wird. ✖

Scientists at the University of Graz have broken new ground in this field for several years now: algorithms have been deduced from the way in which swarms of bees organize themselves and subsequently been implemented in small swarming or schooling robots—such as artificial shells, insects, or fish. It is examined how these "model organisms" interact with "real" animals, what feedback loops emerge from this, and how evolutionary algorithms adjust to this form of "cohabitation." These bio-hybrid ICT systems are expected to generate knowledge about how complex networks function and are regulated in nature. Scientists reckon that their work will impact on agriculture, animal husbandry, and environmental protection. ×

Klima und Dekarbonisierung

Das Klimageschehen ist ein komplexes System par excellence – mit einer Vielzahl an Verknüpfungen und Rückkopplungsschleifen. Gleiches gilt für alle Anstrengungen, das Weltklima im Lot zu halten und unseren Lebensstil zu dekarbonisieren.

Das Klimageschehen auf der Erde ist ein hochkomplexes System, das sich aus vielen Teilsystemen zusammensetzt, die miteinander verknüpft sind (Darstellung nach Österreichischem Sachstandsbericht AAR14):

- **Atmosphäre:** die Lufthülle der Erde. Sie macht zwar nur einen winzigen Teil der von der Sonne erwärmten Masse aus, ihre Zusammensetzung, insbesondere ihr Kohlendioxid-, Wasserdampf- und Aerosolgehalt, hat jedoch wesentlichen Einfluss auf die Temperatur der Erdoberfläche, weil sie terrestrische Strahlung absorbieren und auf die Erdoberfläche zurückstrahlen kann. Ebenso können die enthaltenen Wolken und Aerosole solare Strahlung reflektieren und absorbieren. Die Atmosphäre hat eine vergleichsweise nur geringe Speicherkapazität für Energie, allerdings kann sie einige für den Energie- und Strahlungshaushalt sehr wesentliche Spurenstoffe wie Kohlendioxid (CO_2), Methan und Lachgas über Jahrzehnte oder noch länger speichern.
- **Hydrosphäre:** Wasser in Ozeanen, Seen und Flüssen, Grundwasser, aber auch Wasserdampf und Wolkentropfen. Sie hat aufgrund der großen Masse und der hohen spezifischen Wärmekapazität des Wassers eine sehr hohe Speicherkapazität für Energie, wodurch sie jahreszeitliche, aber auch längerfristige Temperaturschwankungen stark dämpft. Wie die Atmosphäre ist auch der Ozean ein wichtiger Speicher für klimarelevante Spurenstoffe. Die Hydrosphäre enthält die für das menschliche Wohlergehen so wichtigen Trink- und Nutzwasservorräte, deren Änderungen nicht nur klimabedingt, sondern auch durch Dammbauten, Bewässerung und andere direkte menschliche Eingriffe bedingt sind.
- **Kryosphäre:** Wasser in fester Form, Gletscher und Inlandeis, Permafrostböden, die Schneedecke, Meereis sowie gefrorene Wolken- und Niederschlagspartikel. Die Kryosphäre wächst bzw. schrumpft auf Kosten bzw. zugunsten der Hydrosphäre, indem Wasser gefriert oder

3.2

Klima

FOCUS: CLIMATE

Climate and Decarbonization

The climate system is a complex system par excellence—with a large number of links and feedback loops. The same applies to all efforts to keep the global climate in balance and to decarbonise our lifestyle.

Climatic events on Earth depend on a highly complex system consisting of multiple interrelated subsystems (quoted according to AAR14):

- **Atmosphere:** the layer of air surrounding Earth. Although it represents only a tiny part of the mass warmed by the Sun, its composition, especially its contents of carbon dioxide, water vapor, and aerosols, has a considerable impact on the temperature of the Earth's surface because the atmosphere absorbs terrestrial radiation and reflects it back. Similarly, the clouds and aerosols the atmosphere contains reflect and absorb solar radiation. The capacity of the Earth's atmosphere to store energy is comparatively low, but it is capable of storing a number of trace gases crucial for the Earth's energy and radiation budget, such as carbon dioxide (CO_2), methane, and nitrous oxide, over decades or even longer.

- **Hydrosphere:** water in oceans, lakes, and rivers, groundwater, as well as water vapor and cloud droplets. Due to its huge mass and the high specific heat capacity of water, its capacity to store energy is extremely high so that it is capable of substantially stabilizing both seasonal and more long-term changes in temperature. Similar to the atmosphere, the ocean is an important reservoir for climate-relevant trace elements. The hydrosphere contains the drinking and processing water so essential for human well-being. Changes in water supplies are not only due to the climate but also the result of direct human interference, such as through the building of embankment dams and irrigation.

- **Cryosphere:** water in solid form, including glaciers and ice sheets, permafrost grounds, the snow cover, sea ice, as well as frozen cloud and precipitation particles. The cryosphere grows or shrinks at the cost or to the benefit of the hydrosphere through water freezing or melting. In polar regions it can lead to increasing

schmilzt. In Polargebieten führt sie durch ihre hohe Albedo (Reflexionsvermögen für solare Strahlung) und ihre Fähigkeit, den Energiestrom zwischen warmem Ozean und kalter Atmosphäre zu unterbinden, zu verstärkten Temperatur- und Niederschlagsschwankungen bzw. Schwankungen im Spurenstoffaustausch.

- **Lithosphäre:** der feste, unbelebte Teil der Erde. Sie hat trotz ihrer enormen Masse eine nur relativ geringe effektive Wärmekapazität, weil Wärme nur langsam und in geringe Tiefen transportiert wird. Sie ist bei Weitem das größte Reservoir von Kohlenstoff in Form von Kalk, Kohle, Erdgas und Erdöl. Während natürliche Prozesse lithosphärischen Kohlenstoff nur langsam in die Atmosphäre freisetzen können, geschieht dies durch anthropogene Prozesse wie Verbrennung in vergleichsweise kurzer Zeit. Auch ihre sonstige chemische Zusammensetzung und ihre Topografie haben starke Auswirkung auf das Klima, vor allem regional und lokal, sowie auf die darauf befindliche Biosphäre.
- **Biosphäre:** Flora und Fauna, die sich in den vier obigen Sphären findet. Auch der Mensch ist als Teil der Biosphäre zu betrachten. Trotz ihrer relativ geringen Masse hat sie durch ihre Fähigkeit, wichtige Spurenstoffkreisläufe wie den von CO_2 oder CH_4 zu kontrollieren, große Bedeutung für das globale Klima. Menschliche Aktivitäten verändern die Biosphäre direkt durch Landnutzung oder Verbauung, aber auch indirekt durch die Emission von Spurengasen und deren Folgen.

Ein wesentlicher Teil der Klimaforschung beschäftigt sich mit der Bestimmung der Reservoirs und Flüsse von klimarelevanten Substanzen zwischen den Subsystemen. Behandelt werden vor allem Energie-, Wasser- und Kohlenstoffkreisläufe. Die Vorgänge werden in hohem Ausmaß vom Energieaustausch der Erde mit dem Weltraum und somit vom Strahlungshaushalt der Erde beeinflusst. Dieser stellt sich als die Differenz zwischen der von der Sonne empfangenen Strahlungsenergie und der von der Erde wieder in den Weltraum abgestrahlten Energie dar. Dieses Verhältnis wiederum wird im Wesentlichen von drei Größen beeinflusst: von der Solarkonstante, vom planetaren Albedo-Effekt und vom Gehalt der Treibhausgase in der Atmosphäre.

Schon diese kurze Zusammenstellung zeigt, wie unheimlich komplex das Klimasystem ist. Um mit dieser Unzahl von relevanten Einflussfaktoren und deren Verknüpfungen und Wechselwirkungen umgehen zu können, werden Simulationsmodelle konstruiert.

Modelle versuchen, die Komplexität überschaubar zu machen

Ein Simulationsmodell ist eine quantitative, näherungsweise Beschreibung des natürlichen Systems. Dabei wird versucht, die physikalischen und biogeochemischen Prozesse in den verschiedenen Teilsystemen (Atmosphä-

variations in temperature and precipitation and to fluctuations in the exchange of trace elements due to its high albedo (reflection of solar radiation) and ability to block the energy flow between the warm ocean and the cold atmosphere.

- **Lithosphere:** the rigid, inanimate crust of Earth. Despite its enormous mass, its heat capacity is relatively low because heat is transported only at a slow pace and to low depths. It is by far the largest reservoir of carbon in the form of lime, coal, natural gas, and mineral oil. Whereas lithospheric carbon is released into the atmosphere through natural processes only very slowly, this happens within comparatively short time through anthropogenic processes like combustion. Its other chemical components and its topography also have a strong impact on the climate, particularly regionally and locally, as well as the biosphere, for which the lithosphere provides a habitat.

- **Biosphere:** the flora and fauna existing in the four spheres mentioned above. Humans are also regarded as part of the biosphere. Although its mass is relatively low, it has a powerful effect on the global climate because of its capacity to control important cycles of trace elements like CO_2 or CH_4. Human activities influence the biosphere directly through land use and development, as well as indirectly through the emission of trace gases and their consequences.

An important aspect of climate research has to do with the identification of the reservoirs of climate-relevant substances and their flows back and forth between the subsystems. Energy, water, and carbon dioxide cycles are particularly relevant in this respect. These processes are influenced to a high degree by Earth's energy exchange with the universe and thus by the Earth's radiation budget. The latter is the difference between the radiation energy received from the sun und the energy radiated back into the universe from Earth. This relationship in turn depends largely on three parameters: the solar constant, the planetary albedo effect, and the content of greenhouse gases in the atmosphere.

Even this brief summary shows how unbelievably complex our climate system is. Simulation models are constructed in order to be able to handle this myriad of influencing factors and their interrelationships and mutual reactions.

re, Hydrosphäre etc.) so genau wie möglich zu beschreiben und die Kopplung zwischen den Teilsystemen entsprechend abzubilden. Solche Modelle sind keine statistische Extrapolation aus der Vergangenheit, sondern simulieren das Verhalten des Systems aufgrund allgemein gültiger physikalischer Gesetze. Dabei stellen sich mehrere große Herausforderungen: Zum einen ist die Parametrisierung der Modelle auf Basis von realen Messdaten entscheidend, zum anderen müssen die zahlreichen Rückkopplungsschleifen ausreichend genau und vollständig formuliert werden. Diese Rückkopplungen sind in hohem Ausmaß nicht linear; eine Berechnung der sogenannten »tipping points«, jener Punkte, an denen der Zustand des Systems in einen anderen kippt, ist derzeit extrem schwierig. Überdies müssen Modelle notwendigerweise vereinfachende Annahmen treffen.

Es gibt bereits eine große Anzahl von unterschiedlichen Modellen. Die Fortschritte in der Klimaforschung beruhen in einem großen Ausmaß darauf, dass die Modelle immer umfassender werden und immer mehr Parameter einbeziehen. In manchen Teilbereichen, etwa beim Verhalten von Aerosolen in der Atmosphäre, gibt es noch viele Unsicherheiten. Ein wirklich umfassendes und ausgereiftes Modell des gesamten »Systems Erde« gibt es noch nicht.

Eine zentrale Einschränkung bei Klimamodellen ist derzeit die räumliche Auflösung in der Größenordnung von 100 Kilometern, die aufgrund der numerischen Lösungsverfahren und der zur Verfügung stehenden Rechnerkapazität beschränkt ist. Um feiner aufgelöste Daten zu erhalten – was etwa im Alpenland Österreich unerlässlich ist, um regionale Aussagen über die Folgen der künftigen Klimaentwicklung machen zu können –, werden Downscaling-Verfahren eingesetzt – so etwa statistische Methoden oder »Nesting«-Verfahren, bei denen die Ränder eines regionalen Modells durch Werte des globalen Modells definiert werden. Dabei müssen allerdings viele Einschränkungen in Kauf genommen werden.

Simulationen des zukünftigen Klimas basieren auf sogenannten »Szenarien«, in denen mögliche Zukünfte im Hinblick auf Bevölkerungswachstum, Wirtschaftsentwicklung, Landnutzungsänderungen, Innovationstätigkeit, internationale Kooperation usw. formuliert werden. Daraus ergeben sich Werte für die zu erwartenden Emissionen von Treibhausgasen, die schließlich als Input für Klimamodelle dienen. Die derzeit im Rahmen des UN-Weltklimarates IPCC gebräuchlichen Szenarien wurden übrigens in Österreich entwickelt, nämlich am IIASA (International Institute for Applied Systems Analysis) in Laxenburg.

Mammutaufgabe Dekarbonisierung

Die Emissionspfade, die sich aus den Szenarien und den Klimamodellen ergeben, erfordern vielfältige Maßnahmen, um aus eingetretenen technologischen Pfaden auszubrechen und einen Umschwung zu »grünen« Verfahren der Energiegewinnung und -verwendung einzuleiten. Forscherin-

Models as attempts to make the complexity of the climate system graspable

A simulation model is a quantitative and approximate description of the natural system. It seeks to describe the physical and biochemical processes of the individual subsystems (atmosphere, hydrosphere, etc.) as precisely as possible and depict the interconnection between the subsystems accordingly. Such models do not represent statistic extrapolations from the past but simulate the behavior of the respective system on the basis of generally valid physical laws. This confronts researchers with a number of major challenges: on the one hand, the parameterization of models on the basis of real measuring data is decisive; on the other hand, the numerous feedback loops must be formulated sufficiently accurately and exhaustively. These feedbacks are mostly nonlinear; it is currently extremely difficult to calculate the so-called "tipping points," i.e., those points at which critical changes in the state of the system occur. In addition, models necessarily have to make simplified assumptions.

By now, a large number of different models exist. Progress made in climate research depends to a considerable extent on models that have become increasingly comprehensive and take more and more parameters into account. In some subareas, for example as to the behavior of aerosols in the atmosphere, there are still many uncertainties. A truly holistic and fully developed model of the entire "System of Earth" does not exist yet.

Currently, a central limitation of climate models is a spatial resolution in the order of 100 kilometers, which is restricted due to numerical procedures and available computing capacities. In order to obtain data of a higher resolution—which is indispensible in an alpine country like Austria in order to be able to make regional predictions about the consequences of the future climate development—downscaling methods have been employed, such as statistical methods or the method of nesting, by which the margins of a regional model are defined through values of the global model. However, numerous inadequacies have to be put up with.

Simulations of the future climate are based on so-called "scenarios" in which possible forms of future developments with regard to population growth, economic development, changes in land use, innovation, international cooperation, etc. are formulated. This results in values for the expected emissions of greenhouse gases that will eventually serve as input for climate models. By the way, the scenarios currently used by the UN's Intergovernmental Panel on Climate Change (IPCC) were developed in Austria, namely at the IIASA (International Institute for Applied Systems Analysis) in Laxenburg, Lower Austria.

nen und Forscher am IIASA haben diese Herausforderung systematisch so zusammengefasst: »Die Dekarbonisierung von Energiesystemen erfordert integrierte Ansätze für Stromerzeugung und -übertragung, Gebäude, Verkehr und Industrie, die in drei verschiedene Bereiche unterteilt sind.

- Der erste befasst sich mit der Dekarbonisierung der Stromerzeugung durch Umstellung von fossilen Brennstoffen auf kohlenstofffreie Quellen, darunter Wind-, Solar-, Wasser-, Geothermie- und Gezeitenenergie. Einige Länder könnten auch die Kernenergie ausbauen oder eine fortgesetzte Nutzung fossiler Brennstoffe mit Kohlenstoffabscheidung und -speicherung (ccs) in Betracht ziehen. Smart-Grid-Management und Stromübertragung über große Entfernungen können Schwankungen ausgleichen, Unterbrechungen beheben, den Stromspeicherbedarf reduzieren und die Effizienz von Stromnetzen steigern.
- Zweitens müssen die Länder die Effizienz beim Endenergieverbrauch wie beim Transport, Heizen und Kühlen von Gebäuden sowie in der Industrie und bei Haushaltsgeräten erhöhen.
- Drittens geht es um die Elektrifizierung der derzeitigen Nutzung fossiler Brennstoffe außerhalb der Stromerzeugung. Das betrifft den Ersatz von Fahrzeugen mit Verbrennungsmotoren durch Elektro- oder Wasserstofffahrzeuge, Kessel und Heizgeräte sowie verschiedene industrielle Prozesse wie die Stahl- und Zementherstellung. Biokraftstoffe und Biomasse können saubere Wärmeenergie liefern, ihre Verwendung muss jedoch die Übereinstimmung mit der Ernährungssicherheit, dem Erhalt der biologischen Vielfalt und anderen ›Nachhaltigen Entwicklungszielen‹ gewährleisten.«

Welche Mammutaufgabe das ist, wird im Lauf der weiteren Ausführungen deutlich: »Das Design und die Implementierung dieser Transformation sind komplex. Ein negativer Trade-off-Effekt könnte sich ergeben, wenn der Zugang zu Energie und die Leistbarkeit parallel zur Dekarbonisierung vernachlässigt werden. Ein solches Versagen kann zu öffentlichem Widerstand gegen die Klimapolitik führen. [...] ein effizienteres und kostengünstigeres Energiesystem kann einen erheblichen Rebound-Effekt erzeugen, bei dem das Nachfragewachstum die erhöhte Ressourceneffizienz kompensiert. Die Verwendung anderer knapper Ressourcen wie knapper Metalle kann schwerwiegende ökologische und soziale Folgen haben.«

Komplexe industrielle Energiesysteme

Dekarbonisierung erfordert also einen umfassenden Ansatz, wie ihn beispielsweise der Innovationsverbund NEFI (»New Energy for Industry«) verfolgt, in dem rund 100 Partner aus Unternehmen, Forschungseinrichtungen und öffentlichen Institutionen in Österreich zusammenarbeiten. NEFI ist eine sogenannte »Vorzeigeregion Energie« des Klima- und Energiefonds,

The Mammoth Task of Decarbonization

Emission pathways resulting from the scenarios and climate models that have been developed require a diversified set of measures in order to break away from well-trodden technological paths and initiate a turnaround toward "green" methods of energy generation and use. IIASA researchers have systematically summed up this challenge as follows: "Decarbonizing energy systems calls for integrated approaches across power generation and transmission, building, transport, and industry, which fall into three distinct areas.

- The first covers the decarbonization of electricity generation by shifting from fossil fuels to zero-carbon sources, including wind, solar, hydro, geothermal, and tidal energy, among others. Some countries may also expand nuclear power or consider continued fossil fuel use with carbon capture and storage (CCS). Smart-grid management and long-distance power transmission can address intermittency, remedy interruptions, reduce electricity storage needs, and increase the efficiency of power grids.
- Second, countries need to improve energy efficiency in final energy use, including transport, the heating and cooling of buildings, industrial energy use, and household appliances.
- The third is the electrification of current uses of fossil fuels outside power generation, such as the replacement of the internal combustion engine through electric or hydrogen vehicles, boilers and heaters, as well as various industrial processes, including steel and cement production. Biofuels and biomass can provide clean thermal energy, but their use must ensure consistency with food security, biodiversity conservation, and other Sustainable Development Goals."

By what is pointed out further, it becomes clear what a mammoth task this is: "The design and implementation of this transformation are complex. A negative trade-off effect could arise from neglecting the access to and affordability of energy while concentrating on decarbonization. Such failure might lead to public resistance to climate policies. A more efficient and low-cost energy system may generate a substantial rebound effect in which demand growth compensates for increased resource efficiency. The use of other scarce resources, such as scarce metals, might result in serious ecological and social consequences."

in deren Rahmen mit innovativen Energietechnologien aus Österreich Musterlösungen für intelligente, sichere und leistbare Energie- und Verkehrssysteme der Zukunft entwickelt und demonstriert werden, und basiert auf einer Initiative und Förderungen der Länder Oberösterreich und Steiermark. Die Koordination des Innovationsverbundes liegt beim AIT Austrian Institute of Technology und der Montanuniversität Leoben, dem Energiesparverband Oberösterreich und der oberösterreichischen Standortagentur Business Upper Austria.

Im Rahmen einer Reihe konkreter Einzelprojekte werden Methoden entwickelt und in der Praxis erprobt, mit denen die Energieeffizienz in der Güterproduktion erhöht und CO_2-Emissionen stark gesenkt werden können. Das erfordert neben neuen Einzeltechnologien auch technische und ökonomische Lösungen zum systematischen Roll-out, neue regulatorische Rahmenbedingungen sowie neue Geschäftsmodelle, die über die bestehenden betrieblichen Aktivitäten der Unternehmen hinausgehen. Überdies braucht es Änderungen des übergeordneten Energiesystems, etwa einen Ausbau erneuerbarer Energieträger, eine sektorübergreifende Energieinfrastrukturplanung, eine konsequente Nutzung von Abwärmepotenzialen und eine optimierte Bereitstellung und Nutzung energetischer Flexibilitäten. NEFI verfolgt daher einen systemischen Ansatz, der Industrie und Gewerbe aus unterschiedlichen Sparten als zentralen Teil eines integrierten Energieverbundes sieht. Als Schlüsseltechnologien werden Wärmepumpen zur Abwärmenutzung, innovative Speichertechnologien sowie neue Lösungen zur Nutzung erneuerbarer Energie in industriellen Energiesystemen eingesetzt.

Eines der NEFI-Projekte ist SANBA: In der ehemaligen Martinek-Kaserne in Baden bei Wien mit denkmalgeschützten Gebäuden aus den 1930er-Jahren soll ein Niedertemperaturheiz- und Kühlnetz entwickelt werden, wobei Abwärme aus dem Abwasser der benachbarten NÖM-Molkerei sowie lokal verfügbare erneuerbare Wärmequellen wie Geothermie verwendet werden. Erforscht werden Möglichkeiten zur Integration dieser Bausteine in eine dezentrale Energieversorgung auf Quartiersebene.

Ein anderes NEFI-Projekt beschäftigt sich mit der Nutzung von Abwärme im Zementwerk Gmunden. Im Zentrum steht eine Hochtemperatur-Wärmeauskopplung aus dem 400 Grad Celsius heißen Zementabgas. Die gewonnene Energie soll in eine Hochtemperaturleitung zur Dampfversorgung für Großabnehmer im Stadtgebiet eingespeist werden, die mit einem Langzeitwärmespeicher (bis zu zwei Monate) gekoppelt ist. Neben den technologischen Aspekten werden auch die Wirtschaftlichkeit und die gesellschaftliche Akzeptanz evaluiert.

Einen völlig anderen Schwerpunkt hat – um noch ein drittes Beispiel zu nennen – das NEFI-Projekt »Clean Energy for Tourism« (CE4T) in Salzburg, dessen Ziel eine Dekarbonisierung der Wintertourismusbranche unter Verwendung modernster Digitalisierungstechnik ist. Allein für die Basisbe-

Complex industrial energy systems

Decarbonization thus requires a holistic approach such as that pursued by the NEFI (New Energy for Industry) innovation network, in which some 100 partners from the business world, research, and public institutions in Austria collaborate. NEFI is a so-called Energy Model Region supported by the Austrian Climate and Energy Fund and based on an initiative of and funding from the federal states of Upper Austria and Styria. Within its framework, model solutions for intelligent, secure, and affordable energy and transport systems of the future are developed and demonstrated with the aid of innovative energy technologies made in Austria. This innovation network is coordinated by the AIT Austrian Institute of Technology, the Leoben Mining University, the Upper Austrian Energy Saving Association, and the industrial location agency Business Upper Austria.

Methods contributing to the improvement of energy efficiency in the production of industrial goods and to a substantial reduction of CO_2 emissions are developed and put to the practical test within the framework of specific projects. In addition to new individual technologies, this also requires technical and economic solutions for their systematic deployment, as well as new regulatory master conditions and business models going beyond the existing operational activities of businesses and industries. Moreover, adjustments of the overriding energy system are called for: a coherent and immediate development of renewable energy sources, an integrated energy infrastructure planning across sectors, a consistent exploitation of waste heat potentials and an optimized supply and utilization of energetic flexibilities. NEFI therefore pursues a systematic approach that sees industries and trades of various branches as central stakeholders within an integrated energy network. Heat pumps facilitating the utilization of waste heat, innovative storage technologies, and new solutions for the use of renewable energy in industrial energy systems are employed as key technologies.

One of the relevant NEFI projects is SANBA: At the former Martinek barracks in Baden near Vienna, in buildings from the 1930s listed as cultural heritage, a low-temperature heating and cooling grid is about to be developed, using waste heat gained from the waste water of the adjacent NÖM dairy plant and such locally available renewable heat sources as geothermal energy. The project explores the possibilities of integrating these building blocks to ensure a decentralized energy supply system at district level.

Another NEFI project is concerned with the use of waste heat from the Gmunden cement plant. The focus is on high-temperature heat recuperation from 400-degree-Celsius cement waste gas. The energy gained is to be fed into a high-temperature grid for the steam

schneiung (30 Zentimeter) zu Beginn der Wintersaison werden bis zu 15 MWh Energie pro Hektar benötigt. Die damit verbundenen Lastspitzen sind eine Herausforderung für die regenerative Energieversorgung und das Energienetz. Das Projekt beinhaltet den Aufbau eines Energiemonitorings zur Steigerung der Energieeffizienz, eine Dekarbonisierung der Energieaufbringung und die Integration von erneuerbaren Energieerzeugungseinheiten in das Gesamtsystem.

Wasserstoff & Co

Eine zweite Schiene neben der Integration bestehender Technologien in Energiesysteme ist die Entwicklung neuer, disruptiver Technologien. Die EU und die österreichische Bundesregierung setzen beispielsweise stark auf Wasserstoff und andere »grüne« Gase (wie Biomethan oder synthetisches Methan auf Basis erneuerbaren Stroms). Im aktuellen Regierungsprogramm ist festgehalten, dass Österreich Innovationsführer bei Wasserstofftechnologie und zur »Wasserstoffnation Nummer 1« werden solle. Anvisiert wird vor allem die Herstellung der Gase auf Basis von Überschussstrom. Wasserstoff ist ein potenziell unbegrenzt verfügbarer, sicherer und effizienter Energieträger, der aus erneuerbaren Quellen herstellbar ist.

Es gibt zahlreiche Anwendungsmöglichkeiten von Wasserstoff, etwa in industriellen Systemen, im Mobilitätssektor oder als Speichermedium, um einen flexibleren Einsatz und Betrieb bestehender Infrastruktur zu ermöglichen. Als besonders interessant erscheint eine Sektorenkopplung (Strom – Wärme – Gas bzw. Haushalt – Industrie – Verkehr – Landwirtschaft). Entscheidend wird sein, dass die gesamte Wertschöpfungskette (Produktion, Verteilung, Speicherung, Endverbrauch) emissionsfrei gestaltet werden kann. Derzeit wird Wasserstoff fast zur Gänze aus Erdgas hergestellt, was hohe CO_2-Emissionen mit sich bringt. In Zukunft sollen indes ausschließlich erneuerbare Energiequellen wie Wind oder Fotovoltaik zum Einsatz kommen. Bei einzelnen Komponenten einer künftigen Wasserstoffwirtschaft – etwa bei großtechnischen Speichern, Elektrolyseuren, Brennstoffzellen oder Gasmotoren – macht man in der Forschung und Entwicklung Fortschritte. Substanzielle Fragen gibt es allerdings noch hinsichtlich der Systemintegration. Derzeit verhindern eine fehlende Wasserstoffinfrastruktur und die (noch) hohen Gestehungskosten eine großflächige Marktdurchdringung dieser Technologien.

Transformation im Dienst des Klimaschutzes

Nach übereinstimmender Ansicht aller Experten, vom UN-Weltklimarat bis zum Climate Change Centre Austria, vom Österreichischen Wirtschaftsforschungsinstitut (Wifo) bis zur Europäischen Kommission, verlangt das Erreichen des im Pariser Weltklimavertrag festgelegten Zieles, die Erwär-

supply of large consumers in the municipal area and combined with long-term heat storage (up to two months). In addition to technological aspects, economic viability and social acceptance are being evaluated.

To mention a third example, the NEFI project Clean Energy for Tourism (CE4T) in Salzburg has an entirely different focus. Its goal is the decarbonization of the winter tourism industry using state-of-the-art digitization technology. For the basic production of artificial snow (30 centimeters) at the beginning of the winter season alone, up to 15 MWh of energy per hectare are needed. The resulting peak loads pose a challenge to renewable energy supply and the energy system. The project comprises the implementation of energy monitoring for the sake of an improvement of energy efficiency, a decarbonization of energy supplies, and integration of renewable energy production units into the overall system.

Hydrogen and the like

A second line alongside the integration of existing technologies into energy systems is the development of new, disruptive technologies. For instance, the EU and the Austrian government strongly believe in hydrogen and other "green" gases (such as biomethane or synthetic methane based on renewable electricity). The government program states that Austria should become an innovative leader in the field of hydrogen technology and "Hydrogen Nation No. 1." The focus is primarily placed on the production of gases on the basis of excess current. Hydrogen is a secure and efficient energy carrier that is potentially available in unlimited quantities, as it can be produced from renewable sources.

There are numerous applications for hydrogen, including industrial systems, the mobility sector, or as a storage medium, so as to enable a more flexible use and operation of extant infrastructure. Sector coupling (electricity—heat—gas or household—industry—transport—agriculture) appears to be particularly promising. What will be decisive is that it will be possible to devise the entire value creation chain (production, distribution, storage, final consumption) as being emission-free. Currently, hydrogen is produced almost completely from natural gas, which entails high CO_2 emissions. In the future, however, exclusively renewable energy sources like wind or photovoltaics will be used. In research and development progress has been made in the case of individual components of the future hydrogen economy, such as large-scale industrial storage, electrolyzers, fuel cells, or gas engines. On the other hand, considerable problems still have to be coped with when it comes to system integration. Presently, the lack of a hydrogen infrastructure and (still-)high production costs prevent these technologies from penetrating the market on a large scale.

mung auf maximal zwei Grad über dem vorindustriellen Niveau zu begrenzen – was einer Absenkung der Treibhausgasemissionen um 90 Prozent bis
2050 entspricht –, entschlossenes Handeln von vielen Seiten. »Dies erfordert
mehr als inkrementell verbesserte Produktionstechnologien, grünere
Konsumgüter und eine Politik, die marginale Effizienzsteigerungen anstößt«,
heißt es im Österreichischer Sachstandsbericht 2014 (AAR14). Es brauche
vielmehr »eine Transformation der Interaktion zwischen Wirtschaft,
Gesellschaft und Umwelt«. Diese Ansicht steckt auch hinter aktuellen
Konzepten wie der Österreichischen Klima- und Energiestrategie (#mis-
sion2030) oder dem »Europäischen Green Deal«, die auf Basis einer Transformation hin zu einer dekarbonisierten Gesellschaft einen neuen Wachstums-
schub für die österreichische und europäische Wirtschaft bringen sollen.

In den Sozialwissenschaften versteht man unter »Transformationen«
Prozesse, die physische oder qualitative Änderungen in Systemen hervorrufen und deren Form, Struktur oder Bedeutung verändern. Es handelt
sich dabei, wie es etwa in den Berichten des UN-Weltklimarates (IPCC) formuliert wird, um »Änderungen der Grundeigenschaften von Systemen inklusive
des Wertesystems, der regulativen, legislativen oder bürokratischen Regime,
der finanziellen Institutionen sowie technologischer oder biologischer
Systeme«. Ein umfassender Lösungsansatz muss also Wechselwirkungen
komplexer dynamischer Systeme auf verschiedenen Skalenebenen berücksichtigen. Beispiele für solche Interaktionen sind das Zusammenwirken von
Klimawandel, Mobilitätsverhalten und Landnutzungsänderungen, von
Bevölkerungsentwicklung, Gesundheitszustand der Bevölkerung und
Umweltschädigung, von technologischem Wandel und globaler Marktin-
tegration sowie die Tatsache, dass einige Teile der Welt sich rasch verändern,
während andere in Stagnation und Armut verharren. Außerdem wird zunehmend erkannt, dass Nachhaltigkeitsprobleme in den Lebensstilen und
der damit verbundenen derzeitigen Organisationsform von Produktion und
Konsum begründet sind. In struktureller Hinsicht stehen Klimawandel und
übermäßiger Ressourcenverbrauch in engem Zusammenhang mit der
derzeit vorherrschenden wirtschaftlichen Ordnung.

Um gangbare Pfade in Richtung Nachhaltigkeit entwerfen zu können,
sind somit umfassende sozioökonomische Veränderungsprozesse nötig,
die auf Nachhaltigkeit abzielen: eine »sozioökologische Transformation«.
Sozioökologische Systeme sind komplex: Sie verändern sich dynamisch,
setzten sich aus zahlreichen Subsystemen mit vielen Rückkopplungen
zusammen, weisen viele Nichtlinearitäten auf und sind in hohem Maße
pfadabhängig. Sie sind durch Ungewissheit charakterisiert, ihre Lenkbarkeit
durch herkömmliche politische oder administrative Steuerungsinstrumente
ist schwierig bis unmöglich.

Transformation for the Benefit of Climate Protection

According to what all experts—from the UN's Intergovernmental Panel on Climate Change and the Climate Change Centre Austria to the Austrian Institute for Economic Research and the European Commission—unanimously agree upon, meeting the target established by the Paris Agreement of limiting global warming to a maximum of two degrees Celsius above preindustrial levels (which comes up to a 90 percent reduction of greenhouse gas emissions by 2050) calls for resolute action on the part of many. "This requires more than incrementally improved production technologies, greener consumer goods, and a policy encouraging marginal increases of efficiency," says the 2014 Austrian Assessment Report (AAR14). What is rather needed is "a transformation of the interaction between the economy, society, and the environment." This view is also behind current concepts like the Austrian Climate and Energy Strategy (#mission2030) or the European Green Deal, which are to bring a new growth spurt for the Austrian and the European economy on the basis of a transformation toward a decarbonized society.

Social sciences understand "transformations" as processes bringing about physical or qualitative changes in systems by altering their form, structure, or relevance. As is pointed out in IPCC reports, transformations are "alterations of fundamental attributes of a system, including value systems, the regulative, legislative, or bureaucratic regimes, financial institutions, and technological or biological systems." A comprehensive solution also has to take into account interdependencies between complex dynamic systems at different scale levels. Examples of such interactions are the interrelationships between climate change, mobility behavior, and modified land use, between demographic development, the public state of health, and environmental damage, between technological change and global market integration, as well as the fact that some parts of the world are changing rapidly while others stagnate and continue to live in poverty. Moreover, it is increasingly recognized that sustainability problems are rooted in contemporary lifestyles and the organizational forms of production and consumption related to them. From a structural point of view, climate change and an excessive consumption of resources are closely connected to the currently prevalent economic order.

In order to be able to design feasible paths toward sustainability, comprehensive socioeconomic transformation processes specifically aimed at sustainability are consequently required: a type of "socioecological transformation." Socioecological systems are complex: they change dynamically, are composed of numerous subsystems involving multiple feedback loops, show multiple nonlinearities, and are path-

Transformationsforschung

Die relativ neue Wissenschaftsdisziplin der Transformationsforschung versucht, Methoden und Wege zur Gestaltung der »Großen Transformation« zu entwickeln. Dazu gehört neben der Beschreibung und Erklärung von historischen Transformationen sowie der Darstellung gegenwärtiger Transformationsdynamiken auch das Bewerten gegenwärtiger Lösungsvorschläge. Man unterscheidet dabei grob zwischen »eigendynamischer« und »forcierter« Transformation. Im Selbstverständnis dieser Wissenschaft geht es nicht nur um Erkenntnisgewinn, sondern auch um die direkte Unterstützung gesellschaftlicher Akteurinnen und Akteure im Hinblick auf konkrete Fragestellungen. Diese Ambitionen werden verständlicherweise kontrovers diskutiert und bedürfen einer kritischen Reflektion.

Forscherinnen und Forscher des IIASA haben allgemeine Kriterien erarbeitet, um im Dickicht von gegenseitigen Abhängigkeiten und einander widersprechenden Nachhaltigkeitszielen einen Kurs zu finden: Erstens müssen die als sinnvoll erachteten Transformationen die Standards technischer Machbarkeit erfüllen. Zweitens müssen sie Kompromisse ansprechen und schließen. Drittens müssen sie durch eine Kombination aus öffentlichen und privaten Mitteln finanziert werden. Viertens müssen die Transformationen die Entwicklung und den Einsatz neuer Technologien beschleunigen. Fünftens ist politische Kohärenz zwischen verschiedenen Politikbereichen (horizontal), zwischen Regierungsebenen (vertikal) und im Laufe der Zeit (zeitlich) erforderlich, um Kompromisse zu bewältigen und eine rechtzeitige Umsetzung sicherzustellen. Sechstens können Unternehmen eine Kofinanzierung bereitstellen und viele der erforderlichen organisatorischen und technologischen Änderungen vorantreiben. Daher muss jede Transformation die Geschäftswelt durch kohärente Richtlinien, Marktanreize und Vorschriften einbeziehen. Und schließlich erfordern Transformationen das Engagement der Zivilgesellschaft und öffentliche Debatten über nachhaltige Entwicklungspfade.

Zur Konkretisierung solcher allgemeinen Überlegungen kann die Komplexitätsforschung einiges beitragen. Eine wertvolle Hilfe sind etwa komplexe Modelle, die erfassen, wie wirtschaftliche Subjekte (Unternehmen, Händler, Konsumenten etc.) durch Lieferketten verknüpft sind. So kann man etwa untersuchen, welche systemischen Auswirkungen es hat, wenn man unterschiedliche Arten der Bepreisung von CO_2-Emissionen vornimmt. Welche Folgen hätte die Einführung einer CO_2-Endbesteuerung von Produkten auf die gesamte Lieferkette? Wie ist es um die Konsequenzen im Vergleich zu anderen Varianten von CO_2-Abgaben bestellt? An welchen Punkten ergeben sich dann Probleme? Wie könnte die öffentliche Hand unterstützend eingreifen, um den Schaden für die existierende Wirtschaft möglichst gering zu halten? Wie könnte man die erwünschte Transformation mit vielen kleinen Schritten erreichen, ohne dass man drakonische Maßnahmen setzen muss? Solche umfassenden Wirtschaftsmodelle gibt es

dependent to a high degree. They are characterized by uncertainty and difficult or even impossible to control through conventional political or administrative instruments.

Transformation Research

A relatively young scientific discipline, transformation research seeks to develop methods and ways of designing the "Great Transformation." Apart from describing and explaining transformations of the past and depicting contemporary transformation dynamics, it also encompasses the evaluation of presently suggested solutions. One roughly differentiates between "self-reinforcing" and "forced" transformation. Transformation research sees its goals not merely in gaining knowledge, but also in directly supporting societal actors with regard to concrete problems. These ambitions are understandably discussed controversially and need critical reflection.

Researchers of IIASA have established general criteria in order to find a way through the thicket of mutual dependencies and contradictory sustainability goals: First, the transformations considered reasonable must meet the standards of technical feasibility. Second, trade-offs must be discussed and reached. Third, transformations must be financed through a combination of public and private funds. Fourth, transformations must accelerate the development and deployment of new technologies. Fifth, policy coherence is needed across branches of government (horizontal), between levels of government (vertical), and over time (temporal) to manage trade-offs and ensure timely implementation. Sixth, businesses can provide cofinancing and drive many of the necessary organizational and technological changes. Each transformation must therefore engage the business community through a coherent set of guidelines, market incentives, and regulations. And finally, transformations require civil society engagement and public debates about sustainable development pathways.

Complexity research can contribute to making such general considerations more concrete. Complex models mapping economic subjects (companies, dealers, consumers, etc.) connected by supply chains can be of valuable help. For example, it will be possible to find out about the systemic impacts of different ways of pricing CO_2 emissions. What would be the consequences if a CO_2-based taxation of products were introduced for the entire supply chain? In what way would these consequences differ when compared to those resulting from other variants of CO_2-related charges? At what points could problems occur? How could the government step in with a helping hand in order to keep the damage for the existing economy as small as possible? How could the desired transformation be reached in multiple

noch nicht, aber es wird daran gearbeitet, etwa am Complexity Science Hub (CSH) Vienna. Die Schwierigkeit liegt dabei darin, trotz Datenschutz möglichst valide Daten über konkrete Wirtschaftsstrukturen zu sammeln und zu ordnen. Davon verspricht man sich großen Nutzen: Wenn man all diese Abhängigkeiten, die niemand mehr überblicken kann, wirklich in einem Demonstrator zu simulieren imstande ist, wäre eine ganz andere Form von Wirtschafts- und Umweltpolitik möglich – eine Politik, die auf konkreten Daten beruht und deren Konsequenzen sich vorab genau studieren lassen. ✖

Quellen

Austrian Panel on Climate Change (APCC), Österreichischer Sachstandsbericht Klimawandel 2014 (AAR14), Verlag der Österreichischen Akademie der Wissenschaften, Wien 2014, 1096 Seiten, ISBN 978-3-7001-7699-2; kostenloser Download: *https://ccca.ac.at/wissenstransfer/apcc/apcc-aar14/austrian-assessment-report-2014-aar14*

https://wiki.bildungsserver.de/klimawandel/index.php/Globale_Zirkulationsmodelle

https://www.zamg.ac.at/cms/de/klima/informationsportal-klimawandel/klimaforschung/klimamodellierung/regionale-klimamodelle

Jeffrey D. Sachs, Guido Schmidt-Traub, Mariana Mazzucato, Dirk Messner, Nebojsa Nakicenovic und Johan Rockström, »Six Transformations to achieve the Sustainable Development Goals«, in: Nature Sustainability, Jg. 2019, Nr. 2, S. 805–814, DOI: 10.1038/s41893-019-0352-9

small steps without having to take draconian measures? Such comprehensive economic models do not yet exist but are in the process of being developed, such as at the Complexity Science Hub (CSH) Vienna. The difficulty lies in the necessity to collect and organize as much valid data about actual economic structures as possible, in spite of the protection of data privacy. There is hope to greatly benefit from such models. If it were indeed possible to simulate all these interdependencies, which no one is capable of keeping track of any longer, within a single demonstrator, this would enable a fundamentally different form of economic and environmental policy—a policy based on concrete data the consequences of which could be studied thoroughly in advance. ✕

Sources

Austrian Panel on Climate Change (APCC), *Austrian Assessment Report 2014 (AAR14),* published by the Austrian Academy of Sciences, Vienna, 2014, 1096 pages, ISBN 978-3-7001-7699-2;
free download: *https://ccca.ac.at/wissenstransfer/apcc/apcc-aar14/austrian-assessment-report-2014-aar14*

https://wiki.bildungsserver.de/klimawandel/index.php/Globale_Zirkulationsmodelle

https://www.zamg.ac.at/cms/de/klima/informationsportal-klimawandel/klimaforschung/klimamodellierung/regionale-klimamodelle

Jeffrey D. Sachs, Guido Schmidt-Traub, Mariana Mazzucato, Dirk Messner, Nebojsa Nakicenovic, and Johan Rockström, "Six Transformations to Achieve the Sustainable Development Goals," in: *Nature Sustainability,* 2019, no. 2, 805–814,
DOI: 10.1038/s41893-019-0352-9

Städte und Straßen:
Komplexe Infrastruktur des Zusammenlebens

Bei der Planung von Siedlungen und Verkehrssystemen müssen unzählige Parameter unter einen Hut gebracht werden. Moderne Simulationssysteme helfen dabei ungemein.

Man schrieb das Jahr 2007, als die UNO im *State of World Population Report* bekannt gab, dass erstmals in der Menschheitsgeschichte mehr als die Hälfte aller Menschen (damals 3,3 Milliarden) in Städten leben. Seither hat sich die Urbanisierung weiter beschleunigt. Im *Atlas of the Human Planet 2019* kam das Joint Research Centre der Europäischen Kommission zu dem Ergebnis, dass 76 Prozent der Weltbevölkerung (das entspricht 5,6 Milliarden Menschen) in urbanen Zentren leben. Österreich ist vergleichsweise ländlich geprägt: 58 Prozent der Einwohner leben laut EU-Statistik in sechs urbanen Zentren.

Städte sind nicht nur Ansammlungen vieler Menschen, sondern weisen auch zahlreiche Strukturen auf, die sie zu Zentren der Wirtschaft, der Innovation und des sozialen Lebens machen. Sie bilden auf vielerlei Ebenen Netzwerke, die einander beeinflussen und sich mit der Zeit verändern – sie sind damit komplexe Systeme. Auf der einen Seite weisen Städte physische Netzwerke wie etwa Straßen, Bahnlinien, elektrische Leitungen, Telekommunikationsnetzwerke, Ver- und Entsorgungsstrukturen usw. auf, die quasi den Stoffwechsel der Siedlungen ermöglichen. Auf der anderen Seite sind Städte aber viel mehr als nur ihre Gebäude und sonstige durch Transportsysteme miteinander verbundene Strukturen: Stadtforscher sind sich einig, dass das Wesen von Städten ihre Bewohnerinnen und Bewohner sind: Städte bringen Menschen zusammen, erleichtern ihre Interaktion und führen zur Entwicklung neuer Ideen, die schließlich mehr Wohlstand und eine höhere Lebensqualität hervorbringen. »In Amerika und Europa beschleunigen Städte die Innovation, indem sie die smarten Einwohner*innen miteinander verbinden, aber in den Entwicklungsländern spielen Städte eine noch kritischere Rolle: Sie sind Tore zwischen Märkten und Kulturen«, formulierte der renommierte Harvard-Ökonom Edward Glaeser vor einigen Jahren in seinem bahnbrechenden Buch *Triumph of the City*.

Zwischen den verschiedenen Netzwerken, die eine Stadt ausmachen, gibt es zahlreiche Rückkopplungen, alles hängt auf bestimmte Weise mit allem zusammen. »Gemeinsam bilden sie [die Netzwerke] ein allumfassen-

FOCUS: URBANISATION & MOBILITY

Cities and Streets:
The Complex Infrastructure
of Living Together

When planning human settlements and traffic and transportation systems, countless parameters have to be reconciled. This is where modern simulation systems come in handy.

In 2007, the United Nations announced in its *State of World Population Report* that it was for the first time in the history of humankind that more than half of the global population (3.3 billions at the time) lived in metropolises. Since then, urbanization has accelerated further. In its *Atlas of the Human Planet 2019,* the European Commission's Joint Research Centre has found that 76 percent of the world's inhabitants (i.e. 5.6 billion people) live in urban centers. Austria is a comparatively rural area: according to EU statistics, 58 percent of its inhabitants live in six urban centers.

Cities are not only accumulations of large numbers of people, but they are also characterized by numerous structures that make them centers of the economy, of innovation, and of social life. They form networks on multiple levels, influencing one another and changing over time—which makes them complex systems. On the one hand, cities are furnished with such physical networks as streets, railroad lines, power supply lines, telecommunications networks, supply and disposal systems, etc., all of which, in a way, enable the metabolism of urban settlements. On the other hand, cities are much more than the sum of their buildings and other structures connected by transportation systems: urbanists agree that the essence of cities is made up by their inhabitants: cities bring people together, they facilitate their interaction and lead to the development of new ideas, which finally bring about more wealth and a higher quality of life. "In America and Europe, cities speed innovations by connecting their smart inhabitants to each other, but cities play an even more critical role in the developing world: They are gateways between markets and cultures," the renowned Harvard economist Edward Glaeser pointed out several years ago, in his groundbreaking book *Triumph of the City.*

There are multiple feedbacks among the various networks a city consists of. Everything is connected in one way or another. In his book *Scale: The Universal Laws of Growth, Innovation, Sustainability, and*

des, überaus komplexes adaptives System, das permanent Energie, Ressourcen und Informationen aufnimmt und verarbeitet. Das Ergebnis ist das außerordentliche kollektive Phänomen, das wir als Stadt bezeichnen und das aus der Dynamik und der Organisation der Art und Weise erwächst, wie Menschen durch soziale Netzwerke miteinander interagieren«, schreibt der us-Komplexitätsforscher Geoffrey West in seinem kürzlich auch auf Deutsch erschienenen Buch *Scale. Die universalen Gesetze des Lebens von Organismen, Städten und Unternehmen.*

Wachstumsgesetze

West hat gemeinsam mit Kolleginnen und Kollegen in jahrelanger Detailarbeit grundlegende Gesetze erforscht, welche die Komplexität von Städten – ähnlich wie von Lebewesen oder Unternehmen – erfassen. Man hat sogenannte »Skalengesetze« entdeckt, die beschreiben, wie gewisse Eigenschaften mit der Größe einer Stadt zusammenhängen. Eine Gruppe von Eigenschaften betrifft die Infrastruktur, also etwa die Zahl der Straßen und Gebäude oder die Länge der Kanalisation: Wenn sich die Bevölkerung einer Stadt verdoppelt, braucht man nicht doppelt so viel Infrastruktur, sondern nur um rund 85 Prozent mehr. Eine Stadt ist also effizienter als andere Formen des Zusammenlebens von Menschen. Völlig anders verhalten sich hingegen sozioökonomische Eigenschaften – im Positiven etwa die Höhe von Gehältern oder die Anzahl von Patenten, im Negativen beispielsweise die Kriminalitätsraten, die Zahl der hiv-Infizierten oder die Umweltbelastung: Bei einer Stadt mit doppelt so vielen Einwohnern ist deren Ausmaß um 115 Prozent größer. Daneben gibt es noch eine dritte Gruppe von Merkmalen: Die Zahl der Jobs oder von Wohnungen wächst linear mit der Bevölkerungszahl.

Zusammengenommen erklären diese Gesetzmäßigkeiten den großen Erfolg der Stadt als Form des Zusammenlebens von Menschen. Das Bemerkenswerte dabei: »Das gilt für Städte weltweit im selben Ausmaß, unabhängig von Geschichte, Geografie und Kultur einer Stadt. Diese außerordentliche Universalität liegt darin begründet, dass soziale Interaktionen im Grunde überall auf der Welt gleich ablaufen. Hinter dem komplexen Chaos, das uns umgibt, scheint eine eindrucksvolle Einfachheit zu stecken«, so West.

Intelligente Stadtplanung

Stadtplanung muss mit dieser ungeheuren Komplexität von städtischen Strukturen umgehen können. Ein völlig neuer Ansatz, der am ait Austrian Institute of Technology entwickelt wurde, versucht dem auf innovative Weise gerecht zu werden: Im »City Intelligence Lab« werden die komplexen Auswirkungen der Planung von Stadtteilen, Straßennetzen,

the Pace of Life in Organisms, Cities, Economies, and Companies, which recently also appeared in German, US complexity scientist Geoffrey West describes how all "urban characteristics" together form "an overarching multiscale quintessentially complex adaptive system that is continuously integrating and processing energy, resources, and information. The result is the extraordinary collective phenomenon we call a city, whose origins emerge from the underlying dynamics and organization of how people interact with one another through social networks."

Laws of growth

Together with his colleagues, West has, over years of in-depth research, explored fundamental laws defining the complexity of cities—which are similar to those of living organisms or companies. They discovered so-called "scaling laws," which describe how specific properties relate to the size of a city. A set of properties concerns infrastructure, i.e. the number of streets and buildings or the length of the sewage system: when the population of a city doubles, there is no need for twice as much infrastructure, but only for approximately 85 percent more of it. A city is therefore more efficient than other forms of coexistence. However, socioeconomic properties behave completely differently—such as, in a positive sense, the height of income or the number of patents, and, in a negative sense, crime rates, the number of HIV-infected persons, or environmental damage: in a city with twice as many inhabitants, they will have increased by 115 percent. In addition, there is a third group of hallmark features: the number of jobs or of apartments, for example, will grow in linear proportion to the population increase.

In their entirety, these laws account for the big success of the city as a form of human coexistence. What is particularly remarkable about it: according to West, this applies in equal measure to cities around the globe, regardless of their history, geography, and culture. This extraordinary universality has to do with the fact that social interactions basically take place in the same way everywhere around the globe. "There appears to be a striking simplicity behind the complex chaos that surrounds us," West says.

Intelligent city planning

City planning must be able to cope with this enormous complexity of urban structures. An entirely new approach developed at the AIT Austrian Institute of Technology attempts to do justice to this fact in an innovative fashion. At its City Intelligence Lab, the complex impacts

Gebäuden usw. auf Wirtschaft, Umwelt und Mobilität transparent und sichtbar gemacht. Vom frühesten Planungsstadium an können vielfältige Szenarien entworfen und sofort evaluiert werden. Mithilfe von Schlüsseltechnologien wie Augmented Reality (AR) oder künstliche Intelligenz (KI) werden physikalische Berechnungen und komplexe Simulationen erstellt und visualisiert – man kann praktisch in Echtzeit eruieren, welche Konsequenzen eine Planänderung für den Energieverbrauch, die Verkehrserschließung und Zugänglichkeit eines Stadtteils oder für die sommerliche Überhitzung hat. Dieses Labor ermöglicht es, den Ansatz einer kokreativen Entwicklung zu verfolgen, mit dem gemeinsam neues Wissen geschaffen wird: Planer, Auftraggeber und Nutzer arbeiten an interaktiven Projektionswänden und 3-D-Modellen gemeinsam Projekte und Planungsszenarien aus, und das System berechnet innerhalb wenigen Minuten die Auswirkungen und stellt diese anschaulich dar. Dies ermöglicht eine radikal neue Form der nahtlosen Zusammenarbeit zwischen mehreren Partnern.

Grundbedürfnis Mobilität

Ein zentrales Bedürfnis des Menschen ist Mobilität. Historiker haben nachgewiesen, dass das schon immer so war. Durch unseren Lebensstil und die modernen Verkehrstechnologien hat sich dieses Bedürfnis noch verstärkt – in der Coronakrise wurde uns deutlich vor Augen geführt, was uns fehlt, wenn wir unsere Mobilität einschränken müssen. Unsere Verkehrsinfrastrukturen sind komplexe Netzwerke, die einer Vielzahl von Einflussfaktoren unterliegen. »Das Nebeneinander von Personenmobilität, Gütertransport und zugehöriger Verkehrsinfrastruktur wird immer mehr durch ein systemisches Zusammenspiel abgelöst, basierend auf neuen Technologien und übergreifenden Stakeholder-Interessen und Geschäftsmodellen«, heißt es in einem aktuellen Perspektivenpapier des AIT Center for Mobility Systems. Und weiter: »Eine integrierte Betrachtung von Personenverkehr und Logistik, verbunden mit einer flexiblen Nutzung der Infrastruktur, eröffnet neue Perspektiven für die Gestaltung der Mobilität der Zukunft. Gleichzeitig soll das Mobilitätssystem ökologisch verträglich, effizient, sicher und resilient sein sowie den Bedürfnissen der Menschen gerecht werden. Für wirtschaftlich und gesellschaftlich sinnvolle Lösungen bedarf es daher einer ganzheitlichen Betrachtungsweise sowie der engen Kooperation aller Beteiligten.«

In der Verkehrsplanung und -steuerung müssen folglich unzählige Parameter unter einen Hut gebracht werden. Dabei helfen Methoden aus der Komplexitätsforschung ungemein. Auch in diesem Fall sind möglichst realitätsnahe Mobilitätsdaten bei Computermodellen und -simulationen das Um und Auf. Moderne Medien und Technologien erlauben es, sehr viel mehr über das tatsächliche Kommunikations- und Mobilitätsverhalten der Menschen zu erfahren als in früheren Zeiten: Sensoren in Smartphones oder

of the planning of urban neighborhoods, road networks, buildings, etc. on the economy, the environment, and mobility are rendered transparent and visible. Multiple scenarios can be devised and instantly evaluated from the earliest planning phase onward. With the aid of such key technologies as augmented reality (AR) or artificial intelligence (AI), physical calculations and complex simulations are carried out and visualized—it is possible to find out practically in real time how a change of plan would affect energy consumption, the traffic infrastructure, and the accessibility of a particular neighborhood—or the excessive heat of summer. This lab makes it possible to pursue an approach of co-creative development by which new knowledge is generated in a collaborative effort: planers, awarding authorities, and users work together on interactive projection walls and 3D models as they jointly flesh out projects and planning scenarios, the impacts of which can immediately be calculated and distinctly visualized by the system within a few minutes. This facilitates a radically new form of seamless collaboration among multiple partners.

Mobility as a basic need

Mobility is a central human need. Historians have proven that it has always been like this. This urge has even become stronger through our lifestyle and modern transportation technologies. During the coronavirus crisis we have clearly felt what we lack when we are forced to restrict our mobility. Our traffic and transport infrastructures are complex networks that are subject to a multitude of influencing factors. "While the mobility of people, the transportation of goods, and the associated infrastructure used to exist side by side, this system is increasingly replaced now by systemic interaction—based on new technologies, as well as stakeholder interests and business models spanning across fields," it says in a recent AIT Center for Mobility Systems perspective paper and continues as follows: "An integrated view of personal transport and logistics—together with a flexible use of infrastructure—opens up new perspectives for the mobility of the future. At the same time, the mobility system ought to be ecologically sustainable, efficient, safe, and resilient, and to satisfy individual human needs. A holistic view and the close cooperation of all stakeholders are required to find sensible solutions in both economical and societal terms."

When planning and controlling traffic and transportation systems, countless parameters have to be reconciled. This is where methods borrowed from complexity science come in extremely handy. Here, too, mobility data reflecting reality as closely as possible are essential for the construction of computer models and simulations.

Fahrzeugen etwa liefern heute eine wahre Flut an Informationen, aus denen mithilfe von Big-Data-Algorithmen räumlich und zeitlich sehr fein aufgelöste Mobilitätsdaten ermittelt werden können. Beispiel sind die Echtzeit-Stauwarnungen in den Karten des weltgrößten Suchmaschinenanbieters. In vielen Staaten können Handy-Positions- und -Verbindungsdaten relativ einfach genutzt werden. Forscher in den USA beispielsweise können daraus verblüffende Dinge bis hin zu Frühwarnungen für eine Grippewelle herauslesen. Aus Datenschutzgründen wesentlich schwieriger ist dies in Europa. Doch auch in Österreich werden Handy-Daten (in anonymisierter Form) bisweilen zur Analyse des Bewegungsverhaltens der Menschen genutzt. Geschehen ist dies etwa auf dem Höhepunkt der Coronakrise, als ein großer Handynetzbetreiber den durchschnittlichen Bewegungsradius der Menschen ermittelte und dadurch die Wirkung der von der Politik verhängten Beschränkungen beim Betreten des öffentlich Raums nachweisen konnte: Kurz nach Lockdown-Beginn sank der durchschnittliche Bewegungsradius von zuvor zwölf auf acht Kilometer, bevor er dann auf rund zehn Kilometer stieg.

Lenken von Fußgängerströmen

Dass die Erhebung von hochqualitativen Mobilitätsdaten auch datenschutzkonform möglich ist, beweisen Crowd-Sourcing-Apps: Von Freiwilligen auf dem Smartphone installiert, kann etwa das am AIT entwickelte System MODE automatisch alle zurückgelegten Wege erfassen und dabei sogar das benutzte Verkehrsmittel erkennen. Nach einer Auswertung auf einem vertrauenswürdigen Server können diese Daten für viele Anwendungen genutzt werden. So kann etwa die Effizienz eines bestimmten Mobilitätssystems gesteigert werden. Möglich wird so auch die Gestaltung von resilienten Netzen, die bei ungeplant auftretenden Ereignissen funktionsfähig bleiben.

Eine besonders harte Nuss ist der Fußgängerverkehr, denn die Bewegungen von Personen als Individuen, in der Gruppe oder sogar in Menschenmassen sind sehr dynamisch und daher nur schwer vorherzusagen. Hier spielt die Psychologie der Massen eine große Rolle, agiert doch »das Herdentier Mensch« in vielen Situationen trotz alledem vorhersehbar: Wie man einander ausweicht oder wie viele Gehspuren sich auf einem Weg bilden, sind selbstorganisierende Effekte, die sich auf viele Situationen übertragen lassen. Am AIT wurde in diesem Zusammenhang das System SIMULATE entwickelt, in dem die Auswirkungen von Lenkungsmaßnahmen berechnet werden können – etwa eine Vereinzelung von Personenströmen beim Eingang in eine U-Bahn-Station (um Gedränge am Bahnsteig zu vermeiden) oder eine veränderte Wegeleitung durch Absperrbänder etc. Dadurch kann z. B. von vornherein verhindert werden, dass Situationen entstehen, in denen Massenpanik auftreten könnte.

Modern media and technologies permit us to learn much more about the actual human communicative and mobility behavior than in the past: today, for example, sensors in smartphones or vehicles supply us with a genuine flood of information from which mobility data that have been fine-tuned in terms of space and time can be ascertained with the aid of big data algorithms. An example are the real-time traffic jam alerts in the maps of the world's leading search engine operator. In many countries, cellphone positional tracking and call detail data can be used relatively easily. US researchers are able and permitted to elicit astonishing things from them, including early warnings against flu epidemics. For reasons of data protection, this is considerably more difficult in Europe. However, cellphone data (in anonymized form) are occasionally also referred to in Austria to analyze human mobility behavior. For example, this happened at the peak of the coronavirus crisis when a leading mobile network operator managed to find out about the average radius of people's movements and was thus in a position to prove the effect of the restrictions imposed on the population by the government as to entering public space: shortly after the lockdown had begun, the average range of movement decreased from twelve to eight kilometers before it rose to approximately ten kilometers.

Controlling pedestrian flows

That high-quality mobility data can also be gathered in a way that is in compliance with legal data protection regulations is proven by crowd sourcing apps: installed on their smartphones by volunteers, the system MODE, for example, which has been developed at the AIT, is capable of registering all distances covered and even of identifying the means of transport that has been used. Having been analyzed on a trustworthy server, these data subsequently lend themselves to numerous applications. For instance, the efficiency of a specific mobility system can be improved. This also enables the design of resilient networks that will continue to function even in the case of unexpected events.

An especially tough nut to crack is pedestrian circulation, for the movements of persons as individuals, within a group, or even in a crowd are highly dynamic and therefore difficult to envisage. Crowd psychology plays an important role here, as human "herd animals" do act predictably in many situations, in spite of everything: how people move out of one another's way or how "walking lanes" form automatically along a walkway are self-organizing effects that can be transferred to many situations. In this context, the system SIMULATE has been contrived at the AIT, with the aid of which it is possible to deter-

Dieses Berechnungsverfahren fand in der Coronkrise eine ganz neue Anwendungsmöglichkeit bei der Optimierung von Maßnahmen, um den Mindestabstand zwischen Personen einzuhalten und die Kontaktzeit von Menschen zu minimieren. In Umsteigestationen des öffentlichen Verkehrs kann beispielsweise durch Kennzeichnungen am Boden, Umleitungen mit Absperrbändern oder die Änderung der Bewegungsrichtungen von Rolltreppen erreicht werden, dass die Dichte an Fußgänger*innen niemals zu groß wird. Ähnliches ist auch in Supermärkten etwa durch Zugangsbeschränkungen, die Veränderung von Durchlässen zwischen Regalen oder ein Einbahnsystem im Geschäft umsetzbar. Derzeit noch nicht ganz klar ist, ob und wie sich das Bewegungsverhalten der Menschen durch Corona verändert hat. Vermutet wird, dass Menschen derzeit frühzeitiger ausweichen als vor der Krise – doch das gilt es erst noch empirisch zu belegen. ✖

Quellen

AIT Center for Mobility Systems, *Nachhaltig, sicher & digital: Perspektiven für ein menschenzentriertes Mobilitätssystem,* Wien, 2020; Download: *https://www.ait.ac.at/fileadmin/mc/mobility/Center/Perspektiven.pdf*

European Commission, Joint Research Centre, *Atlas of the Human Planet 2019. A compendium of urbanisation dynamics in 239 countries,* Luxembourg, 2020; Download: *https://ec.europa.eu/jrc/en/publication/eur-scientific-and-technical-research-reports/atlas-human-planet-2019*

Edward L. Glaeser, *Triumph of the City. How Our Greatest Invention Makes Us Richer, Smarter, Greener, Healthier, and Happier,* The Penguin Press, New York, 2011

Geoffrey West, *Scale. Die universalen Gesetze des Lebens von Organismen, Städten und Unternehmen,* C.H. Beck, München, 2019

mine the effects of control measures—such as isolating individuals from a pedestrian flow at the entrance to a subway station (in order to prevent crowding on the platform), or redirecting people through barrier tapes, etc. Thanks to such measures it is possible to prevent situations that could end up in a mass panic form the very start.

This computational procedure has now been harnessed for an entirely new application during the coronavirus crisis with regard to the optimization of measures, so as to be able to ensure the necessary minimum distance between people and minimize the exposure to human contact. In public transport stations offering transfer options, for example, such measures as floor markings, redirections by means of barrier tapes, or changes of escalator directions ensure that the density of pedestrians will never become too high. Similar things can be accomplished in supermarkets through access restrictions, the changing of passageways between shelves, or a one-way system throughout the store. At the moment it is not fully clear whether people's mobility behavior has changed because of the coronavirus pandemic. It is assumed that people now move out of one another's way earlier than before the crisis—but this will yet have to be proven empirically. **×**

Sources

AIT Center for Mobility Systems, *Sustainable, Safe and Digital: Perspectives for a Human-Centered Mobility System,* Vienna, 2020; download: *https://www.ait.ac.at/fileadmin/mc/mobility/Center/ Perspectives.pdf*

European Commission, Joint Research Centre, *Atlas of the Human Planet 2019. A compendium of urbanisation dynamics in 239 countries,* Luxembourg, 2020; download: *https://ec.europa.eu/jrc/en/ publication/eur-scientific-and-technical-research-reports/atlas-hu- man-planet-2019*

Edward L. Glaeser, *Triumph of the City. How Our Greatest Invention Makes Us Richer, Smarter, Greener, Healthier, and Happier,* New York, 2011

Geoffrey West, *Scale: The Universal Laws of Growth, Innovation, Sustainability, and the Pace of Life in Organisms, Cities, Economies, and Companies,* New York, 2017

Von der Entwicklung und Widerstandsfähigkeit der Wirtschaft

Immer genauere Einblicke in das Wirtschaftssystem ermöglichen ein besseres Verständnis dessen, wie Wachstum erfolgt, wie Krisen verlaufen und wie ein Kollaps vermieden werden kann.

Traditionell vertrat man die Ansicht, dass die Performance und Entwicklung einer Volkswirtschaft von drei Produktionsfaktoren abhängen: von Kapital, Arbeit und Boden. Im Lauf der Zeit – als die Landwirtschaft einen kleiner und kleiner werdenden Teil zur Wirtschaftsleistung beitrug – haben Ökonomen den Boden aus dieser Gleichung gestrichen und Kapital und Arbeit begrifflich präzisiert: Unter dem Begriff »Sachkapital« wurden alle physischen Gegenstände zusammengefasst, die zur Produktion von Gütern und Dienstleistungen erforderlich sind – etwa Maschinen, Gebäude oder Transportmittel. Unter den Begriff »Humankapital« subsumierte man die Ausbildung, das Wissen und das Know-how der Menschen, die in einer Volkswirtschaft tätig sind. Und der Begriff »Sozialkapital« beschrieb die Fähigkeit einer Gesellschaft, Beziehungen herzustellen, um Wissen weiterzugeben und auf diese Weise Know-how zu akkumulieren.

Diese detailliertere Betrachtungsweise ermöglichte große Fortschritte beim Verstehen ökonomischer Zusammenhänge, erwies sich aber als nicht vollständig. Das fand auch in der Definition einer »Totalen Faktorproduktivität« (TFP) seinen Niederschlag, welche die Lücke zwischen empirisch beobachteten Daten und durch Wirtschaftsmodelle erfassten Bereichen schloss. Als Maß für die Produktivität gibt die TFP an, welcher Teil des Wachstums der Produktion sich nicht auf eine Zunahme des Einsatzes der Produktionsfaktoren Arbeit und Kapital zurückführen lässt, sondern sozusagen als unerklärter Rest übrig bleibt (und häufig mit dem Einsatz von Technologien erklärt wurde). Dieser Rest blieb lange Zeit eine Black Box, in die man nicht weiter hineinschauen konnte.

Komplexitätskapital

Erst mit dem Aufkommen des Systemdenkens und von Netzwerktheorien sowie der Verfügbarkeit von detaillierten Daten ab der Millenniumswende kam man einen Schritt weiter. Forscher um Ricardo Hausmann (Harvard University) und César Hidalgo (damals MIT, heute Universität

On the Economy's Development and Resilience

Increasingly detailed insights into the economic system facilitate a better understanding of how growth is brought about, how crises proceed, and how collapse can be prevented.

Traditionally, it was argued that the performance and development of an economy depended on three factors of production: capital, labor, and land. Over time—with agriculture contributing less and less to economic performance—economists eliminated land from this equation and defined the terms of capital and labor more precisely: The term "physical capital" encompassed all real objects required for the production of goods and services such as machinery, buildings, and means of transportation. The term "human capital" subsumed the education, training, knowledge, and know-how of people working in a national economy. And the term "social capital" described a society's ability of forming interpersonal relationships in order to share knowledge and accumulate know-how.

Taking this more detailed look at things ensured that substantial progress was made in the understanding of economic interconnections, although it turned out to be incomplete nevertheless. This led to the definition of "total factor productivity" (TFP), which was meant to close the gap between empirically observed data and areas defined by economic models. A measure of productivity, TFP indicates what proportion of growth in output cannot be accounted for by an increase in the use of the factors of labor and capital and is left as an unidentified remainder. For a long time, this remainder was a black box that could not be looked into.

Complexity capital

It was not possible to go one step further until systems thinking and network theories emerged and detailed data were made available starting at the turn of the millennium. Researchers in the teams of Ricardo Hausmann (Harvard University) and César Hidalgo (then MIT, today University of Toulouse) coined the term "economic complexity" and defined an index that can be established for all countries in the

Toulouse) entwickelten den Begriff »Wirtschaftskomplexität« und definierten einen Index, der sich für alle Staaten der Welt ermitteln lässt. Die Daten dafür stammen aus Außenhandelsstatistiken. 2011 wurde erstmals The *Atlas of Economic Complexity* herausgegeben, der seither regelmäßig aktualisiert wird. In diesem »Komplexitätskapital« wird die Wirtschaftsstruktur hinsichtlich ihres Branchenmixes und ihrer Exporte abgebildet: Ein Bestimmungsfaktor ist die »Diversität«, welche die Vielzahl verschiedener Produkte, die in einem Land hergestellt werden, abbildet. Der zweite Faktor ist die »Ubiquität«, die misst, wie viele andere Länder ein bestimmtes Produkt produzieren. Der Index lässt also erkennen, wie vielfältig eine Volkswirtschaft ist, in wie viele Staaten deren Güter exportiert werden und in welchem Ausmaß Produkte hergestellt werden, die in nicht vielen anderen Staaten produziert werden können. Er ist damit ein Maß für das geballte Know-how einer Gesellschaft und bildet die wirtschaftliche Komplexität einer Volkswirtschaft ab.

Dieser Ansatz, der explizit wirtschaftliche Netzwerke einbezieht, erwies sich als äußerst mächtig: Mithilfe der Kategorie Komplexitätskapital kann nicht nur die unterschiedliche wirtschaftliche Entwicklung von Staaten erklärt, sondern auch der künftige Weg gut vorhergesagt werden. Österreich ist in dieser Hinsicht sehr gut aufgestellt: Unter den 27 EU-Staaten nimmt Österreich hinter Deutschland und Tschechien den dritten Platz ein. Eine noch höhere wirtschaftliche Komplexität weist die Schweiz auf; die USA liegen dagegen hinter Österreich. Im aktuellen *Forschungs- und Technologiebericht* der österreichischen Bundesregierung wird daher festgehalten, dass Österreich gut vorbereitet sei, um zukünftige Innovationen nicht nur erzeugen, sondern sie auf einem weltweiten Markt auch erfolgreich positionieren zu können.

Liefer- und Wertschöpfungsketten im Brennpunkt

Mithilfe von Methoden der Komplexitätsforschung werden nun noch detailliertere Einblicke in die Struktur der Wirtschaft möglich. Ein großes Forschungsgebiet ist derzeit die Analyse von Liefer- und Wertschöpfungsketten, über die alle Wirtschaftssubjekte auf vielen Ebenen (Information, Zahlungsströme, Güterströme usw.) miteinander verknüpft sind – wobei sich die Verbindungen wie die Eigenschaften von Unternehmen, Konsumentinnen und Konsumenten dynamisch verändern. Es handelt sich also um ein »klassisches« komplexes System.

Wenn eine Lieferkette unterbrochen und der Lagerbestand aufgebraucht ist, muss die Produktion eingestellt werden. Dadurch können sich Lieferausfälle in Kaskaden durch das ganze Lieferkettennetzwerk fortpflanzen und im schlimmsten Fall zu einem Komplettausfall ganzer Industriezweige, einem sogenannten »Lieferkettenkollaps«, führen. Wie zentral Lieferketten für eine funktionierende Volkswirtschaft sind, sah man erst

world, the necessary data deriving from export statistics. *The Atlas of Economic Complexity* was published for the first time in 2011 and has been updated regularly ever since. This "complexity capital" reflects a country's economic structure in terms of its mix of industries and its exports: One determining factor is the "diversity" indicating the multitude of different products manufactured in a country. The second factor is "ubiquity," measuring how many other countries produce a specific product. The index thus reveals how versatile an economy is, into how many countries its goods are exported, and to what extent products are manufactured that cannot be produced in other countries. It is therefore a measure of a society's concentrated know-how and mirrors a national economy's economic complexity.

This approach, which explicitly incorporates economic networks, has turned out to be extremely powerful: with the aid of the category of complexity capital it is not only possible to explain why national economies develop differently but also to predict in a plausible way what directions they will take in the future. Austria is excellently positioned in this respect: among the 27 EU member states, the country ranks in third place after Germany and Czechia. The economic complexity of Switzerland is even higher, whereas the United States lags behind Austria. The Austrian government's most recent *Research and Technology Report* states that Austria is well prepared to not only produce future innovations but to also position them successfully on a global market.

Focusing on supply and value creation chains

The methods of complexity science now permit even more detailed insights into the economic structure. Currently, a major field of research is the analysis of supply and value creation chains, by which all economic subjects are concatenated on multiple levels (information, flows of payments and goods, etc.)—with interactions changing dynamically, as do the properties of companies and consumers. It is therefore a "classic" complex system.

When a supply chain is interrupted and the stock has been depleted, production is forced to stop. In this way, delivery shortfalls may cascade throughout the supply chain, which in the worst case will lead to a complete standstill of entire industries, a so-called "supply chain collapse." The vital importance of supply chains for a functioning national economy made itself felt only recently, during the coronavirus crisis. In previous decades, globalization and the outsourcing of production had led to significant improvements in efficiency, but at the same time the whole system had become more vulnerable, i.e. less resilient, to failure. Due to restrictions in global

jüngst in der Coronakrise. In den Jahrzehnten davor hatten Globalisierung und Auslagerung der Produktion zwar zu einer massiven Effizienzsteigerung geführt, doch gleichzeitig war das gesamte System für Störungen anfälliger, weniger resilient geworden. So kam es infolge von Einschränkungen des globalen Handels beispielsweise zu einer temporären Einstellung der Autoproduktion in der EU oder in Korea. In den USA brach zeitweise die Fleischversorgung zusammen, weltweit gab es Probleme bei Medizingütern, und in Österreich kam es kurzfristig zu einem Ausfall von Hefelieferungen (wodurch Brauereien, Bäckereien und Backfans zu Hause in Schwierigkeiten gerieten).

An vielen Forschungseinrichtungen werden zurzeit Lieferantennetzwerke modelliert – wobei das Schwierige daran das Erheben der Daten ist. In Ungarn wird das etwa anhand von Mehrwertsteuerdaten versucht, in Brasilien über Angaben zum Zahlungsverkehr. In Österreich hat »Fraunhofer Austria« kürzlich im Rahmen des Projekts PRESIDE (Prognosemodelle zur Sicherung der Daseinsvorsorge) gemeinsam mit einem großen Lebensmittelgroßhändler eruiert, aus welcher Region Waren in welche Gebiete geliefert werden. Auf diese Weise lässt sich darstellen, welche Auswirkungen eine Quarantäne oder eine Grenzschließung auf die Lebensmittelversorgung hätte.

Wesentlich weiter geht das im Vorjahr gestartete »Josef-Ressel-Zentrum für Echtzeitvisualisierung von Wertschöpfungsnetzwerken« an der FH Oberösterreich in Wels. Unter der Leitung von Markus Gerschberger wird in Kooperation mit BMW und Hofer ein Simulationssystem entwickelt, das Lieferantennetzwerke in Echtzeit darstellt, überwacht und frühzeitig Störungen erkennen soll. Dazu werden diejenigen Unternehmen bzw. Lieferbeziehungen identifiziert, die besonders kritisch für das gesamte System sind. Das Ergebnis soll ein »Control Tower« sein, von dem aus relevante Netzwerkdaten an einem Ort überwacht, Daten auf intelligente Weise verteilt und Entscheidungsträger optimal unterstützt werden. Im Zuge der Coronakrise wurde in Kooperation mit Partnern auch ein Tool zur »Systemischen Risikoanalyse für die Lebensmittel-Versorgungssicherheit in Österreich« (SYRI) entwickelt.

Wie resilient ist ein System?

Ein sehr umfassendes Ziel verfolgt man am Complexity Science Hub (CHS) Vienna. Dort hat man das Fernziel im Auge, die gesamte österreichische Wirtschaft in einem Simulationsmodell abzubilden. Daraus würden sich sehr viele Schlüsse ziehen lassen: etwa welchen (systemischen) Wert ein einzelnes Unternehmen für eine Region hat, was passieren würde, wenn sich ein neuer Produzent ansiedeln würde, wie ein Wirtschaftszweig von Zoll- oder Steuererhöhungen betroffen wäre, wo Bedarf an welchen Arbeitskräften besteht usw. Zum Aufbau eines solchen Simulators werden

trade, it came to a temporary cessation of automobile production in both the European Union and Korea, for example. In the United States, meat supply was disrupted for some time, and global problems could be observed in the case of medical equipment; in Austria, the supply of yeast was interrupted for a brief period of time (which brought about problems for breweries, bakeries, and baking aficionados in private households).

Many research institutions are currently modeling supplier networks—the difficulty about it being the collection of data. They try to solve the problem by using value added tax data in Hungary and payment transaction information in Brazil. In our country, Fraunhofer Austria has recently initiated the project PRESIDE (prognosis models for securing services of public interest) to establish in collaboration with a major food wholesaler which goods are delivered from A to B. In this way, the impact of quarantine or closed borders on food supplies can be determined.

The Josef Ressel Center for the Real-Time Visualization of Value Creation Networks installed last year at the University of Applied Sciences Upper Austria in Wels goes considerably further. Led by Markus Gerschberger and in cooperation with BMW and the Hofer supermarket chain, a simulation system is being developed that is to depict and monitor supplier networks in real time and identify deficits at an early point in time. For this purpose, those companies and supply relationships are identified that are particularly critical for the system as a whole. The result is expected to be a kind of "control tower" functioning as a single station from which to monitor relevant network data, distribute data intelligently, and support decision-makers in the best possible way. Moreover, in the course of the coronavirus crisis a tool for "Systemic Risk Analysis for Food Supply Security in Austria" (SYRI) has been developed together with partners.

How resilient is a system?

An extremely holistic goal is pursued at the Complexity Science Hub (CHS) Vienna. Its long-term objective is the visualization of the entire Austrian economy within a simulation model. This would allow a multitude of conclusions to be drawn: what (systemic) value a specific enterprise has for a region; what would happen if a new manufacturing company established itself; in what ways an economic sector would by affected by increases in taxes or custom duties; where there will be a need for specifically skilled workforce, etc. Presently, data are being gathered to set up a relevant simulator. In cooperation with the Austrian Economic Chambers (WKO), more than 100,000 WKO members where asked via a questionnaire to name their central

derzeit Daten erhoben. In Zusammenarbeit mit der Wirtschaftskammer Österreich wurden während der Coronakrise mehr als 100.000 Mitglieder der WKO per Fragebogen gebeten, ihre zentralen Zulieferer und Abnehmer sowie ihre typischen Lagerstände zu nennen. Außerdem wurde erhoben, wie viele Mitarbeiterinnen und Mitarbeiter ausfallen können, bevor die Produktion gefährdet ist, und wie viele im Zuge der Coronakrise verfügbar waren. Eine erste statistische Auswertung der Daten von knapp 6000 Unternehmen zeigte, dass die österreichischen Zulieferketten insgesamt nur beschränkt robust sind: Jede dritte befragte Firma gab an, mindestens einen Lieferanten zu haben, dessen Ausfall nach Aufbrauchen der aktuellen Lagerbestände einen kompletten Stillstand des Betriebs bewirken würde. Für 55 Prozent dieser zentralen Lieferanten gibt es keine Alternativen, rund 40 Prozent stammen aus dem Ausland. Gleichzeitig sind die Lagerbestände der Unternehmen in Österreich jedoch relativ hoch – als Puffer für Lieferschwierigkeiten reichen sie im Schnitt einen Monat lang. Die Forscherinnen und Forscher sehen dringenden Bedarf einer genaueren Analyse mit wesentlich mehr Daten, um Schwachstellen identifizieren und die Resilienz der österreichischen Wirtschaft insgesamt erhöhen zu können.

Mit Methoden der Komplexitätsforschung kann die Resilienz eines Wirtschaftssystems mittlerweile quantitativ beziffert werden. Forscherinnen und Forscher um Peter Klimek (CSH Vienna) haben dazu ein Modell konstruiert, das auf einem Ansatz der Physik, der sogenannten »Linearen Widerstandstheorie«, beruht: Diese beschäftigt sich damit, wie etwa magnetische Materialien reagieren, wenn sie von einem starken externen Magnetfeld beeinflusst werden. Es stellte sich heraus, dass die Struktur dieses Problems der Frage der Krisenanfälligkeit einer Wirtschaft infolge von äußeren Disruptionen ähnelt. Durch die Störung entsteht ein Ungleichgewicht, den das System erst nach einiger Zeit überwindet. Das mathematische Modell wurde mit Daten von 56 Industriesektoren aus 43 Ländern zwischen den Jahren 2000 und 2014 parametrisiert. In der Folge konnte gezeigt werden, wie ein Schock wellenartig das ganze System durchläuft und allen wechselseitigen Verbindungen folgt. Das machte u. a. verständlich, warum es nach der Finanzkrise 2008/09 so lange dauerte, bis alle Branchen wieder zur Normalität zurückfanden.

Im Kampf gegen Finanzkrisen

Solche Modelle lassen viele interessante weitere Untersuchungen zu. Stefan Thurner, Leiter des CSH Vienna, hat ein Modell der Finanzmärkte mit Banken als Netzwerkknoten und Finanztransaktionen als Verbindungen erstellt. Die Frage war, wie sich Schocks in diesem Modell ausbreiten – und wie sich dies verhindern ließe. In dem Modell wurde etwa eine Bank in die Insolvenz geschickt und beobachtet, wie andere Banken davon betroffen sind. Vergleichbar ist das Geschehen dem Entstehen eines Lochs in einem

suppliers and buyers and indicate their typical stock inventories. In addition, inquiries were made as to how many employees could be released without putting production at risk, and how many were available during the coronavirus crisis. A first statistical evaluation of the data obtained from just under 6,000 companies has revealed that Austria's supply chains as a whole are only robust to a limited extent: every third company questioned stated that it had at least one supplier whose cessation of activities would cause the company's complete standstill after current stock supplies had been used up. For 55 percent of these central suppliers there are no alternatives, and about 40 percent are located abroad. At the same time, however, stock supplies of companies in Austria are relatively high—they would last a month on average as buffers to compensate for delivery problems. Researchers see the urgent need for a more detailed analysis relying on more data in order to identify weak points and be able to improve the resilience of the Austrian economy as a whole.

Using methods of complexity science, it has meanwhile become possible to quantify the resilience of an economic system. Researchers working with Peter Klimek (CSH Vienna) have constructed a model based on an approach borrowed from physics, the so-called "linear theory of resistance": it looks into how magnetic materials react when influenced by a strong external magnetic field. It has turned out that the structure of this problem is similar to that of an economy's vulnerability to crisis due to outside disruption. Disturbances cause an imbalance that the system will only be able to overcome after some time. The mathematical model was parameterized with data obtained from 56 industrial sectors in 43 countries from the years between 2000 and 2014. The research team has thus succeeded in showing how a shock runs through the whole system in waves, seizing all interrelated junctions. Among other things, this makes it understandable why it took so long until all industries had returned to normal after the financial crisis of 2008/9.

Struggling against financial crises

Such models permit us to carry out many additional fascinating analyses. Stefan Thurner, president of the CSH Vienna, has drawn up a model of financial markets, with banks as network nodes and financial transactions as connecting lines. The question was posed as to how shocks would propagate within this model—and how this could be prevented. In the model, a bank was declared bankrupt, and then it was observed how this would impact on other banks. Such an event can be compared to a hole in a sweater that grows larger and larger due to some snowball effect and spreads to larger and larger parts of

Pullover, das durch einen Schneeballeffekt immer größer wird und immer weitere Teile der Strickarbeit erfasst. Irgendwann verliert das Netzwerk dann seine Funktion – wie es bei einem Bankencrash der Fall ist. Um das zu verhindern, muss ein lokales Problem eingedämmt werden, muss lokal beschränkt bleiben. Durch zahlreiche Simulationen hat Thurner herausgefunden, dass das durch eine „systemic risk tax" – eine kleine Steuer, die abhängig vom systemischen Risiko einer Institution ist – möglich ist, die für die Banken einen Anreiz schafft, ihr lokales Netzwerk vernünftig zu gestalten. Im Idealfall muss niemand diese Steuer bezahlen – weil alle vernünftig handeln. Das gesamte System könnte dadurch um den Faktor 10.000 stabiler werden. ✖

Quellen

César Hidalgo, *Wachstum geht anders. Von kleinsten Teilchen über den Menschen zu Netzwerken,* Hoffmann und Campe, Hamburg 2016, 288 Seiten, ISBN 978-3-455-50308-1

The Atlas of Economic Complexity; http://atlas.cid.harvard.edu

the knitting. At some point, the network will lose its function—as is the case in a banking crash. In order to prevent this, a local problem has to be contained and remain limited to a specific region. Basing his work on numerous simulations, Thurner has found out that this can be achieved with a modest tax depending on the systemic risk of an institution (systemic risk tax) that creates an incentive for banks to manage their local network reasonably. In the ideal case, this tax will not have to be paid by anyone—because everyone has acted reasonably. The stability of the entire system could be improved by the factor of 10,000. ✕

Sources

César Hidalgo, *Why Information Grows: The Evolution of Order, from Atoms to Economies,* New York, 2015

The Atlas of Economic Complexity; http://atlas.cid.harvard.edu

»Man braucht Flexibilität und Anpassungsfähigkeit«

»Cyber Physical Systems« wie etwa autonome Fahrzeuge weisen eine immense Komplexität auf – sowohl in sich als auch in Beziehung zu ihrer Umwelt. Um mit den vielen Unwägbarkeiten umgehen zu können, müssen diese Systeme adaptiv und resilient gestaltet werden. Wie das geschehen kann, erläutert Mario Drobics, Forscher am AIT Austrian Institute of Technology.

Unter »Internet of Things« (IoT) versteht man die zunehmende Vernetzung von Gegenständen, die per Sensoren Daten aus ihrer Umgebung aufnehmen und elektronisch mit anderen Teilnehmern im Netz teilen. Man verspricht sich davon immense Fortschritte etwa im Bereich der Medizin, bei der Verkehrsplanung und -steuerung, der Betreuung älterer Menschen, beim sorgsameren Umgang mit Ressourcen, bei der Optimierung der Produktion, der Wartung von Maschinen, der Senkung des Energieverbrauchs sowie beim Monitoring der Umwelt. Man schätzt, dass die Zahl der über das IoT vernetzten Gegenstände bereits die 10-Milliarden-Marke überstiegen hat – und das Wachstum wird weitergehen.

Das IoT ist schon in sich ein komplexes System mit vielen Ebenen, Verbindungen und Rückkopplungen, die sich mit der Zeit verändern. Zusätzliche Komplexität kommt ins Spiel, wenn die elektronischen Sensornetzwerke direkt mit der physischen Welt und uns Menschen interagieren, wie das bei sogenannten »Cyber Physical Systems« (CPS) der Fall ist. »Wir haben es mit komplexen Systemen zu tun, die sich durch große soziale, technische und organisatorische Abhängigkeiten auszeichnen«, erläutert Mario Drobics, Leiter der Competence Unit »Cooperative Digital Technologies« am AIT. Es sei unmöglich, die Abhängigkeiten bis ins letzte Detail zu verstehen und für einen konkreten Fall zu überlegen, welche Konsequenzen es hat, wenn etwas Unvorhergesehenes passiert. Vielmehr müsse man auf den Resilienzgedanken setzen – also darauf, im System die Fähigkeit zu verankern, mit Veränderungen, egal welcher Art, umzugehen und gegebenenfalls das Gesamtsystem neu auszurichten. »Kurz gesagt: Man braucht Flexibilität und Anpassungsfähigkeit«, so Drobics.

Als für das Design resilienter Systeme hilfreich erachtet der Forscher die sieben Prinzipien, die das Stockholm Resilience Centre ausgearbeitet hat *(https://www.stockholmresilience.org/research/research-news/2015-04-08-seven-principles-for-building-resilience.html)*.

"We need flexibility and adaptability"

"Cyberphysical systems" such as autonomous vehicles are immensely complex—both in themselves and in relation to their environment. In order to be able to cope with their many imponderables, systems of this kind must be designed to be adaptive and resilient. Mario Drobics, researcher at the AIT Austrian Institute of Technology, explains how this can be achieved.

"Internet of Things" (IoT) refers to the increasing networking of objects that use sensors to record data from their surroundings and share it electronically with other participants in the network. This is expected to lead to enormous progress in areas such as medicine, traffic planning and control, care for the elderly, the more circumspect use of resources, the optimization of production, maintenance of machines, reduction of energy consumption, and environmental monitoring. It is estimated that the number of items networked via IoT has already exceeded the 10 billion mark—and keeps growing.

IoT is in itself a complex system with many levels, connections, and feedbacks that change over time. Additional complexity comes into play when electronic sensor networks interact directly with the physical world and us humans, as is the case with so-called "cyberphysical systems" (CPS). "We are dealing with complex systems that are characterized by major social, technical, and organizational dependencies," explains Mario Drobics, head of AIT's Cooperative Digital Technologies Competence Unit. He regards it as simply impossible to understand these dependencies down to the last detail and to assess the consequences for a specific case if something unforeseen happens. One must rely on the idea of resilience rather—in other words, on anchoring in the system the ability to deal with changes of whatever kind and, if necessary, realign the entire system. "In short, we need flexibility and adaptability," says Drobics.

The researcher considers the seven principles developed by the Stockholm Resilience Centre to be helpful for the design of resilient systems *(https://www.stockholmresilience.org/research/research-news/2015-04-08-seven-principles-for-building-resilience.html)*.

1. **»Maintain diversity and redundancy«:** Man braucht Vielfalt und Redundanz, um bei Veränderungen oder Ausfällen Alternativen zur Hand zu haben.

2. **»Manage connectivity«:** Es bedarf eines ausgewogenen Maßes an Vernetzung, sodass Störungen aufgefangen werden können und möglichst nicht weitergetragen werden.

3. **»Manage slow variables and feedbacks«:** Man muss seine Aufmerksamkeit auch auf langsame Veränderungen richten. Wenn man z. B. die langsame Erhöhung der Temperatur im Zuge des Klimawandels ignoriert, wird der Druck auf das System irgendwann plötzlich so groß, dass es schwierig sein wird, darauf zu reagieren und das System wieder in einen stabilen Zustand zu bekommen.

4. **»Foster complex adaptive systems thinking«:** Man muss immer das Gesamtsystem im Blick haben, Inseldenken funktioniert nicht mehr.

5. **»Encourage learning«:** Beim Umgang mit komplexen Systemen gibt es keine fertigen Kochrezepte. Man muss ständig aus dem lernen, was man tut.

6. **»Broaden participation«:** Man benötigt eine breite Basis, auf der man lernen kann. Alle Stakeholder sollten ein gemeinsames Verständnis und gemeinsame Perspektiven entwickeln und dadurch gegenseitiges Vertrauen aufbauen.

7. **»Promote polycentric governance«:** Entscheidungsfindung und Steuerung müssen Vielfalt zulassen. In festen Bahnen zu denken und in alten Abhängigkeiten zu verharren, kann für den Aufbau resilienter Systeme nicht hilfreich sein.

Dieser Ansatz lässt sich sehr gut auf technische Systeme übertragen, so Drobics. Er nennt als Beispiel ein Projekt, in dem es um die Vertrauenswürdigkeit von Cyber Physical Systems, konkret von autonomen Fahrzeugen, geht. »Die Frage ist: Wie können wir technische Systeme an der Schnittstelle zur physischen Welt so gestalten, dass sie vertrauenswürdig sind?« Um die enorme Komplexität in den Griff zu bekommen, sind in Drobics' Augen zwei Aspekte wesentlich: Einerseits muss das System in sich adaptiv sein, damit es stets seine Funktion erfüllen kann; andererseits muss man die Interaktionen mit der Außenwelt entsprechend berücksichtigen. »Man muss sich also überlegen, welche Maßnahmen man treffen muss, um mit Unvorhergesehenem umzugehen«, so Drobics. Manche Dinge könne man im Vorfeld überlegen, viele möglicherweise auftretende Probleme kenne man aber gar nicht. Dennoch muss es das Ziel sein, das System auf solche Probleme vorzubereiten, sodass es entsprechende Reaktionen setzen kann.

Wenn beispielsweise ein Teil der Elektronik ausfällt, muss das System zumindest so weit abgesichert sein, dass es zu keinem fatalen Schaden kommt. »Wenn das Fahrzeug am Fahrbahnrand stehen bleibt, ist es ausfallsicher (fail-safe). Es passiert also nichts Schlimmes. Wenn wir uns aber auf

1. **Maintain diversity and redundancy.** Diversity and redundancy are essential to have alternatives at hand in case of changes or failures.

2. **Manage connectivity.** A balanced degree of networking is required so that disturbances can be absorbed and, if possible, not passed on.

3. **Manage slow variables and feedbacks.** You have to pay close attention to slow changes as well. If you ignore the slow increase in temperature due to climate change, for instance, the pressure on the system will at some point suddenly become so great that it will be difficult to respond to it and get the system back to a stable state.

4. **Foster complex adaptive systems thinking.** You always have to keep a wary eye on the overall system; insular thinking no longer works.

5. **Encourage learning.** When dealing with complex systems there are no ready-made recipes. You have to constantly learn from what you do.

6. **Broaden participation.** You need a broad basis on which to learn. All stakeholders should come to a common understanding and shared perspectives to build mutual trust.

7. **Promote polycentric governance.** Decision-making and management must allow for diversity. Moving along the same old track and sticking to old dependencies cannot be helpful for the development of resilient systems.

This approach can be efficiently transferred to technical systems, says Drobics, citing a project that is about the trustworthiness of cyber-physical systems, specifically autonomous vehicles. "The question is: How can we design technical systems at the interface with the physical world in such a way that they are trustworthy?" In Drobics's view, two aspects are essential to get a handle on the enormous complexity: On the one hand, the system must be adaptive in itself so that it can always fulfil its function; on the other hand, interactions with the outside world must be weighed accordingly. "You have to think about which measures will help you deal with the unforeseen," he says. Some things can be considered in advance, but many potential problems are unknown. Nevertheless, the goal must be to prepare the system for such problems so that it can react accordingly.

If, for example, a part of the electronics fails, the system must be protected at least to the extent that no fatal damage occurs. "If the vehicle stops at the edge of the road, it is fail-safe. Nothing bad will happen. But if we really want to rely on the system, it must continue to function even in the event of a mistake. We describe this as fail-

das System wirklich verlassen wollen, muss es auch im Fall eines Fehlers weiter funktionieren. Wir sprechen von ›fail-operational‹.« Gemeinsam mit Kolleginnen und Kollegen der TU Wien und von TTTech untersuchen AIT-Forscherinnen und -Forscher, wie man Ausfälle von Sensoren etwa dadurch kompensieren kann, dass man versucht, die notwendigen Informationen aus anderen Quellen zu bekommen (auch wenn diese vielleicht weniger genau sind). »Das System muss adaptiv sein und innerhalb weniger Millisekunden eine Alternative gefunden haben.«

Noch weniger absehbar sind Einflüsse auf autonome Fahrzeuge von außen. Was soll das System tun, wenn plötzlich ein Hindernis auftaucht, das Wetter umschlägt oder – noch problematischer – ein Cyberangriff auf die Software stattfindet. »In komplexen, sich ständig verändernden Systemen kann man nicht mehr von einem ›normalen‹ Verhalten des Systems sprechen. Ein Angriff lässt sich nicht sofort klassifizieren.« Das bedeutet, dass das System so gestaltet werden muss, dass es auf der einen Seite langsame Veränderungen antizipiert, auf der anderen Seite aber festzustellen in der Lage ist, wenn etwas aus dem Ruder läuft. »Wenn etwas völlig Atypisches eintritt, muss das System reagieren.« Für das Erkennen derartiger Anomalien können Steuerbefehle, Logdateien oder sogar verschlüsselte Datenkanäle herangezogen werden. »Dabei versteht man zwar nicht immer, was kommuniziert wird, kann aber trotzdem gewisse Muster herauslesen.«

Technisch gesehen sind zum Aufbau von resilienten, adaptiven Systemen drei Grundmomente wesentlich: »Erstens geht es um eine funktionale Redundanz, bei der im Fall des Falles andere Systeme einspringen können. Redundanz bedeutet hier nicht, dass man, um Ausfallsicherheit zu gewährleisten, alles doppelt ausführen muss, wie man das etwa bei den Mondmissionen getan hat.« Zweitens müssen Systeme lernen können: »Man braucht Lernalgorithmen, um zu erkennen, wann etwas nicht mehr so läuft, wie es sollte – obwohl sich die Umwelt und teils auch die Systeme selbstständig verändern.« Das setzt drittens Kommunikation voraus. »Wenn Fahrzeuge untereinander und mit der Umgebung vernetzt sind und Daten austauschen, können die Komponenten des Systems voneinander lernen.« Kommunikation ermöglicht überdies weitere Redundanzen: »Wenn etwa ein Sensor eines Fahrzeugs ausfällt, kann beispielsweise ein Sensor des voranfahrenden Autos angezapft werden.«

Der Forscher betont, dass parallel dazu eine gesellschaftliche Diskussion zu führen sei: Inwieweit wollen wir technischen Systemen vertrauen? Was tun, wenn wir ihnen nicht mehr vertrauen können? Wer hat dann die Verantwortung? »Das ist eine zentrale Frage. Da bedarf es gesellschaftlicher und technischer Normen, die Hand in Hand gehen und regeln, wie wir diese Systeme in den Alltag integrieren und wer dann die Verantwortung übernehmen soll«, so Drobics. ✖

operational." Together with colleagues from the Vienna University of Technology and TTTech, AIT researchers are investigating how to compensate for sensor failures by trying to obtain the necessary information from other sources (even if they may be less accurate). "The system must be adaptive and must have found an alternative within a few milliseconds."

Even less foreseeable are external influences on autonomous vehicles. What should the system do if an obstacle suddenly appears, if the weather changes or—even more problematic—if a cyberattack on the software occurs? "In complex, constantly changing systems, one can no longer speak of a normal behavior of the system. An attack cannot be immediately classified." This means that the system must be designed to be able to anticipate slow changes and to detect something getting out of hand. "If something completely atypical occurs, the system must respond." Control commands, log files, or even encrypted data channels may be used for the detection of such anomalies. "Though it is not always possible to understand what is being communicated, you can identify certain patterns."

From a technical point of view, three basic moments are essential for the construction of resilient, adaptive systems: "First, it is a matter of functional redundancy; other systems can step in if necessary. Redundancy here does not mean that everything has to be done twice in order to guarantee fail-safe operation, as was the case with the moon missions, for example." Second, systems must be able to learn: "We need learning algorithms to recognize when something is not working as it should, even though the environment and sometimes the systems themselves are changing." Third, communication is called for. "If vehicles are networked with each other and with their environment and exchange data, the components of the system can learn from each other." Communication also enables further redundancies: "If a sensor in a vehicle fails, for example, a sensor in the car in front can be tapped."

The researcher emphasizes that a social discussion must be conducted in parallel: To what extent do we want to trust technical systems? What do we do if we can no longer trust them? Who will be in charge then? "This is a crucial question. There is a need for social and technical standards that go hand in hand and regulate how we integrate these systems into everyday life and who should then take responsibility," says Drobics. ✕

»Die neue rechnergestützte Sozialwissenschaft bietet unglaubliche Möglichkeiten«

Professor Alex »Sandy« Pentland leitet die MIT Connection Science und Human Dynamics Labore und war zuvor am Aufbau des MIT Media Lab und des Media Lab Asia in Indien beteiligt. Er ist einer der meistzitierten Computer-Wissenschafter, „Forbes" bezeichnete ihn als einen der „sieben einflussreichsten Computer-Wissenschafter der Welt". Er ist Gründungsmitglied von Beratungsgremien für Google, AT&T, Nissan und den UN-Generalsekretär. Pentland gründete mehr als ein Dutzend Unternehmen, ist Mitglied in der US National Academy of Engineering und im World Economic Forum aktiv.

Alex »Sandy« Pentland, ein Pionier der Vermessung von sozialen Netzwerken und individuellen Verhaltensmustern, ist überzeugt, dass wir durch Nutzung von Daten eine bessere Gesellschaft aufbauen können.

Schon in der griechischen Antike befasste man sich mit der Frage, wie die Gesellschaft funktioniert und was sie zusammenhält. Welche Faktoren sind wesentlich, damit Menschen gemeinsam große Aufgaben bewältigen? Wie organisiert man das Zusammenleben am besten? Wie sollten Institutionen gestaltet sein, damit sie den gemeinsamen Interessen der Menschen am dienlichsten sind? Solche Fragen standen auch am Beginn der Aufklärung, als es darum ging, moderne Staaten zu errichten. Auguste Comte träumte beispielsweise davon, eine exakte Wissenschaft von Sozialsystemen aufzubauen: eine »Soziophysik«, wie er es nannte. Auch bei Adam Smith oder Karl Marx standen die Organisation des Zusammenlebens und die Koordination zwischen Individuen und Menschengruppen im Zentrum aller Überlegungen. Viele Theorien wurden erdacht, viele mögliche Mechanismen des Zusammenlebens formuliert – und auf ihrer Basis neue Gesellschaftsformen und Institutionen geschaffen.

3.5

Soziale Systeme

"This new computational social science offers incredible possibilities"

Professor Alex "Sandy" Pentland directs the MIT Connection Science and Human Dynamics labs and previously helped create and direct the MIT Media Lab and the Media Lab Asia in India. He is one of the globally most-cited computational scientists, with Forbes declaring him one of the "seven most powerful data scientists in the world". Pentland is a founding member of advisory boards for Google, AT&T, Nissan, and the UN Secretary General, a serial entrepreneur who has co-founded more than a dozen companies. He is a member of the US National Academy of Engineering and leader within the World Economic Forum.

Alex "Sandy" Pentland, a pioneer in measuring social networks and individual behavior patterns, is convinced that using data will help us build a better society.

The question of how society functions and what holds it together was already addressed in Greek antiquity. Which factors are essential for people to master great tasks together? How is living together best organized? How should institutions be designed so that they are most conducive to people's common interests? Such questions also stood at the beginning of the Enlightenment when the aim was to build modern states. Auguste Comte, for example, dreamed of establishing an exact science of social systems: a "sociophysics," as he called it. With Adam Smith or Karl Marx, too, the organization of coexistence and the coordination between individuals and groups of people were at the center of all considerations. Many theories were conceived, many possible mechanisms of coexistence were formulated—and new forms of society and institutions were created on their basis.

Sensoren zeichnen Verhalten und Sozialkontakte auf

Allerdings: Die Theorien blieben Theorien, man konnte ihre Richtigkeit im Grunde kaum beweisen. Das ändert sich derzeit, zumindest in den Augen von Forschern, die sich mit »Computational Social Science« beschäftigen. Ein Pionier unter diesen Wissenschaftern ist Alex »Sandy« Pentland, einer der Gründer des MIT Media Lab und derzeit Leiter der MIT Connection Science Research Initiative. Er begann schon in den 1980er-Jahren mit der Entwicklung von Methoden, um das tatsächliche Verhalten von Menschen anhand realer Daten zu untersuchen. Pentland war beispielsweise am Bau von sogenannten »Soziometern« beteiligt, die mithilfe von Sensoren das Leben von freiwilligen Versuchspersonen, insbesondere deren Verhalten und Sozialkontakte, aufzeichnen. Heutige Smartphones können all das und noch viel mehr, und mit ausgereiften Methoden zur Auswertung von Big Data – etwa von Handy- oder Kreditkartendaten – können sehr weitreichende Schlüsse auf das Verhalten von Menschen gezogen werden.

An den traditionellen Sozialwissenschaften kritisiert Pentland vor allem zwei Dinge: Zum einen findet er es falsch, den Menschen vorwiegend als rationales Individuum zu betrachten – denn dadurch übersehe man die immense Bedeutung der Mitmenschen (peers) in der unmittelbaren Umgebung. Zum anderen, und eng damit zusammenhängend, ist Pentland der Ansicht, dass Adam Smith und Karl Marx nur halb recht hatten: Die Konzentration auf Klassen und Märkte – beides Aggregate, die den Durchschnitt einer großen Zahl von Menschen abbilden – verstelle den Blick auf die Muster der individuellen Beziehungen zwischen Menschen auf der Mikroebene. Und auf diese kommt es Pentland zufolge an: Menschliches Verhalten sei stark von Peer-to-Peer-Kontakten und den Brücken zwischen Individuen mitbestimmt, pflegt er in seinen zahlreichen Artikeln, Büchern und Interviews zu betonen. Als Beleg dafür wertet er beispielsweise eine Studie der Harvard University, in der nachgewiesen wurde, dass jene Menschen, die über ein größeres soziales Netzwerk verfügen, ein höheres Einkommen haben. Sie haben nämlich Zugriff auf einen reicheren Fundus an Ideen und Möglichkeiten und können diese auch umsetzen. Nebenbei bemerkt: Menschen mit schwächer ausgeprägten sozialen Netzwerken haben laut dieser Studie ein höheres Risiko, früher zu sterben.

»Wenn wir uns selbst besser verstehen, können wir bessere Gesellschaften aufbauen«, so Pentlands Überzeugung. Die heutigen Institutionen stammen größtenteils aus dem 19. Jahrhundert und beruhen daher auf einem alten Bild des Menschen, das sich nun im Lichte der detaillierteren Einsichten durch Big Data als nur halbrichtig erwiesen habe. »Das ist das erste Mal in der Geschichte der Menschheit, dass wir genug über uns selbst zu sehen imstande sind, um hoffen zu können, tatsächlich soziale Systeme aufzubauen, die qualitativ besser funktionieren als die Systeme, die wir immer hatten«, so Pentland.

Sensors record behavior and social contacts

However: The theories remained theories, their correctness could hardly be proven. This is currently changing, at least in the eyes of researchers working on "computational social science." A pioneer among these scientists is Alex "Sandy" Pentland, one of the founders of the MIT Media Lab and currently head of the MIT Connection Science Research Initiative. He began developing methods to study the actual behavior of people using real data back in the 1980s. Pentland was, among other things, involved in the construction of so-called "socio-meters," which use sensors to record the lives of volunteers, especially their behavior and social contacts. Today's smartphones can do all this and much more, and with sophisticated methods for evaluating big data—such as mobile phone or credit card data—very far-reaching conclusions can be drawn about people's behavior.

Pentland's criticism of the traditional social sciences is twofold: First, he thinks it is wrong to view people primarily as rational individuals—because by doing so, one overlooks the immense importance of peers in their immediate environment. Second, and closely related to this, he believes that Adam Smith and Karl Marx were only half right: Their concentration on classes and markets, both aggregates that represent the average of a large number of people, obscures the patterns of individual relationships between people at the micro-level. And that's what Pentland says it's all about: Human behavior is strongly influenced by peer-to-peer contacts and the bridges forged between individuals, he likes to emphasize in his numerous articles, books, and interviews. As proof of this, he cites, for example, a Harvard University study that shows that people with a larger social network have a higher income. After all, they have access to a richer pool of ideas and opportunities and can put them into practice. People with weaker social networks, by the way, have a higher risk of dying earlier according to this study.

"Once we understand ourselves better, we can build better societies," Pentland believes. Most of today's institutions date back to the nineteenth century and are therefore based on an old image of man that, in the light of more detailed insights provided by big data, has now been shown to be only half correct: "This is the first time in human history that we have the ability to see enough about ourselves that we can hope to actually build social systems that work qualitatively better than the systems we've always had," says Pentland.

Bürger*innen sollen volle Kontrolle über ihre Daten haben

Entscheidend in diesem Zusammenhang sind ein sorgsamer Umgang mit Daten und der Aufbau von Vertrauen in die digitale Gesellschaft. »Wir brauchen gesellschaftliche Systeme, denen wir alle vertrauen können.« Findet man keine Lösung, würde das zu einer »unglaublich invasiven Big-Brother-Welt« führen, die sich nicht einmal George Orwell in seinen kühnsten Fantasien für das Buch 1984 hätte ausdenken können. Pentlands Gruppe am MIT kämpft gezielt dagegen an und hat eine Open-Algorithms-Architektur (OPAL) entwickelt, die umfassenden Datenschutz gewährleistet und den Bürgerinnen und Bürgern jederzeit die volle Kontrolle über ihre Daten sichert. Die Forscherinnen und Forscher bauen derzeit gemeinsam mit Partnern in Kolumbien und im Senegal ein solches System auf. Dabei werden auch alle Stakeholder zusammengebracht, die entscheiden sollen, welche – privaten oder öffentlichen – Daten für wen und für welche Zwecke zugänglich sein sollen.

Die Vision zielt auf die Etablierung eines sozialen Systems, das durch Rückkopplungen ständig Echtzeitwissen über den Erfolg oder Misserfolg von Maßnahmen liefert – quasi eine neuartige Art der (seit Adam Smith sprichwörtlichen) »unsichtbaren Hand«, die für die Koordinierung der Gesellschaft sorgt. Das soll Pentland zufolge eine »neue Datenwelt ermöglichen, eine Welt, die fairer, effizienter und inklusiver ist und mehr Chancen als je zuvor bietet«. ✕

Quellen

Thomas Hardjono, David L. Shrier und Alex Pentland (Hg.), *Trusted Data. A New Framework for Identity and Data Sharing,* The MIT Press, Cambridge/Mass. und London 2019. ISBN 9780262043212

Alex Pentland, »Data for a New Enlightenment«, in: *Towards a New Enlightenment? A Transcendent Decade,* BBVA OpenMind 2019; *https://www.bbvaopenmind.com/en/articles/data-for-a-new-enlightenment/*

Citizens should have full control over their data

Careful data handling and building trust in the digital society are crucial in this context. "We need civic systems that we can all trust." If no solution is found, this would lead to an "incredibly invasive Big Brother world," which not even George Orwell would have come up with in his wildest fantasies for the book 1984. Pentland's group at MIT is specifically fighting against this and has developed an Open Algorithms Architecture (OPAL) that ensures comprehensive data protection and gives citizens full control over their data at all times. The researchers are presently setting up such a system together with partners in Colombia and Senegal. This will also bring together all the stakeholders who are to decide which data, whether private or public, should be accessible to whom and for what purposes.

The vision is aimed at establishing a social system that constantly provides real-time knowledge about the success or failure of measures through feedback—a new type of (since Adam Smith proverbial) "invisible hand" that safeguards the coordination of society. This should, according to Pentland, allow for a "new world of data, a world that is more fair, efficient, and inclusive, and that provides greater opportunities than ever before."×

Sources

Thomas Hardjono, David L. Shrier, and Alex Pentland, eds., *Trusted Data. A New Framework for Identity and Data Sharing*, Cambridge/Mass. and London, 2019.

Alex Pentland, "Data for a New Enlightenment," in *Towards a New Enlightenment? A Transcendent Decade*, BBVA OpenMind, 2019; *https://www.bbvaopenmind.com/en/articles/data-for-a-new-enlightenment/*

Matthias Weber und Thomas Scherngell,
Center for Innovation Systems & Policy,
AIT Austrian Institute of Technology

Die neue Rolle von Forschung, Technologie und Innovation in der Gesellschaft

Innovationssysteme werden immer komplexer. Neben technologischen Innovationen rücken zunehmend soziale und organisatorische Innovationen in den Vordergrund. Forschung, Technologie und Innovation müssen stärker denn je auf gesellschaftliche Bedarfe und Belange eingehen. Dafür sind neue Methoden erforderlich.

Forschung, Technologie und Innovation (FTI) waren die vergangenen Jahrzehnte hindurch ein wichtiger, wenn nicht gar der zentrale Treiber für gesellschaftliche Veränderung. Aufbauend auf einem forschungs- und technologiezentrierten Verständnis von Innovation hat dies zu einer sehr erfolgreichen ökonomischen Entwicklung geführt. Auch Österreich zählt zu den Ländern, die davon stark profitiert haben.

Heute sind wir indes vermehrt mit technologischen Entwicklungen konfrontiert, die in ihrer Geschwindigkeit und ihren Auswirkungen unsere Gesellschaft vor große Herausforderungen stellen. Obwohl die Digitalisierung in vielerlei Hinsicht mit großen Hoffnungen verbunden wird, stellt sie etablierte Geschäftsmodelle in Frage und führt zu Umwälzungen in globalen Wertschöpfungsketten. Neue medizinische Entwicklungen liefern nicht nur neue Diagnose- und Therapiemöglichkeiten, sondern werfen zugleich grundlegende ethische Fragen auf. Die Coronapandemie hat aufgezeigt, dass Wissenschaft und Forschung extrem gefordert sind, rascher als in der Vergangenheit neue Lösungsansätze zur Bewältigung unerwarteter Krisensituation bereitzustellen.

Diese Beispiele zeigen, dass FTI stärker denn jemals zuvor auf gesellschaftliche Bedarfe und Belange eingehen müssen. Wir beobachten zurzeit einen grundlegenden Wandel der Rolle von FTI in unserer Gesellschaft – weg von einem weitgehend autonomen Faktor, der die Entwicklungsrichtung unserer Gesellschaft sehr stark bestimmt hat, hin zu einer Kraft, die zielgerichtet für die Bewältigung gesellschaftlicher Herausforderungen eingesetzt wird. Kurz gesagt: Die Wechselwirkungen zwischen FTI und Gesellschaft verstärken einander.

Matthias Weber and Thomas Scherngell,
Center for Innovation Systems & Policy,
AIT Austrian Institute of Technology

The New Role of Research, Technology, and Innovation in Society

Innovation systems are becoming more and more complex. In addition to technological innovations, social and organizational innovations are gaining increasing importance. Research, technology, and innovation must respond to social needs and concerns with more power than ever before. This calls for new methods.

Research, technology, and innovation (RTI) have been an important, if not the central driver of social change over the past decades. Based on a research- and technology-centered understanding of innovation, this has led to a very successful economic development. Austria is one of the countries that have benefited substantially from this.

Today, however, we are increasingly confronted with technological developments that present our society with major challenges in terms of their speed and impact. Although digitization is invested with great hopes in many respects, it casts doubt on established business models and leads to upheavals in global value chains. New medical developments not only offer new diagnostic and therapeutic options but also raise fundamental ethical questions. The coronavirus pandemic has shown that science and research are extremely challenged to provide new solutions to unexpected crisis situations more quickly than in the past.

These examples show that RTI has to respond more than ever before to societal needs and concerns. We currently observe a fundamental change in the role of RTI in our society—away from a largely autonomous factor that has determined the direction of societal development to a force that is purposefully deployed to meet social challenges. In short, the interactions between RTI and society reinforce each other.

The present debate on "mission-oriented" research reflects this. This does not mean that RTI should be pursued exclusively in a purpose-oriented sense. Exploratory scientific research also plays a central

Die aktuelle Debatte über »missionsorientierte« Forschung spiegelt das wider. Das bedeutet zwar nicht, dass FTI ausschließlich in einem zweckorientierten Sinne durchgeführt werden sollen – explorative wissenschaftliche Forschung spielt auch im Rahmen dieser Neuausrichtung eine zentrale Rolle für das Generieren neuer Erkenntnisse und einer großen Bandbreite methodischer und technologischer Lösungsansätze. Dennoch verschiebt sich das Koordinatensystem, in dem sich FTI-Akteure bewegen, und zwar grundlegend und in mehrfacher Hinsicht: Erstens werden Forschung und Technologie zunehmend nur noch als zwei Bausteine von Innovation unter zahlreichen anderen gesehen; soziale und organisatorische Innovationen rücken stärker in den Brennpunkt. Zweitens erfordern FTI die Einbeziehung eines deutlich breiteren Spektrums von Partnern über die etablierten FTI-Akteure aus Wissenschaft, Wirtschaft und Politik hinaus. Vor allem Städte stehen als Orte der Innovation stärker im Vordergrund, weil sie häufig Träger jener Systeme sind, die in Zukunft eine Transformation durchlaufen müssen (Mobilität, Energieversorgung, Stoffströme usw.). Drittens hat das Folgen für die zukünftige Positionierung von FTI-Politik: Zum einen kommt dem Zusammenspiel von FTI-Politik und jenen Politikfeldern, die innovative Lösungen für ihre jeweiligen Ziele suchen, größere Bedeutung zu. Zum anderen ist das Zusammenspiel dieser verschiedenen Politikfelder gerade auf urbaner Ebene besonders intensiv und führt zu einer Stärkung integrierter, auf Systemveränderungen ausgerichteter Strategien.

Ein höherer Integrationsgrad bedeutet aber auch, dass die Komplexität des Innovationssystems massiv zunimmt und daher neue Methoden zu dessen Analyse und zur Politikgestaltung benötigt werden. Das reicht von neuen Daten und Analyseverfahren (z. B. Mikrodaten, Big Data Analytics und semantischen Methoden) bis hin zu einer Ausweitung partizipativer Ansätze, in die eine Vielzahl von Akteur*innen und Stakeholdern in die Politikentwicklung eingebunden werden. Das AIT Center for Innovation Systems & Policy entwickelt neue Methoden und Ansätze entlang dieses Spektrums.

Auf Mikrodaten basierende Indikatoren ermöglichen neue Einsichten

Ein Beispiel für neue Methoden am einen Ende dieses Spektrums sind Arbeiten zu Mikrodaten im Rahmen der europäischen Forschungsinfrastruktur RISIS (»Research Infrastructure for Science and Innovation Policy Studies«, risis2.eu), die seit einigen Jahren aufgebaut wird. Ausgangspunkt war die Erkenntnis, dass Innovation heute in Netzwerken von forschenden und innovierenden Organisationen geschieht. In den letzten Jahren sind solche Innovationsysteme komplexer geworden, da die sie tragenden Netzwerke nicht nur an Größe, sondern auch an Diversität zunehmen – etwa hinsichtlich des thematischen, institutionellen und geografischen Hintergrunds der teilnehmenden Organisationen.

role in generating new knowledge and a wide range of methodological and technological approaches to solving problems in the context of this reorientation. Nevertheless, the coordinate system in which RTI actors operate is shifting fundamentally and in several respects: First, research and technology are increasingly seen as just two building blocks of innovation among many others. Social and organizational innovations are moving more into the foreground. Second, RTI require the involvement of a much broader spectrum of partners beyond the established RTI actors from science, business, and politics. Cities, in particular, are becoming more prominent as places of innovation because they are often the carriers of the systems that will have to undergo transformation in the future (mobility, energy supply, material flows, etc.). Third, this has consequences for the future positioning of RTI policy: on the one hand, the interaction between RTI policy and those policy fields that seek innovative solutions for their respective goals are taking on greater significance; on the other hand, the interplay of these different policy fields is particularly intense at the urban level and leads to a strengthening of integrated strategies geared to systemic changes.

However, a higher degree of integration also means that the complexity of the innovation system is increasing on a massive scale, which is why new methods for its analysis and policy making are needed. This ranges from new data and analytical methods (e.g., microdata, big data analytics, and semantic methods) to an expansion of participatory approaches that involve a large number of actors and stakeholders in policy development. The AIT Center for Innovation Systems & Policy develops new methods and approaches along this spectrum.

Indicators based on microdata provide new insights

An example of new methods at one end of this spectrum is work on microdata in the context of the European Research Infrastructure for Science and Innovation Policy Studies RISIS (risis2.eu) being established for several years now. The starting point was the recognition that innovation today takes place in networks of organizations doing research and implementing innovations. In recent years, such innovation systems have become more complex as the networks supporting them have increased not only in size but also in diversity—regarding the thematic, institutional, and geographical background of the participating organizations, for example.

Traditional models and indicators of empirical innovation research (such as input-output analyses or the indication of R&D expenditure as a percentage of GDP) can no longer adequately reflect the

Traditionelle Modelle und Indikatoren der empirischen Innovations-forschung (etwa Input-Output-Analysen oder die Angabe der F&E-Ausgaben in Prozent des BIP) können die unterschiedlichen Facetten und Wirkungsme-chanismen von Innovationssystemen nicht mehr adäquat abbilden. Ins Zentrum der wissenschaftlichen Debatte sind neue Datenbasen und Indi-katoren gerückt, die F&E-Aktivitäten auf einer Mikroebene von Einzelorgani-sationen und deren Kollaborationen erfassen.

Während in der Vergangenheit Forschungs- und Innovationsaktivitä-ten vor allem mithilfe standardisierter statistischer Kategorien erfasst wurden (z. B. NACE-Kategorien von Sektoren oder NUTS-Kategorien von räum-lichen Ebenen), ermöglichen Mikrodaten ein wesentlich differenzierteres Bild der Entwicklung von Innovationsmustern. Im RISIS-System werden verschiedene Outputdaten, z. B. Publikationen, Patente oder F&E-Koopera-tionen von Universitäten, Forschungsorganisationen oder Unternehmen, standardisiert und qualitätsgesichert gesammelt; eine Geokodierung erlaubt eine flexible räumliche Analyse. Mithilfe semantischer Methoden können zudem unterschiedliche thematische Schwerpunkte wie etwa die Aktivitäten im Bereich neuer Schlüsseltechnologien oder im Hinblick auf große gesellschaftliche Herausforderungen untersucht werden.

Mikrodaten lassen sich zur Entwicklung neuer Indikatoren heranzie-hen, welche die Komplexität der Wissensbasis einer Organisation und/oder einer Region erfassen. Damit lassen sich auch Modelle konstruieren, die den Einfluss von Innovation auf die sozioökonomische Entwicklung zu erklären versuchen.

In jüngster Zeit ist insbesondere ein neuer Index zur Messung der sogenannten »Wissenskomplexität« von Regionen in den Vordergrund gerückt: Eine Region mit hoher Wissenskomplexität produziert demnach Erkenntnisse und Wissen (die sich z. B. in Patenten niederschlagen) in vielen verschiedenen technologischen Feldern (das heißt, sie weist eine hohe Diversität auf) und gleichzeitig in solchen, für die nur von wenigen anderen Regionen produziert werden können. Erste Analysen haben ergeben, dass die Bereiche digitale Kommunikation, Computertechnologie und Telekom-munikation die höchste Wissenskomplexität aufweisen und die Regionen, in denen diese Technologien entwickelt und produziert werden, typischer-weise andere sind als die traditionellen europäischen Kernregionen. Unter den Regionen mit der höchsten Wissenskomplexität finden sich etwa die Bretagne, Madrid oder Südirland und nicht, wie in herkömmlichen Rankings, beispielsweise Oberbayern oder die Großregion Paris. Das zeigt, dass die Überwindung von gewachsenen Disparitäten in Europa möglich ist.

Mit Modellen, die auf solchen neuen Indikatoren beruhen, kann beispielsweise auch die Frage geklärt werden, wie groß der Einfluss der Fähigkeit, komplexes Wissen zu produzieren, auf das Produktivitätswachs-tum einer Region ist. In empirischen Simulationsmodellen wird zudem

different facets and mechanisms of innovation systems. New databases and indicators that capture R&D activities at a microlevel of individual organizations and their collaborations have become the focus of scientific debate.

Whereas research and innovation activities were mainly recorded using standardized statistical categories (e.g., NACE categories of sectors or NUTS categories of spatial levels) in the past, microdata allow for a far more differentiated picture of the development of innovation patterns. In the RISIS system, various output data, such as publications, patents, or R&D collaborations of universities, research organizations, or companies, are collected in a standardized and quality-assured way; geocoding allows a flexible spatial analysis. Semantic methods can also be employed to explore different thematic focal themes such as activities in the field of new key enabling technologies or with regard to societal grand challenges.

Microdata can be used to develop new indicators that capture the complexity of the knowledge base of an organization and/or a region. They may also provide means to construct models aimed at explaining the impact of innovation on socioeconomic development.

Recently, a new index for measuring the knowledge complexity of regions has come to the fore: according to this index, a region with high knowledge complexity produces knowledge and expertise (which is reflected in patents, for instance) in many different technological fields (which means that the region has a high diversity) and at the same time in those for which only a few other regions are qualified. Initial analyses have shown that the fields of digital communications, computer technology, and telecommunications are the most complex areas of knowledge and that the regions in which these technologies are developed and produced are typically different from Europe's traditional core regions. Brittany, Madrid, or Southern Ireland, for example, and not, as in traditional rankings, regions such as Upper Bavaria or the Île-de-France rank among those with the highest knowledge complexity. This shows that it is possible to overcome deep-rooted disparities in Europe.

Models based on such new indicators can, for instance, also be used to determine the extent to which the ability to produce complex knowledge influences the productivity growth of a region. Empirical simulation models moreover attempt to identify exogenous factors influencing the capacity of organizations or regions to produce knowledge—such as the way RTI policy interventions affect this capacity.

versucht, exogene Einflussfaktoren auf die Kapazität von Organisationen oder Regionen zur Wissensproduktion zu bestimmen – etwa wie sich Interventionen der FTI-Politik auswirken.

Systematische Vorausschau und Einbindung von Stakeholdern

Ein zweites Beispiel für den Umgang mit komplexen Zusammenhängen sind »Foresight-Prozesse« zur Gestaltung von Politikstrategien. Darunter versteht man eine systematische und strukturierte Auseinandersetzung mit komplexen Zukünften. Man will einen offenen Blick in die Zukunft werfen, um mögliche, machbare, wahrscheinliche oder wünschenswerte Entwicklungen zu formulieren und zu analysieren. Foresight-Prozesse setzen auf eine Kombination von quantitativen, qualitativen und partizipativen Methoden. Solche Vorausschaustudien wurden z. B. bei der Entwicklung des nächsten EU-Forschungsrahmenprogramms »Horizon Europe« für die Jahre 2021 bis 2027 eingesetzt, um sicherzustellen, dass die Strategie tatsächlich einen Beitrag zur Bewältigung der großen gesellschaftlichen Herausforderungen leisten kann, denen sich Europa gegenübersieht. Im Herbst 2019 wurden fünf »Mission Boards« eingerichtet, die spezifische Missionen entwickeln und vorschlagen sollen. Die Mitglieder dieser Boards kommen aus unterschiedlichsten Bereichen (Wissenschaft, Politik, Wirtschaft, Zivilgesellschaft) und sind bei der Entwicklung von möglichen Missionsthemen in hohem Maß unabhängig. Um zu gewährleisten, dass die Missionen einen zukunftsorientierten und zukunftsfähigen Charakter haben, werden sie jeweils durch von der EU-Kommission finanzierte Vorausschauprojekte unterstützt, die vom AIT Center for Innovation Systems & Policy koordiniert werden. In einigen dieser Foresight-Prozesse werden verschiedene Formen der Beteiligung von Fachleuten und Stakeholdern umgesetzt. Darüber hinaus sind auch Konsultationen unter Einbeziehung von Bürgerinnen und Bürgern in den EU-Staaten geplant – ganz wie es die neue Rolle von FTI in der Gesellschaft nahelegt. ✖

Systematic foresight and stakeholder involvement

A second example for dealing with complex interrelationships are "foresight processes" for the design of policy strategies. This approach describes a systematic and structured examination of complex futures. The goal is to take an open look into the future in order to formulate and analyze possible, feasible, probable, or desirable developments. Foresight processes rely on a combination of quantitative, qualitative, and participatory methods. Such foresight studies have been used, for example, in the development of "Horizon Europe," the Ninth EU Framework Program for Research and Innovation for the years 2021 to 2027 in order to ensure that the strategy can actually contribute to addressing the societal grand challenges facing Europe. In fall 2019, five Mission Boards were set up to develop and propose specific missions. The members of these boards come from a wide range of backgrounds (science, politics, business, civil society) and are highly independent in developing possible mission themes. In order to guarantee that the missions have a future-oriented and forward-looking character, they are each supported by foresight projects financed by the EU Commission and coordinated by the AIT Center for Innovation Systems & Policy. Some foresight processes provide for further forms of participation of experts and stakeholders. In addition, consultations involving citizens in the EU countries are planned—just as the new role of RTIS in society suggests. ✕

Wenn Komplexität zu menschlicher Überforderung und Unsicherheit führt

Menschen stehen bei der Benutzung von Maschinen oft vor komplexen Aufgaben, denen sie sich nicht gewachsen fühlen. Unter dem Schlagwort »Deconstructing Complexity« entwickelt die User-Experience-Forschung Methoden, die den Umgang mit der Technik erleichtern sollen.

Die Nutzung von technischen Artefakten ist für uns Menschen oft schwierig, weil wir im Allgemeinen die Geräte nicht kennen, nicht gleich verstehen, wie sie funktionieren, oder uns nicht merken (wollen), wie man sie bedient. »Deshalb ergibt sich für Anwenderinnen und Anwender eine gewisse Komplexität«, sagt Manfred Tscheligi, Universitätsprofessor am Center for Human-Computer Interaction der Universität Salzburg und Leiter des Center for Technology Experience am AIT Austrian Institute of Technology. »Besonders komplex wird die Sache, wenn ein Gerät nicht unmittelbar das tut, was man will – und man keine Ahnung hat, warum das so ist.«

Der Komplexitätsbegriff, den Tscheligi hier verwendet, ist stark in der Wahrnehmungspsychologie bzw. im Bereich der Materialität von (realen oder virtuellen) technischen Gegenständen verwurzelt. Dabei geht es darum, wie Menschen Gegenstände in ihrer Umgebung wahrnehmen und begreifen. »Der Mensch kann ein System aus vielen Einzelteilen mit vielen Verknüpfungen und einer verästelten Struktur nicht sofort erfassen und interpretieren«, so der Forscher. Das hat Folgen, die von Unsicherheit und mangelndem Vertrauen in Technik über das Gefühl des Kontrollverlusts bis hin zur Furcht vor Technologie und deren Ablehnung reichen. »Etwas kann technisch super funktionieren, aber wenn ich als Mensch damit nicht umgehen kann – ›es mir zu komplex ist‹ –, kann ich nichts damit anfangen«, so Tscheligi. Bei der Gestaltung von Technologien und den Schnittstellen zu den Anwenderinnen und Anwendern muss daher auf den Menschen Rücksicht genommen werden. Klingt logisch, ist aber in der Praxis noch keineswegs überall Standard. »Komplexität muss sowohl aus technischer Sicht als auch aus Sicht der Nutzerinnen und Nutzer betrachtet werden. Die zweite Dimension kommt bei der Entwicklung neuer Technologien oftmals

When Complexity Leads to Distress and Insecurity in Humans

Using machines, humans are frequently confronted with complex tasks by which they feel overwhelmed. Under the slogan of "deconstructing complexity," user experience research develops methods intended to facilitate our handling of technology.

The use of technical artifacts frequently proves challenging for us humans, as we are probably unfamiliar with the devices in question, do not understand straightaway how they function, or fail (or refuse) to remember how to operate them. "This leads to users being faced with a certain degree of complexity," says Manfred Tscheligi, university professor at the Center for Human-Computer Interaction at the University of Salzburg and head of the Center for Technology Experience at the AIT Austrian Institute of Technology. "Matters become particularly complex when a device does not do what it is expected to do—and you have no idea why."

The concept of complexity Tscheligi refers to here is mostly rooted in perceptual psychology and in the materiality of (real or virtual) technical objects. It is about how humans perceive and grasp objects in their surroundings. "Humans are not capable of comprehending and interpreting a system consisting of a myriad of components, shortcuts, and ramifications on the spot," the scientist points out. Implications range from insecurity and a lack of trust in technology to a feeling of having lost control and a fear of technology and its rejection. "Something might work super easily technically, but when I, being human, am unable to handle it—'It's too complex for me'—it is useless for me," says Tscheligi. The construction and design of technologies and user interfaces therefore has to take human needs into account. This may sound logical but is by no means common standard yet everywhere. "Complexity must be seen from the perspective of both technology and its users. This latter dimension is frequently not duly considered in the development of new technologies," Tscheligi adds.

noch zu kurz. Es bedarf einer Zusammenschau beider Seiten, die man auch gemeinsam testen sollte«, so Tscheligi.

Aus dieser Grundproblematik hat sich eine eigene Wissenschaftsdisziplin entwickelt. In der Experience-Forschung gibt es Verfahren, mit denen etwa die subjektive Komplexität gemessen werden kann oder das komplexe Zusammenspiel von Experience-Faktoren untersucht wird. Überdies wurden Methoden entwickelt, wie man die wahrgenommene Komplexität reduzieren kann. Tscheligi: »Unser hehres Ziel ist es, den Menschen das Leben bei der Nutzung von technischen Artefakten leichter zu machen.« Ein gängiger Ansatz hierfür heißt in der Fachsprache »Deconstructing Complexity«. Dabei werden komplexe Zusammenhänge in ihre einzelnen Bestandteile zerlegt, um so »besser zu verstehen, welche Probleme auftreten können. Auch Verknüpfungen der Teile werden betrachtet. Wenn man die einzelnen Elemente verstanden und verbessert hat, werden sie wieder zusammengesetzt«, so Tscheligi. Das können Produkte oder auch Softwareprogramme, also virtuelle Artefakte, sein. Einen wesentlichen Einfluss haben auch die situativen Bedingungen von »Use« und »Non-Use«.

Die Dekonstruktion der Komplexität bedarf einer Methode des Zerlegens, die reproduzierbar ist. Eines dieser Verfahren nennt sich »heuristische Analyse«: Man durchwandert ein Produkt oder ein Interface nach bestimmten Prinzipien Stück für Stück, um die Grundprinzipien des Designs der Reihe nach abzuarbeiten und zu klären, an welchem Punkt Probleme auftauchen, welche die Benutzbarkeit beeinträchtigen. Tscheligi: »Oft wäre es besser, einen Teil wegzulassen, um die Komplexität eines Produkts zu reduzieren, das dann genauso gut oder sogar noch besser funktioniert.«

Was der Mensch erfassen kann

Die Beschäftigung mit einem technischen System ist aber nur eine Seite. »Nicht nur das System, sondern auch seine Umgebung gilt es zu zerlegen«, erklärt Markus Murtinger, Leiter der Competence Unit Experience Business Transformation am AIT. Man müsse auch fragen: Wer sind die User? Welche Aufgabe haben sie? Welche Informationen brauchen sie etwa direkt auf einem Bildschirm, um eine Aufgabe erledigen zu können? Murtinger nennt ein Beispiel: »Oft werden alle Funktionen, die man zum Bedienen einer Maschine irgendwie brauchen kann, auf einem Display untergebracht. In der Realität sieht man aber, dass es drei ganz unterschiedliche Gruppen von Usern gibt: Einmal in der Woche kommt jemand für die Systemadministration Verantwortlicher, einmal am Tag die Person, welche die Maschine einstellt, und dann gibt es jemanden, der tatsächlich mit und an der Maschine arbeitet: Den unterschiedlichen Personen sollte man jeweils nur jene Funktionen anzeigen, die sie auch wirklich benötigen. Dadurch wird die Arbeit viel einfacher. Perfekt wäre es, wenn die Maschine bzw. das Interface den User und seine Rolle erkennt und sich an die Person anpasst. Das nennt man Adaptive Interface.«

Starting out from this fundamental problem, a scientific discipline in its own right has materialized. User experience research offers practices by which it is possible to measure subjective complexity or by which the complex interplay between experience factors can be analyzed. What is more, methods have been devised to reduce complexity as perceived by users. Tscheligi: "It is our noble goal to make life easier for people when using technical artifacts." Experts call an approach that is widely employed to solve this problem "deconstructing complexity." Complex entities are broken down into their components so as to "better understand the problems that may arise. We also look at the ways in which the parts are interconnected. Once the individual elements have been understood and improved, they are put together again," Tscheligi explains. This approach cannot only be used for products but also for software programs, i.e. virtual artifacts. A major influence can also be ascribed to the situational conditions of "use" and "non-use."

The deconstruction of complexity requires a method of fragmentation that is reproducible. One of them is referred to as "heuristic analysis": a product or an interface is analyzed bit by bit according to specific principles in order to systematically work through the fundamental principles of the design and clarify at what points problems interfering with the usability of the item will arise. Tscheligi: "Frequently, it would be better to omit a part altogether to reduce the complexity of a product, which will then run just as smoothly or even better."

What humans can grasp

But dealing with a technical system is only one side of the story. "It is necessary to not only deconstruct the system, but also its environment," explains Markus Murtinger, head of the AIT's Experience Business Transformation Competence Unit. One also has to find out who the users are, what tasks they have to complete, and what type of on-screen information they need to see to be able to do so. Murtinger gives an example: "Frequently, all functions that may be needed to operate a machine at some point are arranged on a display. In reality, however, it turns out that there are three essentially different groups of users: once a week, the person responsible for the administration of the system drops by; once a day, the person who adjusts the machine turns up; and then there is someone who actually works with or at the machine: each of these different groups of operators should only see those functions they really need. This would make everyone's work much easier. And it would be perfect if the interface were able to recognize the user and his or her role and adapt to the respective system—which is consequently called 'adaptive interface.'"

Wahrnehmungspsychologisch gebe es einige wichtige Komplexitäts-faktoren, auf die man bei der Gestaltung von Interfaces achten müsse. Die zwei wichtigsten sind die Menge an Informationen und die Schnelligkeit. »Je mehr auf User einströmt und je rascher das geschieht, umso weniger können sie wahrnehmen – und das belastet sie«, so Tscheligi. Man müsse beim Design daher genau wissen, wie man ein Interface gestaltet, damit die Anwenderinnen und Anwender die für sie jeweils wichtigen Informationen auch wahrnehmen können. In der Praxis geschieht indes oft das genaue Gegenteil – nämlich etwas, was Murtinger »Featuritis« nennt –, frei nach dem Motto: Ein zusätzliches Feature geht schon noch. Auch das sei ein Ausfluss dessen, dass man sich primär mit technischen Problemen beschäf-tigt und zu wenig mit jenen, die eine bestimmte Technik anwenden. »Man darf sich dann nicht wundern, wenn schließlich alles für den Menschen noch komplexer wird.«

Kann man künstliche Intelligenz verstehen?

Faktoren, die diese Entwicklung noch beschleunigen, sind die zuneh-mende Automatisierung und vor allem der Einsatz von künstlicher Intelli-genz (KI). Da stellt sich schnell die Frage nach dem Vertrauen, hat man doch keinen Einblick in den Prozess des maschinellen Lernens. KI ist einer Blackbox vergleichbar, bei der man nicht weiß, auf welchen Kriterien eine Entscheidung des Systems beruht – was ein Gefühl des Kontrollverlusts entstehen lässt. Dagegen treten Forscher seit einigen Jahren unter dem Motto »explainable AI« an: »Was die Erklärbarkeit, also den Versuch zu ver-stehen, angeht, was eine Maschine macht, sind zwei Seiten zu bedenken«, meint Sepp Hochreiter, Professor für Machine Learning an der Johannes-Kepler-Universität Linz. »Die Frage, ob man wirklich verstehen will, wie Maschinen Entscheidungen treffen, hängt davon ab, wofür ein System eingesetzt wird.« Als Beispiel führt er zwei Szenarien an: Im ersten wird etwa ein System in einem selbstfahrenden Auto eingesetzt, um die Zahl der Unfälle zu reduzieren. »Es kann sein, dass das System so gut ist, dass es die Zahl der Verkehrstoten auf ein Hundertstel reduziert. Man versteht aber nicht, warum. Will man nun alles durchschauen, was das System macht, geht die Zahl der Verkehrstoten wieder stark nach oben. Es gibt zwar jetzt wieder mehr Tote, aber man versteht, warum sie tot sind. Die andere Möglichkeit ist die, dass man sich damit begnügt, viele Leben gerettet zu haben, aber nicht versteht, warum.« Das zweite Szenario: »Mein Arbeitskol-lege bekommt infolge einer KI-Bewertung eine Gehaltserhöhung, ich aber nicht. In diesem Fall liegt auf der Hand, dass man wissen will, was die Maschine macht.«

KI-Systeme können Hunderte Faktoren zugleich berücksichtigen, haben größere Datenmengen zur Verfügung, führen diese auf komplexere Weise zusammen und sind daher in der Lage, präziser zu arbeiten. Den

Several central complexity factors have to be considered from the point of view of perceptual psychology when designing interfaces. The two most important ones are the amount of information and speed. "The more information breaks over users' heads and the faster this happens, the less they are able to take it in—and this is felt to be a burden," Tscheligi says. When designing an interface one therefore has to know exactly what to do so that the respective users will be able to merely perceive the information relevant for them. In practice, however, the exact opposite happens more often than not—namely what Murtinger refers to as "featuritis"—according to the principle: one more feature won't hurt. He also sees this as a product of the fact that the focus is primarily on technical problems and not enough on users applying a certain technology. "One must not be surprised when finally everything becomes overly complex for humans."

Is it possible to comprehend artificial intelligence?

Factors accelerating this development are automation on the rise and, above all, the employment of artificial intelligence (AI). In this latter regard, the issue of trust inevitably comes up, as the process of machine learning lies entirely in the dark. AI can be compared to a black box of which it is unknown what criteria the system refers to for its decisions—which ultimately ends up in the feeling of having lost control. Scientists have sought to counter this problem for several years under the motto of "explainable AI": "As to the explainability—i.e. the attempt to understand—what a machine does, two aspects have to be considered," says Sepp Hochreiter, professor for Machine Learning at the Johannes Kepler University Linz. "The question whether one really wants to understand how a machine makes its decisions depends on what a system is used for." To give an example, he describes two scenarios. In the first, a system has been employed in a self-driving car to reduce the number of accidents. "The system may work that excellently that traffic deaths will be reduced to a hundredth of what they used to be. But one does not understand why. If you wish to see through everything the system does, the number of traffic deaths will rise again considerably. Now there are more dead people again, but at least you will understand why they are dead. The other possibility is to content oneself with having saved many lives, without comprehending why." The second scenario: "Following an AI assessment, my colleague at work will get a pay rise, but not me. In this case it is obvious that one wishes to know what the machine does."

AI systems are capable of considering hundreds of factors simultaneously; larger amounts of data are available to them, which they combine in a complex fashion so that they are able to work more

wesentlichen Unterschied zwischen den beiden Szenarien sieht Hochreiter in Folgendem: »Wenn eine KI große statistische Zusammenhänge herstellt, kann das für das Gemeinwohl besser sein, versteht aber einen einzelnen Fall nicht, weil die Maschine die Daten auf sehr komplexe Weise verknüpft. Geht es aber um einen Einzelfall, muss man ›explainability‹ fordern.«

Technisch sei es durchaus möglich, neuronale Netze zu analysieren und festzustellen, wie die Eingangsgrößen zusammengerechnet wurden. Allerdings fragt Hochreiter, was damit wirklich gewonnen ist. »Kann ein Mensch verstehen, wenn eine Maschine 100 Regeln aufstellt und miteinander kombiniert? 100 Regeln auf einmal zu erfassen schafft man als Mensch nicht. Man kann vielleicht jeden Einzelschritt verständlich machen, aber dann ist die holistische Sichtweise nicht mehr gegeben. Die Semantik hinter dem System geht dabei verloren.«

Zuverlässigkeit und Vertrauen

Die Forschung im Bereich »explainable AI« läuft auf Hochtouren – und die Ergebnisse sind in vielerlei Hinsicht wichtig. Es geht beispielsweise auch um die Frage, wer für eine Fehlleistung eines technischen Systems verantwortlich ist. In gewissen Teilbereichen ist man bereits dabei, Antworten zu finden. Im Rahmen des Forschungsprojekts CALIBRAITE entwickeln Forscherinnen und Forscher am AIT zurzeit sogenannte Reliability Displays, die das Vertrauen von Menschen in KI-Systeme heben sollen, indem sie den Usern vermitteln, wie zuverlässig eine intelligenten Funktion ist. Den Usern soll so transparent gemacht werden, ob eine KI ausreichend Informationen zur Einschätzung einer Lage hat und auf welcher Datenqualität die Maschine ihre Bewertungen vornimmt – ob im Fall eines autonomen Fahrzeuges z. B. alle Sensoren zuverlässige Daten liefern oder ob ein Sensor ausgefallen ist.

Dadurch soll es möglich werden, dass die Anwenderinnen und Anwender ihre Erwartungshaltung an die Fähigkeit einer KI anpassen und deren Verlässlichkeit weder unter- noch überschätzen. Das ist ein wichtiger Beitrag, um das Gefühl der Unsicherheit und des Kontrollverlustes zu reduzieren und die Akzeptanz von KI-Systemen langfristig zu steigern. ✕

accurately. Hochreiter describes the essential difference between these two scenarios as follows: "When AI establishes statistical connections on a larger scale, this can prove to be beneficial for a society's common well-being, even if the individual cases cannot be understood as the machine combines data in a very complex fashion. But if an individual case is concerned, explainability is called for."

According to Hochreiter, it is perfectly possible to analyze neural networks and find out how input quantities have been added up. But he wonders what will actually have been gained. "Can a human being understand how a machine has defined 100 rules and combined them? A human being is not capable of grasping 100 rules at once. It may be possible to explain each individual step, but only at the cost of giving up the holistic view. The semantic quality behind the system will get lost."

Reliability and trust

Research into the field of explainable AI is advancing at full speed—and the findings gained are relevant in many respects. For example, there is the problem of who is responsible for a mistake made by a technical system. In certain subareas, scientists are already close to finding answers. Within the framework of the CALIBRaiTE research project, AIT researchers are currently developing so-called reliability displays intended to raise people's trust in AI systems by conveying to users how reliable an intelligent function can be. In this way, it should be made transparent to users if an AI has sufficient information at hand to assess the situation and on the basis of what data quality its evaluations are in fact made—whether, for example, all sensors are supplying reliable data in the case of an automated vehicle, or if one of the sensors has failed.

Thanks to this it should become possible for users to adjust their expectations to the actual abilities of an AI so as to neither under- nor overestimate its reliability. This is an important contribution to reducing the feeling of insecurity and a loss of control and to improving the acceptance of AI systems in the long run. ×

Positionen der Kunst

Positions of Art

Gerald Bast im Gespräch

»Wir müssen wissenschaftliche und künstlerische Methoden zusammenbringen«

Künstlerinnen und Künstler sind geübt darin, mit dem Ungewissen und mit Mehrdeutigkeit umzugehen, aus eingefahrenen Denkstrukturen herauszutreten und das Neue zu suchen. Diese Kompetenzen will Gerald Bast, Rektor der Universität für angewandte Kunst Wien, in die Welt der Wissenschaft einbringen, denn mit herkömmlichen Denkmethoden lassen sich die komplexen Zukunftsprobleme nicht lösen.

Gerald Bast, Studium der Rechts- und Wirtschaftswissenschaften an der Johannes-Kepler-Universität Linz, von 1980 bis 1999 im Bundesministerium für Bildung und Forschung, seit 2000 Rektor der Universität für angewandte Kunst Wien. Mitglied der Europäischen Akademie der Wissenschaften und Künste, stv. Vorsitzender des Dachverbandes der österreichischen Universitäten, Kuratoriumsmitglied des Europäischen Forums Alpbach. Autor und Vortragender insbesondere zur Bildungs- und Kulturpolitik sowie zur Verbindung von Wissenschaft, Kunst und Innovation.

Wenn wir von der Coronakrise einmal absehen: Wie beurteilen sie die derzeitige Entwicklung der Welt?

Gerald Bast: Ein Kennzeichen der Entwicklung, welche die Welt in den letzten Jahren genommen hat, ist, dass sich immer schwerer Voraussagen treffen lassen, wie die nächsten zwei Monate oder fünf Jahre aussehen werden. Es war früher schon schwierig genug, lineare Interpolationen aus der Vergangenheit vorzunehmen. Das kann man mittlerweile über weite Strecken vergessen. Noch vor wenigen Monaten hätte niemand daran gedacht, dass die ganze Welt durch ein Virus, das sich global verbreitet, zum Stillstand kommt.

Für mich ist nur eines sicher: dass es massive gesellschaftliche, politische und ökonomische Veränderungen geben wird und dass diese Veränderungen immer schneller stattfinden werden. Daraus ergibt sich die Notwendigkeit, dass wir versuchen müssen, auf allen Wegen Methoden zu finden, mit solchen Veränderungen umzugehen und sie bewältigen zu können. Die wahrscheinlich größte Herausforderung dabei besteht darin, in einer Welt der permanenten und gravierenden Veränderung nicht nur zu überleben, sondern trotz allem noch gestaltend eingreifen zu können.

Gerald Bast studied law and economics at the Johannes Kepler University Linz. He worked for the Austrian Federal Ministry of Education and Research from 1980 to 1999 and has held the position of rector at the Vienna University of Applied Arts since 2000. Member of the European Academy of Sciences and Arts, vice chairman of the National University Federation, board member of the European Forum Alpbach. Author and lecturer with a focus on educational and cultural policies and the interconnectedness of science, art, and innovation.

An interview with Gerald Bast

"We must bring scientific and artistic methods together"

Thinking out of the box, artists are perfectly used to dealing with uncertainties and ambivalences while being on the lookout for new things and ways to be inspired. Rector Gerald Bast of the Vienna University of Applied Arts seeks to integrate these competencies into the world of science, for complex problems of the future can certainly not be solved with conventional methods of thought.

Aside from the coronavirus crisis: what do you think about the world's current development?

Gerald Bast: A typical sign of the way the world has developed during the past few years is that it has become more and more difficult to predict what the following two months or five years will be like. Earlier, it was difficult enough to make interpolations based on the past. Meanwhile you can largely forget about this. As recently as several months ago no one would have thought that the whole world would come to a standstill because of a virus that is spreading globally.

For me, only one thing is clear: that there will occur severe social, political, and economic changes, and that these changes will take place more and more rapidly. From this, the necessity arises that we must try and find methods in all possible ways to deal with these changes and be able to cope with them. What will probably be the biggest challenge of all is not only to survive in a world of permanent and profound change but also to intervene creatively in spite of it.

Die alten Methoden, in den Lauf der Welt einzugreifen, funktionieren in einer immer komplexer werdenden Welt offenkundig nicht mehr.

Bast: Die alten Methoden funktionieren nur mehr zum Teil. Man soll das Alte aber deswegen nicht gleich wegwerfen. Die alten, bewährten Methoden werden Podeste und Sprungbretter für die Anwendung völlig neuer Methoden und Skills sein. Es ist nicht so, dass wir die Welt und uns und unsere Strategien von Grund auf neu erfinden müssen: Wir müssen auf dem Wissen, das wir haben – das zum Großteil lineares Wissen ist –, aufbauen und es für eine vernetzte und komplexere Art des Denkens nutzen.

Was meinen Sie genau mit »komplexere Art des Denkens«?

Bast: Wir alle haben in der Schule und an den Universitäten gelernt, in konsekutiven Logiken zu denken: wenn A, dann B; ja oder nein; richtig oder falsch. Diese Logiken werden zunehmend obsolet. Eigentlich hätte uns das die Wissenschaft – konkret: die Quantenphysik – schon vor 100 Jahren klargemacht. Wir hätten Bereiche, in denen es Unschärfen, Gleichzeitigkeiten und mehrere miteinander vernetzte Handlungs- und Wirkungsebenen gibt, stärker in den Blick nehmen müssen. Das haben wir viel zu wenig getan.

Haben Sie eine Vermutung, warum dies nicht geschehen ist?

Bast: Es ist immer schwierig, von erfolgreichen Denkstrukturen abzuweichen. Das ist so in der Wirtschaft, in der Politik und etwas abgemildert auch im Bildungs- und Forschungssystem. Überall gibt es Strukturen, die sehr prägend sind und die alten Denk- und Handlungsweisen massiv festigen. Beim herkömmlichen Fächersystem in Schulen und an Universitäten wird jedes Fach separat unterrichtet. Man tut so, als ob die einzelnen Fächer nichts miteinander zu tun hätten. Versuche, das in den letzten Jahren aufzubrechen – etwa mit der Möglichkeit, Projektunterricht zu machen – sind, großflächig betrachtet, gescheitert.

Das Gleiche spielt sich in der akademischen Welt ab: Wir haben zu weit mehr als 90 Prozent monodisziplinäre Studiengänge. Es gibt in den letzten Jahren zwar zarte Versuche, ein bisschen Interdisziplinarität und disziplinenübergreifende Blickweisen in das System einzubringen. Das ist aber noch viel zu schwach. Und zwar deshalb, weil die Karrierepfade der Wissenschafterinnen und Wissen-

It appears that the old methods of interfering with the way of the world do not function any longer in a world that is growing ever more complex.

Bast: The old methods continue to function only partly. But one should not discard the old immediately because of that. The old, well-tried methods will be stepping stones or springboards for the application of entirely new methods and skills. It does not mean that we will have to reinvent the world, as well as us and our strategies, from scratch: we must build on the knowledge we have—which is largely a linear type of knowledge—and make use of it for a networked and more complex way of thinking.

What exactly do you mean by a "more complex way of thinking"?

Bast: At school or university, all of us learned how to think according to the principle of consecutive logics: if there is A then B will apply; yes or no; true or false. These types of logics are becoming increasingly obsolete. Actually, science—quantum physics, to be more concrete—would have made this clear to us as long as one hundred years ago. We should have focused more on areas characterized by a lack of definition, by concurrencies and interconnected levels of action and impact. We have done far too little in this respect.

Do you have any idea why we have failed to do so?

Bast: It is always hard to deviate from successful patterns of thought. This holds true for the economy, for politics, and, to a somewhat lesser degree, for the educational and research systems. Everywhere we can find highly formative patterns firmly cementing our old ways of thinking and acting. At schools and universities practicing a conventional teaching system, each subject is taught separately. Teachers act as if the individual subjects had nothing to do with one another. All in all, efforts undertaken in recent years to break this system open by resorting to a project-related interdisciplinary approach have actually not proven extremely successful.

The same problem prevails in the academic world: more than ninety percent of our degree courses are monodisciplinary. In recent years, feeble attempts have been made to introduce some multidisciplinarity and points of view reaching across disciplines into

schafter von monodisziplinären Standards geprägt sind: Alle müssen immer schneller und immer mehr publizieren, und das macht man in monodisziplinär ausgerichteten Journals, durch die man viele Punkte, wissenschaftliche Reputation und Anerkennung in der Scientific Community, in der Gesellschaft und in der Politik bekommt. Wenn man versucht, disziplinenübergreifende Forschungsprojekte durchzuführen, schadet man der eigenen Karriere. Solange es uns nicht gelingt, diesen herkömmlichen Strukturen andere Strukturen für komplexe Forschungsfelder an die Seite zu stellen, wird sich kaum etwas ändern.

Sie haben kürzlich gemeinsam mit der Johannes-Kepler-Universität Linz das Manifest »Innovation durch Universitas« veröffentlicht, in dem die Bedeutung der Interdisziplinarität und eines holistischen Denkens betont wird. Wie könnte man diese Ideen zum Leben erwecken?

Bast: Wir wollen das auf drei Wegen erreichen: Erstens versuchen wir, in den nächsten Jahren disziplinenübergreifende Studienangebote zu entwickeln und einzuführen. Die Angewandte hat damit schon begonnen: Bei uns läuft seit drei Jahren mit großem Erfolg das Studium »Cross Disciplinary Strategies«, in dem wir zwischen künstlerischen Methoden, Basics in paradigmatischen naturwissenschaftlichen und technischen Feldern bis hin zu Philosophie und den großen Global Challenges einen großen Bogen spannen. Diese Grundidee wollen wir in Kooperation zwischen den beiden Universitäten weiterverfolgen. Zweitens wollen wir gemeinsam themenzentrierte Forschungsprojekte angehen. Und drittens wollen wir versuchen, ein »International Journal for Cross-Disciplinary Research« aufzubauen, das wissenschaftliche Anerkennung sicherstellen soll. Dieses soll auf höchster qualitativer Ebene angesiedelt sein – mit Topleuten, die wir als Peer Reviewers gewinnen wollen, und mit einem internationalen Board, das versteht, was wir wollen. Wenn man Leute findet, die dem Vorhaben höchste wissenschaftliche Wertigkeit verleihen, wird es funktionieren.

Verstehe ich Sie richtig, dass die Interdisziplinarität, von der Sie reden, über das hinausgeht, was gemeinhin darunter verstanden wird – denn Sie wollen ja zusätzlich zu verschiedenen wissenschaftlichen Fächern bzw. Methoden auch künstlerische Methoden einbeziehen?

Bast: Ja, wir wollen wissenschaftliche und künstlerische Methoden zusammenbringen.

the system. But these have been far too weak because academic career paths depend on monodisciplinary standards: scientists are forced to publish more and more at a faster and faster pace, which happens in journals with a monodisciplinary outlook. You will thus earn many credits, gain an academic reputation, and receive recognition from the scientific community, as well as from society and politics. People trying to realize multidisciplinary research projects sabotage their own careers. As long as we do not manage to pair these conventional structures with new ones suitable for more complex fields of research, hardly anything will change.

You have recently published the manifesto "Innovation through Universitas" together with the Johannes Kepler University in Linz, which emphasizes the significance of interdisciplinarity and holistic thinking. How could these ideas be brought to life?

Bast: We want to reach this goal in three different ways. First, attempts will be made by us to develop and introduce an offering of multidisciplinary study programs in the next few years. The "Angewandte," the Vienna University of Applied Arts, has already begun: for three years, we have now successfully run a course called "Cross-Disciplinary Strategies," which spans from artistic methods and basics in paradigmatic scientific and technological fields of studies to philosophy and the big global challenges. We would like to pursue this basic idea within a collaborative framework between our two universities. Second, we would like to tackle theme-centered research projects as a team. And third, we will pursue the idea of establishing an "International Journal for Cross-Disciplinary Research," which is to guarantee academic recognition. We intend to place this journal on the highest level of quality—seeking to win over top people as peer reviewers and working with an international board that understands our goals. If we succeed in finding people who lend highest academic and scientific credibility to this project, everything will work out.

Was ist aus Ihrer Sicht der Mehrwert, wenn man wissenschaftliche und künstlerische Methoden miteinander kombiniert? Oder anders gefragt: Was kann die Kunst einbringen?

Bast: Wir haben eine spezielle Definition von angewandter Kunst, die in unserer institutionellen Tradition begründet ist. Angewandte Kunst bedeutet für uns, dass wir versuchen, mit Methoden, die Künstlerinnen und Künstler anwenden, und mit kreativen ästhetischen Prozessen die Entwicklung und Gestaltung der Gesellschaft zu beeinflussen. Es geht also nicht um L'art pour l'art, sondern um das genaue Gegenteil: Wir glauben, dass Kunst mehr kann, als in Galerien, Museen oder Auktionshäusern wirksam zu sein. Das ist für uns wichtig: Kunst spielte immer auch eine Rolle für die gesellschaftliche Entwicklung.

Welche Methoden wenden Künstlerinnen und Künstler an?

Bast: Wenn man sich genau anschaut, wie Künstlerinnen und Künstler arbeiten, dann sind das Prozesse, die etwas mit dem Umgang mit dem Ungewissen und mit Mehrdeutigkeit zu tun haben und bei denen diese nicht als bedrohend, sondern als produktiv wahrgenommen werden. Im traditionellen Bildungssystem ist Ungewissheit etwas ganz Böses. Bildung war immer unter das Motto gestellt: Wir wollen Ungewissheit beseitigen. Das ist in dieser Engführung jedoch völlig verfehlt: Es geht nicht darum, Ungewissheit auszuräumen – das wäre völlig vermessen und funktioniert gar nicht. Sondern es geht darum, Ungewissheit und Mehrdeutigkeit produktiv werden zu lassen. Und das ist eben das Feld, wie Künstlerinnen und Künstler arbeiten.

Weiters geht es um die Abstraktion von bestehenden Situationen. Abstrahieren kann man nicht nur auf einem Zeichenblatt, abstrahieren kann und muss man auch immer mehr im Kopf. Wenn wir abstrahieren, was zum Beispiel jetzt die Coronakrise bedeutet, dann kommen wir zu einem bestimmten Ergebnis, das uns in der Bewältigung der Krise weiterhilft und vielleicht auch positive Konsequenzen haben kann.

Dann geht es um den Anspruch, aus eingefahrenen Denkstrukturen herauszutreten und ganz bewusst das Neue zu suchen, gegen Traditionen zu arbeiten und das Bestehende in Frage zu stellen. Künstlerinnen und Künstler arbeiten daran, Perspektiven radikal zu verändern.

Solche Strategien haben nicht nur tiefgreifende Umwälzungen in der Kunst mit sich gebracht. Wenn man

Do I understand you correctly that the interdisciplinarity you are talking about goes beyond what is generally understood by it—for you aim to integrate artistic methods in addition to various scientific disciplines and methods.

Bast: Yes, it is our goal to bring scientific and artistic methods together.

What is, from your point of view, the additional value gained by combining scientific and artistic methods? Or, asked differently: what can art contribute?

Bast: We have a special way of defining applied arts, which is rooted in the tradition of our institution. For us, the concept of applied arts means to try to influence the development and layout of society with methods employed by artists and through creative aesthetic processes. This is not about "art for art's sake," but about the exact opposite: we believe that art can do more than exercising its impact in galleries, museums, or auction houses. This is very important to us: art has always played a role in the development of society.

What are the methods employed by artists?

Bast: Taking a closer look at the way artists work, we can see that certain processes are involved. These processes have something to do with dealing with uncertainties and ambivalences that are not perceived as threatening but as productive. In traditional educational systems, uncertainty is evil through and through. Learning has always followed the motto: "We seek to eliminate uncertainty." However, this close association between the two concepts is entirely out of place: there is no point in eliminating uncertainty—this would be entirely presumptuous and not work at all.

But this is also about abstracting from given situations. You cannot only abstract while drawing on a sheet of paper, you can also and are increasingly expected to do it in your mind. By abstracting, for example, the meaning of the current coronavirus crisis, we will arrive at a specific result that will help us cope with the crisis and may also have positive implications.

Equally important is the necessity to step out of well-tried patterns of thought and consciously em-

sich überlegt, wie die Welt von den Ägyptern bzw. nach der Entdeckung der Zentralperspektive dargestellt wurde, die vielleicht nicht ganz zufällig mit dem Wechsel vom geozentrischen zum heliozentrischen Weltbild einherging, oder sich vor Augen hält, wie die Kubist*innen die Welt gesehen, zeitliche und optische Dimensionen aufgelöst und Bilder gemalt haben, die Objekte von allen Seiten gleichzeitig zu zeigen scheinen – das sind radikale Änderungen der Perspektive, die wir auch über die Kunst hinaus dringend brauchen, und das gerade in Zeiten wie diesen, in denen sich alles wahnsinnig rasch verändert und wir versucht sind, nur mehr zu reagieren und nicht zu agieren.

Kann man diese Teilbereiche des künstlerischen Arbeitens, die Sie nun aufgezählt haben, unter dem Überbegriff »Kreativität« zusammenfassen?

Bast: Das wäre etwas verkürzt, zumal der Begriff »Kreativität« etwas schwammig ist. Ich verwende daher den wesentlich präziseren Begriff »künstlerische Methoden«, so wie es naturwissenschaftliche, geisteswissenschaftliche und statistische Methoden gibt. Die Wahl der Methoden kommt oft einem Paradigmenwechsel gleich. Ich erinnere mich noch gut, als in den 1970er- und 1980er-Jahren quantitative Methoden in die akademische Welt Einzug gehalten haben. Das war ein Paradigmenwechsel, der nicht nur einzelne Arbeiten bestimmter Wissenschafterinnen und Wissenschafter beeinflusst, sondern ganze Wissenschaftsdisziplinen verändert hat. Allerdings zum Teil auch verkürzt hat, denkt man an die Veränderungen in der Ökonomie, die weltweit auf quantitative Forschungen zu setzen begonnen hat – mit im Nachhinein betrachtet manchmal etwas zweifelhaften Ergebnissen. Die quantitativen Methoden haben auch in die Psychologie, in die Medizin usw. Einzug gehalten. Eine solche Veränderung kann sehr prägend für die Richtung ein, welche die Entwicklung einer Wissenschaft nimmt.

Was ich mir wünsche und einfordere, ist, dass wir jetzt wieder einen solchen Paradigmenwechsel vollziehen: dass künstlerische Methoden in die gesamte akademische Welt Einzug halten. Vielleicht mit dem Unterschied, dass künstlerische Methoden – anders als statistische – die wissenschaftlichen Disziplinen nicht übernehmen sollen, sondern dass wir additiv und auf Augenhöhe zu einer

brace what is new by counteracting tradition and questioning what exists. Artists work hard to radically change perspectives.

Such strategies have not only brought about profound revolutions in the visual arts. Consider how the world was represented by the Egyptians as opposed to after the discovery of central perspective, which, probably not entirely without coincidence, went hand in hand with the transition from geocentrism to heliocentrism; or remember how the Cubists saw the world, dissolving temporal and visual dimensions by painting pictures showing objects from multiple viewpoints simultaneously—these are radical changes in perspective that are also urgently needed beyond art, especially in times like ours, when everything is changing immensely fast and we are tempted to merely react rather than act.

Could these aspects of artistic work you have just enumerated be summarized under the term "creativity"?

Bast: This would be somewhat simplified, as the term "creativity" is a bit vague. I therefore use the expression "artistic methods," which is considerably more precise, for there are also scientific, humanistic, and statistical methods. The choice of method frequently comes up to a paradigm shift. I can still remember what it was like when quantitative methods found their way into the academic world in the 1970s and 1980s. This was a paradigm change that influenced not solely individual projects conducted by individual academics but entire academic disciplines; it also truncated them, thinking of the changes in the field of economics, which began relying on quantitative research globally—with results that have sometimes turned out questionable in retrospect. These quantitative methods have also established themselves in psychology, in medicine, etc. Such changes can be highly determinative for the direction an academic or scientific discipline will take.

What I wish and call for is for us to accomplish such a paradigm shift once again now: that artistic methods will find their way into the academic world as a whole—the only difference probably being that artistic methods, unlike statistical ones, should not seek to take over academic disciplines but contribute

Sicht beitragen, die diese Vernetztheit und Komplexität widerspiegelt, in der wir heute leben.

Mir fällt auf, dass Sie bisher die emotionale Komponente, die in der Kunst so wichtig ist und in der Wissenschaft eher nicht, noch nicht ins Spiel gebracht haben. Konkret gefragt: Inwieweit halten Sie auch Empathie, soziales Verantwortungsgefühl usw. für eine Wissenschaft der Zukunft für wichtig?

Bast: Emotion, emotionale Intelligenz und Intuition sind etwas ganz Wichtiges. Ich bin überzeugt, dass große Wissenschafterinnen und Wissenschafter sich bewusst sind, dass das wesentliche Elemente ihrer Arbeit sind. Es gibt Naturwissenschafterinnen und -wissenschafter, die sagen, dass sie ohne Intuition niemals in der Lage gewesen wären, zu bestimmten Ergebnissen zu kommen. Edward O. Wilson, einer der ganz großen Biologen, hat einmal gesagt: Ein Wissenschafter muss in der Lage sein, zu denken wie ein Poet und zu handeln wie ein Buchhalter.

Das weitverbreitete Bild, dass der Künstler aus dem Bauch heraus arbeitet und der Wissenschafter aus dem Kopf, ist völlig falsch: In der Wissenschaft spielen Emotion, Zufall und Intuition eine große Rolle. Umgekehrt braucht Kunst natürlich auch intellektuelle Analysefähigkeit, Abstraktionsvermögen und theoretische Reflexion. Schon Leonardo da Vinci hat gesagt: »Ich male nicht mit dem Pinsel, sondern mit dem Kopf.« Kunst und Wissenschaft sind zwei zusammengehörende Geschwister, zwei Seiten ein und derselben Medaille. Sie wurden in den vergangenen zwei Jahrhunderten aus vielen Gründen – nicht immer guten – voneinander getrennt. Das funktioniert jetzt überhaupt nicht mehr. Wir brauchen diese beiden Zugänge heute mehr denn je.

Dazu gehören natürlich auch Empathie und gesellschaftliche Verantwortung. Das hängt auch mit dem neuen Begriff der »Third Mission« von Universitäten zusammen – ein etwas schwammiger Begriff, der vieles vernebelt. Aber im Kern ist klar: Die Wissenschaft hat eine gesellschaftliche Verantwortung, und sie hat eine gesellschaftliche Wirkung, selbst wenn sie das bisweilen bestreitet. Emotionale Intelligenz spielt sowohl in der Politik als auch in der Wissenschaft eine Rolle. Das zeigt sich gerade in Tagen wie diesen wieder sehr deutlich: Bei den Wissenschafterinnen und Wissenschaftern, die jetzt unter unheimlichem Zeitdruck und emotionalem

as one aspect and on an equal footing to a point of view reflecting the interconnectedness and complexity of today's life.

I realize that you have not yet addressed the emotional component, which is so important in art and less so in science. Asked more concretely: in what way do you also consider empathy, social responsibility, and similar qualities essential for a science of the future?

Bast: Emotions, emotional intelligence, and intuition are vital. I am convinced that great scientists are aware of the fact that these are crucial elements of their work. There are scientists saying that without intuition they would never have been able to arrive at certain findings. Edward O. Wilson, one of the leading biologists, once said: "The ideal scientist can be said to think like a poet and work like a clerk."

The widespread image of artists working on a gut level and of scientists relying on their brains is totally wrong: emotions, chance, and intuition play an important role in science. Art, on the other hand, requires such skills as intellectual analysis, abstraction, and theoretical reflection. Leonardo da Vinci once said: "I don't paint with the brush, I paint with the mind." Art and science are two siblings belonging together, two sides of the same coin. During the past two centuries they were separated for many reasons— not all of them good. Now this does not function at all anymore. Today we need these two approaches more than ever.

This, of course, also includes empathy and social responsibility. The "third mission" of universities, a new and slightly ambiguous concept that leaves many things in the dark, also comes into play here. But its core is clear: science has a social responsibility, and it has a social impact, even if it sometimes denies that it does. Emotional intelligence plays a role in both politics and science. In days like these this has become particularly clear once more: lots of emotions are part of the driving force behind scientists doing research into the Corona virus and its possible therapies under unbelievable time pressure and emotional stress.

Stress am Coronavirus und an Therapiemöglichkeiten forschen, sind sehr viele Emotionen als Triebkraft dabei.

Ein anderer Begriff, der gemeinhin eher der Kunst zugeordnet wird, ist »Schönheit«.

Bast: Ja, ein gefährlicher Begriff. Setzt man sich mit Kunstgeschichte auseinander, sieht man, wie wandelbar der Begriff ist. Dinge, die wir heute als hässlich oder fremd empfinden, waren in früheren Zeiten oder anderen Kulturen schön. Ich sage nicht: Kunst darf nicht schön sein – auch unter den Prämissen ihrer Zeit. Schönheit ist ein Stilmittel wie viele andere, wie etwa Provokation oder Erschrecken. Kunst arbeitet mit ästhetischen Codes.

Sind solche ästhetischen Codes auch für die Wissenschaft relevant?

Bast: Da muss man unterscheiden. Es gibt nicht die eine Wissenschaft. Aber gerade wenn man die Geistes- oder Sozialwissenschaften hernimmt: Auch in diesem Bereich wird mit Codes, mit Usancen, mit Denkstrukturen gearbeitet. Das ist sogar in den Formalwissenschaften so.

Aber sind das wirklich ästhetische Codes?

Bast: Ich war in meinem früheren Leben einmal Jurist. Ich habe die Juristerei immer mindestens ebenso sehr als Gesellschaftswissenschaft angesehen wie als pure positivistische Rechtswissenschaft. Ich habe die Leute einmal erschreckt, als ich eine Formulierung in einem Gesetz als schön bezeichnet habe. Das ist mir kürzlich eingefallen, als der österreichische Bundespräsident von der Schönheit der Verfassung gesprochen hat. Das klingt im ersten Augenblick absurd – aber da gibt es schon etwas. Der Neurologe Wolf Singer, der ehemalige Direktor der Abteilung für Neurophysiologie am Max-Planck-Institut für Hirnforschung, hat einmal gesagt: Wenn ich eine Theorie formuliert habe oder eine Formel vor mir sehe, dann weiß ich sofort, ob sie richtig ist oder nicht: wenn ich sie als schön empfinde. Dazu muss man aber ein Bewusstsein für Schönheit, für das Denken in ästhetischen Codes haben. Es ist notwendig, dass Kinder und junge Leute die Sprachen der Kunst, also diese Codes, frühzeitig erlernen. Nur dann können sie diese Schicht des Wissens- und Erkenntniserwerbs nutzen. Meine Forderung lautet daher, dass Menschen herangebildet werden müssen, die in der Lage sind, mit künstlerischen und wissenschaftlichen Methoden gleichermaßen zu arbeiten – und dass man Felder

Another concept commonly associated with art is "beauty."

Bast: Yes, a dangerous concept. Dealing with art history, you will realize how volatile it is. Things we feel to be ugly or alien today were considered beautiful in earlier times or in other civilizations. I don't say that art must not be beautiful—on the premises of its age. Beauty is a stylistic device like many others, such as provocation or shock. Art works with aesthetic codes.

Are such aesthetic codes also relevant for science and academia?

Bast: One must differentiate here. There is not only one science or academic discipline. But especially the humanities and social sciences also rely on codes, on usage, on patterns of thought. This even holds true for formal sciences.

But are these really aesthetic codes?

Bast: In my past life I was a lawyer. I always regarded jurisprudence as a field of social studies, at least to the same extent as I saw it as a pure and positivistic discipline of law. I once shocked people by saying about a phrase in a law text that it was beautiful. This came to my mind again only recently, when Austria's Federal President was talking about the beauty of our constitution. This sounds really absurd at first—but there is a lot of truth in it. The neurologist Wolf Singer, the former director of the Department of Neurophysiology at the Max Planck Institute for Brain Research, once said: "When I have formulated a theory or see a formula in front of me, I immediately know whether it is right or wrong: when I feel it to be beautiful." For this, however, you must have a sense of beauty, of thinking in aesthetic codes. It is necessary for children and young people to learn the languages of art, i.e. its codes, at an early stage. Only then can they use this layer of knowledge acquisition. I therefore demand that we should educate people who are capable of working with artistic and scientific methods alike—and that fields should be established in which these two ways of cognitive research can be combined. Today's complex problems can no longer be solved from the perspective of a single discipline. It goes without saying that everyone will continue to have their own expertise—this will also exist in the

schafft, in denen diese beiden Arten von Erkenntnisfor-
schung miteinander kombiniert werden können. Die
komplexen Probleme von heute sind nicht mehr aus der
Sicht einer einzelnen Disziplin zu lösen. Es hat natürlich
weiterhin jeder seine Expertise – das wird es auch in
Zukunft geben. Ich rede nicht einer Abschaffung von
Fachexpertise das Wort. Aber man muss dem Zusammenarbeiten und Zusammendenken dieser beiden Arbeits-
weisen Raum und Plattformen geben.

**Ein aktuelles Beispiel für eine komplexe Problemstellung, bei der man
mit der Expertise von Einzelwissenschaften nicht mehr weiterkommt,
ist die Künstliche Intelligenz (KI). Was folgt aus dem bisher Gesagten
für diesen Fall?**

Bast: Künstliche Intelligenz ist nicht in erste Linie ein
Problemfeld der Informatik. KI zeigt, dass Wissenschaft
und das, was aus der Wissenschaft folgt, eine gesellschaftspolitische Dimension hat. Hier sind künstlerische
Methoden dringend notwendig, etwa das Brechen mit
Traditionen und herkömmlichen Denkstrukturen, Perspek-
tivenwechsel und ein »thinking out of the box«. Das
braucht man auch, um die rein technologische Komponente der KI weiterzuentwickeln. Ich bin immer wieder
erstaunt, dass manche Menschen sagen: Da wir in einem
digitalen Zeitalter leben, müssen alle Kinder und Jugend-
lichen jetzt programmieren lernen. Das geht bis in die
Erwachsenenbildung hinein. Solche Kenntnisse mögen für
manche nützlich sein, sind aber als Lösungsansatz für das
gesellschaftliche und gesellschaftspolitische Problem
völliger Unsinn. Wir brauchen vielmehr Menschen, die in
der Lage sind, ihr Denken an völlig neue Situationen
anzupassen, um völlig neue Möglichkeiten zu schaffen.
Anwendungsmöglichkeiten sind keine Probleme der
Informatik. Um damit umgehen zu können, braucht es
Fantasie, Intuition, emotionale Intelligenz und gesell-
schaftliches Verantwortungsbewusstsein.

Das gilt es im Bildungssystem zu berücksichtigen.
Ich bin überzeugt, dass wir gerade in Zeiten wie diesen
das Bildungssystem gravierend verändern müssen.
Dafür bleibt nicht mehr viel Zeit. Wir müssen von der im
Bildungsbürgertum des 19. Jahrhunderts wurzelnden
Tradition abgehen, enzyklopädisches Wissen zu vermitteln. Eines der großen zu verankernden Bildungsziele
ist die Befähigung, mit Information und Daten intelligent,
intuitiv und kreativ umzugehen und diese auf eine völlig

future. I am not talking in favor of an abolition of technical expertise. But room and platforms must be given to a form of collaboration and thought involving both methods.

A current example of a complex problem where we will get stuck with the expertise of individual academic disciplines is artificial intelligence (AI). What results, in this case, from what has been said?

Bast: AI is not a problem area of computer science or information technology in the first place. AI shows that science and what science entails also have a sociopolitical dimension. Artistic methods are urgently needed here when it comes to breaking with traditions and well-tried patterns of thought, changing perspectives, and thinking out of the box. This is also necessary in order to develop the purely technological component of AI further. I am astonished time and again when some people say: "As we live in the digital age, all kids and youngsters now have to learn how to program." This reaches well into adult education. Such knowledge might be useful for some but is complete nonsense as an approach to solving a social or sociopolitical problem. We need more people who are capable of adapting their thinking to entirely new situations in order to create entirely new possibilities. Possible applications do not pose problems that have to do with computer science. In order to handle them, what is needed is imagination, intuition, emotional intelligence, and social responsibility.

This has to be taken into account by the educational system. I am convinced that our educational system requires profound transformation especially in times like these. But we are running out of time. We must urgently leave behind the tradition of imparting encyclopedic knowledge, which is rooted in the educated bourgeoisie of the nineteenth-century. One of the major educational goals that have to become firmly established is the capability of handling information and data intelligently, intuitively, and creatively and combining them in a completely novel way that has been unthinkable before.

This applies not only to the educational system, but also to the economy. Today the big players are companies that know how to combine information

neuartige, bisher für undenkbar gehaltene Weise zu kombinieren.

Das betrifft nicht nur das Bildungssystem, sondern auch die Wirtschaft. Die Big Player sind heute jene Firmen, die Informationen kombinieren und etwas daraus machen. Das ist in unserem Bildungssystem bisher nicht abgebildet. Wenn es uns nicht gelingt, das in unsrem Bildungssystem umzusetzen, werden in 20 Jahren große Teile der bestehenden staatlichen Universitäten und die Sekundarstufe im Schulsystem irrelevant geworden sein, weil sie den Erfordernissen der Gesellschaft und der Wirtschaft nicht mehr genügen.

Sie sprechen damit auch die »Arbeit der Zukunft« an – dass sich alle Jobs durch die digitalen Technologien völlig verändern und viele komplett wegfallen werden.

Bast: Es ist kein Zufall, dass genau diese großen Datenfirmen ganz offen sagen: Bildung ist das größte Business des 21. Jahrhunderts. Sie entwickeln jetzt schon ein völlig neues Bildungssystem, das ganz anders ist als jenes, das wir jetzt haben. Sie sagen: Die Leute, die sie auf dem regulären Bildungsmarkt bekommen, können nicht, was sie brauchen. Die großen Datenkonzerne werben massenhaft Absolventen der Philosophie und Geisteswissenschaften an – aber nicht dafür, dass sie dort Philosophie betreiben, sondern dafür, dass sie nach einer Ein- und Umschulung das vorhandene deren Wissen weitertreiben und die ungeahnten Möglichkeiten auf die Spitze treiben. Da müssen wir wahnsinnig aufpassen. Die entscheidende Frage ist, ob wir ein Bildungssystem haben wollen, das als oberstem Prinzip einem Shareholder-Value folgt – oder ein Bildungssystem, das nach wie vor einer demokratischen Gesellschaft und deren gedeihlicher Weiterentwicklung verpflichtet ist.

Ich hoffe, dass die Universitäten in 20 Jahren – und das ist schon sehr spät, aber eine Transformation von Bildung braucht lange – so aussehen werden, dass nur ein kleiner Teil von Studierenden und Forscherinnen und Forschern in monodisziplinären Forschungsfeldern und Studienrichtungen aktiv sein wird. Die große Menge sollte in interdisziplinären, themenzentrierten Arbeitsfeldern tätig sein. Wir müssen dabei an beiden Enden des Bildungssystems gleichzeitig ansetzen. In Schulen kann man auf Projektunterricht umstellen, wie es etwa in Finnland geschieht. In einigen Jahren kommen dann junge

and create something out of it. Our educational system does not reflect this situation. If we fail to implement the necessary requirements, large parts of our public universities and secondary school system will have become irrelevant in twenty years because they will no longer meet the demands of society and of the economy.

This also brings up the issue "work of the future"—that all jobs will change fundamentally through digital technologies and that many will become completely redundant.

Bast: It is precisely the huge data companies that openly say that education will be the biggest business of the twenty-first century. This is not a coincidence. They have already begun developing a fundamentally new educational system, entirely different from what we have now. They say that people coming from the regular learning marketplace do not have the skills they need. The big multinational data companies are recruiting armies of graduates in philosophy and the humanities—not for practicing philosophy but for elaborating on extant knowledge and exploring undreamt-of possibilities once they have been trained the basics. We must be very careful and watch out here. The central question is whether we want an educational system that follows some shareholder value as its highest principle—or an educational system that continues to be committed to democratic society and its thriving development.

I hope that in twenty years from now—which may already be very late, but a transformation of education takes time—universities will only be populated by a small group of students and researchers active in monodisciplinary fields of research and studies. The vast majority should be involved in interdisciplinary and theme-centered fields of work. We must start at both ends of the educational system simultaneously. We can switch to project-based learning in schools, similar to what is being done in Finland. In several years, universities will then be attended by young people knowing what interdisciplinarity means.

Menschen an die Universitäten, die etwas damit anfangen können.

Noch einmal zurück zum Thema KI: Unter Expertinnen und Experten scheint derzeit die Meinung vorzuherrschen, dass Maschinen Menschen vor allem repetitive Arbeiten abnehmen werden und wir uns auf das konzentrieren können und sollen, was spezifisch menschlich ist. Ist das auch Ihre Meinung?

Bast: Ja, das passt mit meinem Bild von Bildung und Bildungszielen zusammen. Es gab noch nie in so kurzer Zeit eine so radikale Veränderung durch eine technologische Revolution. Auf diese Geschwindigkeit müssen wir reagieren, das Bildungssystem muss uns darauf vorbereiten. Es gibt ja einen Streit, wie viele Arbeitsplätze durch KI und Robotik vernichtet werden. Es werden auf jeden Fall viele sein: Wenn wir wissen, welches Potenzial KI hat, dann wissen wir auch, dass es viele Bereiche gibt, in denen Menschen weniger präzise, weniger schnell und weniger verlässlich sind. Es ist völlig klar, dass dort Maschinen eingesetzt werden. Das geschieht auch jetzt schon: Die höchsten Roboterisierungsraten gibt es ausgerechnet in jenen Ländern, die früher als Billiglohnländer bezeichnet wurden. Auf der anderen Seite gibt es Bereiche, in denen Roboter und KI – zumindest noch – nicht einsetzbar sind. Das sind die Bereiche Intuition, emotionale Intelligenz und Gebiete, in denen man radikal Perspektiven wechselt, radikal »out of the box« denkt. Wir Menschen müssen uns auf jene Bereiche konzentrieren, die Maschinen schlechter oder noch gar nicht können. Dann haben wir eine Chance, das sprichwörtlich gewordenen »race against the machine« zu gewinnen.

Haben Sie persönlich Sorge, dass wir dieses Rennen verlieren und uns Maschinen über den Kopf wachsen werden?

Bast: Ich bin ein grundsätzlich optimistischer Mensch. Ich habe keine Angst, ich habe aber Sorge, dass Wissenschaft und Politik sich dieser Herausforderung nicht rasch genug stellen. Gerade unter dem Vorzeichen des großen Einflusses von Technologien brauchen wir viel mehr gebildete Menschen – allein um die Demokratie aufrechtzuerhalten. Da wird es nicht genügen, wenn 40 Prozent der Menschen tertiäre Bildungsabschlüsse haben, sondern da werden wir 80 Prozent brauchen. Das werden aber ganz andere Abschlüsse sein. Obwohl ich ja ein Verfechter offener Universitäten bin, habe ich bei einer Diskussion unter

Let's get back to the subject of AI: among experts, the opinion appears to prevail right now that machines will mainly take repetitive work off people's shoulders so that they can and should concentrate on what is specifically human. Do you agree?

Bast: Yes, this fits in with my idea of education and educational goals. Never before has there been such radical change brought about by a technological revolution within such a short period of time. We must respond to this pace, and our educational system will have to prepare us for this. Experts argue about how many jobs will be destroyed by AI and robotics. In any case, it will be many: knowing the potentials of AI, we also know how many areas there are in which humans are less precise, not as fast, and less reliable. It is entirely clear that this is where machines will be employed, a development that has already set in: the highest robotization rates occur in those very states that were formerly referred to as low-wage countries. On the other hand, there are areas in which robots and AI cannot be employed—at least not yet. These are intuition and emotional intelligence, as well as fields characterized by radical changes in perspective, by a radical form of thinking out of the box. We as humans must concentrate on those areas in which machines are inferior or totally incapable. Then we will have a chance to win the proverbial "race against the machine."

Are you personally worried that we will lose this race and that machines will take the upper hand?

Bast: I am an optimist by nature. But although I am not really afraid, I am worried that science and politics do not face this challenge fast enough. Given the major impact of technologies on our lives, we need many more well-educated people—simply to ensure that democracy can be kept up. For this it will not suffice to have forty percent of people having attained a tertiary level of education—we will need eighty percent. But the qualifications to be gained will be entirely different. Even though I am an advocate of open universities, I once proposed in a discussion among university representatives to introduce a stricter access policy for monodisciplinary fields of studies. The truth is that they are still designed to

Universitäten einmal den Vorschlag gemacht, dass wir strenge Zugangsregelungen für die monodisziplinären Studienrichtungen einführen sollten. Diese sind in Wahrheit noch immer darauf ausgelegt, wissenschaftlichen Nachwuchs zu produzieren. Das ist unverzichtbar, aber wir brauchen nicht zigtausende Germanisten, die in 20 Seminaren die Details der Zweiten Lautverschiebung behandeln können. Im Gegenzug sollten wir aber jene Universitäten finanziell belohnen, die ganz neue themenzentrierte und disziplinenübergreifende Studienangebote machen. Die Antwort von Ministern und hohen Beamten war: Das ist eine super Idee und wäre wahrscheinlich sinnvoll, aber das stehen wir politisch nicht durch. Wenn das die wichtigste Dimension ist, dann haben wir den Wettlauf gegen die Maschine verloren.

Paradoxerweise lässt mich die aktuelle Coronakrise jedoch wieder ein bisschen hoffen. Wenn man sich ansieht, was jetzt in kurzer Zeit an politischen Maßnahmen in Kraft gesetzt wurde, und ich rede dabei nicht von den gefährlichen und zweifelhaften Methoden von Big Data, sondern von ganz neuen gesellschaftlichen Solidaritätsaktionen wie der neuen Form der Kurzarbeit, dem Maskentragen oder den Milliarden, die plötzlich für Notfallfonds da sind, um Unternehmen zu stützen: Die Tatsache, dass so etwas möglich ist, zeigt mir, dass es Grund zur Hoffnung gibt und dass das auch in anderen Bereichen, die eine ähnliche, aber viel langfristigere Bedrohung für unsere Zivilisation bedeuten, möglich sein sollte. Etwa bei der Klimakrise. Bisher hieß es immer: Das geht nicht, da bricht alles zusammen, das halten wir politisch nicht aus. Jetzt können plötzlich – »koste es, was es wolle« – über Nacht Milliarden zur Verfügung gestellt werden. ✖

produce young academics—which is indispensable, but we do not need tens of thousands of German philologists able to deal with the details of the High German consonant shift in twenty seminars or so. On the other hand, universities should be rewarded financially when offering theme-centered and interdisciplinary study programs. Federal ministers and high-ranking officials replied: this is a great idea and would probably make sense, but we will not get through with this politically. If this is our principal dimension, we have already lost the race against the machine.

Paradoxically enough, it seems to me that the current coronavirus crisis harbors some hope. Look at the political measures that have been implemented within a brief period of time—I am not talking about the dangerous and dubious methods of big data, but about unheard-of social solidarity campaigns like the new forms of short-time working, wearing masks, or the billions of euros suddenly made available for emergency funds in order to support businesses: the fact that such things are possible shows me that there is reason for hope and that this should also be possible in other areas posing a similar but more long-term threat to our civilization—such as in the case of the climate crisis. So far, we always heard arguments like: this won't work, everything will break down, or this could not be managed politically. All of a sudden, billions can be mobilized over night, "no matter what the cost." ×

Emergente Bilder aus einem unsichtbaren Material

Die Künstlerin Judith Fegerl, derzeit Artist in Residence am AIT Austrian Institute of Technology, nutzt physikalisch-chemische Vorgänge, um ihre Kunstobjekte entstehen zu lassen. Sie gibt die Rahmenbedingungen vor, aus denen ein Bild oder eine Skulptur emergiert.

Einer von Judith Fegerls liebsten Werkstoffen ist unsichtbar. »Man kann sie nicht sehen, man kann sie nicht hören, und man kann sie bis zu einem gewissen Grad auch nicht spüren: Trotzdem ist elektrische Energie die Grundlage unseres modernen, technologisierten Lebens – mit allem, was damit einhergeht, von der Umweltproblematik über die Versorgungssicherheit bis hin zum Energiesparen.«

Das Thema habe ganz banale Seiten, etwa wenn man zu einem Kind sagt: »Dreh das Licht ab, wenn du aus dem Badezimmer gehst«, aber auch hochkomplexe, etwa bei Versorgungsstrukturen. Es geht einerseits um immense Kräfte, die frei werden können, andererseits aber auch um sehr kleine, kaum wahrnehmbare Details. »Das ist die Spanne, die mich seit jeher interessiert. Jeder Mensch ist Hunderte Male am Tag mit diesem Unsichtbaren und Ungreifbaren konfrontiert. Mit elektrischer Energie ist viel Unsicherheit, Unwissenheit, Angst und Gefahr verknüpft. Es gibt eine Barriere des Nichtverstehens.« Und: Sie ist auch auf künstlerischer Ebene eine Herausforderung: »Mir geht es in meiner Kunst letzten Endes um das Erfahrbarmachen von Energie«, sagt Fegerl. Dass die in Wien geborene und tätige Künstlerin zurzeit Artist in Residence am AIT Austrian Institute of Technology ist, passt hervorragend zu ihrer Grundphilosophie. »Für mich sind Technologie, Infrastruktur und wissenschaftliche Strukturen Tools wie andere auch, um meine künstlerischen Beiträge zu formen.«

Überdies ist Energie für Fegerl auch das Material, an dem sie künstlerische Forschung betreibt. »Man darf Kunst nicht als Gegenpol zur Wissenschaft sehen. Sondern Kunst ist eine andere Form der Forschung. Sie ist genauso ernsthaft und akribisch wie andere Disziplinen.« Genauer: »Ich betreibe künstlerische Grundlagenforschung am Material Energie. Das ist notwendig, finde ich, bevor man irgendetwas anderes damit macht.« Um Kunst als Mittel zum Erkenntnisgewinn nutzen zu können, geht künstlerische Forschung wie jede Art von Wissenschaft von einer konkreten Frage-

Judith Fegerl, geb. 1977, studierte in Wien Visuelle Mediengestaltung, Digitale Kunst sowie Kunst und neue Medien. Sie lebt und arbeitet nach Aufenthalten in Berlin und New York seit 2011 in Wien. Im Mittelpunkt ihrer künstlerischen Arbeiten steht die symbiotische Verbindung von Mensch und Maschine.

Emergent Images from
an Invisible Material

Judith Fegerl, born 1977,
studied Visual Media
Design, Digital Art,
and Art and New Me-
dia in Vienna. After
stays in Berlin and
New York she lives and
works in Vienna since
2011. The focus of her
artistic work is the
symbiotic connection
between man and ma-
chine.

Judith Fegerl, currently artist-in-residence at the AIT Austrian Institute of Technology, uses physical-chemical processes to see her art objects come into being. She provides the framework conditions from which a picture or sculpture emerges.

One of the artist Judith Fegerl's favorite materials is invisible. "You cannot see it, you cannot hear it, and to a certain extent, you cannot feel it either: nevertheless, electrical energy is the foundation of our modern, technologized life—with everything that comes with it, from environmental problems to security of supply and energy saving."

Fegerl sees the quite banal sides of the issue such as when somebody tells a child, "Turn off the light when you're done in the bathroom!" But she is also aware of its complex aspects like those regarding supply structures. On the one hand, works of this kind are about the immense forces that can be released, but, on the other, they are also about very small, barely perceptible details. "This is the range that has always interested me. Everyone is confronted with this invisible and intangible phenomenon hundreds of times a day. A lot of uncertainty, ignorance, fear, and danger is associated with electrical energy, and there is a barrier of incomprehension." This energy is also a challenge in artistic terms: "Ultimately, my art is about making energy tangible," says Fegerl. The fact that Fegerl, who was born and works in Vienna, is currently artist-in-residence at the AIT Austrian Institute of Technology fits perfectly with her basic philosophy. "I regard technology, infrastructure, and scientific structures as tools like others when it comes to developing an artistic contribution."

Moreover, energy is also the material Fegerl focuses her artistic research on. "One must not see art as the antithesis of science. Art is another form of research. It is as serious and meticulous as other disciplines." More precisely: "I do basic artistic research on the material energy. I think that this is necessary before you do anything else with it." In order to be able to use art as a means of acquiring knowledge, artistic research, like any kind of science, starts from a concrete question. The question in Judith Fegerl's case is: How can energy be

stellung aus. In Judith Fegerls Fall lautet die Frage: Wie wird Energie erfahrbar? Die Ergebnisse zeigen sich zum einen als theoretische Erkenntnisse und zum anderen als manifeste Kunstwerke, die sich von der interessierten Bevölkerung betrachten, erfahren oder interpretieren lassen.

Wie das in der Praxis aussehen kann, war heuer in der Installation *reservoir* im Foyer des AIT zu sehen. Vordergründig handelt es sich bei dieser Arbeit um eine Versuchsanordnung zur Erzeugung von elektrischem Strom: zwölf Glasbecken mit eingeschobenen Kupfer- und Aluminiumplatten und einem Elektrolyt samt Verkabelung. »Das war eine funktionierende Batterie.« Nach einer gewissen Zeit wurde die Anlage aber abgebaut, die Platten wurden entnommen: »An ihnen wurde sichtbar, wie sich das Material durch den Prozess des Energieerzeugens verändert hat, wie es teilweise verbraucht worden ist.« An diesen nun als eigenständige Kunstwerke zu betrachtenden Metallplatten wird die Wirkung von Energie erfahrbar: Die Platten zeigen ein jeweils individuelles Muster aus feinen, verästelten Korrosionsspuren, aus grünen Verfärbungen und weißen oxidativen Überzügen in allen erdenklichen Nuancen, das der »Werkstoff« Energie im und am Metall hinterlassen hat. »Ich sehe das auch als bildgebendes Verfahren – wie das Entwickeln einer Fotografie«, so Fegerl. Eine Art Elektrografie also, der chemisch-physikalische Prozesse in Form von emergenten Strukturveränderungen eingeschrieben sind. Das Bild ist nicht durch die vorgegebenen Rahmenbedingungen determiniert, sondern emergiert aus dem Zusammenspiel der verschiedenen Faktoren.

Ihre Installationen plant Fegerl penibel: Wie unter Laborbedingungen werden die Rahmenbedingungen genau kontrolliert, was die Komplexität der möglichen Prozesse reduziert. Aber die Künstlerin baut bewusst auch gewisse Freiheitsgrade ein, die ihrerseits wieder Komplexität ermöglichen. »reservoir« war vor dem Aufbau in Wien bereits in Turin, München, Friedrichshafen und New York zu sehen. »Jedes Mal verwende ich lokales Leitungswasser. Das ist meine Variable: Durch seine unterschiedliche mineralische Zusammensetzung sehen die Platten, die vorher exakt gleich waren, nachher immer anders aus. Das Ergebnis ist abhängig von der Temperatur, von der Luftfeuchtigkeit, von der Sonneneinstrahlung usw. – das alles wirkt sich auf das entstehende Bild aus.«

Mit der Installation macht Judith Fegerl bewusst einen Schritt zurück: »Es ist ein Loslassen vom künstlerischen Gestus. Ich kreiere die Rahmenbedingungen, ich schreibe quasi das Programm und habe dabei eine Wunschvorstellung. Meinen künstlerischen Prozess delegiere ich aber an einen elektrochemischen Prozess. Das Bild entsteht spontan aus sich selbst heraus, es emergiert in einem Selbstorganisationsprozess, auf den ich im Detail keinen Einfluss mehr nehme.« Sie könne dann nur mehr zuschauen, was passiert – und hoffen, dass etwas entsteht, das für sie künstlerisch interessant ist.

made experienceable? The results present themselves as both theoretical insights and manifest works of art that can be viewed, experienced, or interpreted by the interested public.

How this can look like in practice could be seen in the foyer of the AIT until recently, where Fegerl showed her installation *reservoir*. At first glance, this work will strike you as an experimental arrangement for generating electric current: twelve glass basins with inserted copper and aluminum plates and an electrolyte including wiring. "This was a functioning battery." After a certain period of time, the installation was dismantled and the plates were removed: "The plates revealed how their material had changed through the process of generating electricity, how part of it had been consumed." These metal plates showing the impact of energy could now be regarded as independent works of art: each plate displays an individual pattern of fine, branching traces of corrosion, green discolorations, and white oxidative coatings in all conceivable nuances, which the "material" energy has left in and on the metal. "I see this also as an imaging process—like developing a photograph," says Fegerl. In other words, a kind of electrography in which chemical-physical processes are inscribed in the form of emergent structural changes. The image is not determined by the given framework conditions but emerges from the interaction of various factors.

Fegerl plans her installations meticulously: Similar to laboratory conditions, the framework conditions are precisely controlled, which reduces the complexity of potential processes. Yet the artist also provides for certain degrees of freedom, which in turn make complexity possible again. Before *reservoir* was set up in Vienna, it was already on view in Turin, Munich, Friedrichshafen, and New York. "I always use local tap water. This is my variable: Due to its varying mineral composition, the panels, which were exactly the same before, always look different afterwards. The result depends on temperature, humidity, sunlight, etc.; all these factors affect the resulting image."

With this installation, Judith Fegerl deliberately takes a step back: "It is a departure from artistic gesture. I create the framework conditions, I write the program, as it were, and in doing so I follow my wishful thinking. But I delegate my artistic process to an electrochemical process. The picture emerges spontaneously from within itself, in a self-organizing process which I do not control in its details." The artist only watches what happens, hoping that something develops that she finds artistically interesting.

Another project of the artist that makes energy visible is *cauter*. Its starting point is that new museum buildings are technically extremely complex. "They are mechanical organisms: every house is

Ein anderes Projekt der Künstlerin, das Energie sichtbar macht, ist *cauter*. Sein Ausgangspunkt ist, dass neue Museumsbauten technisch extrem aufwendig sind. »Sie sind ein maschineller Organismus: Jedes Haus ist eine Riesenmaschine mit Kabeln, Leitungen, Klimaanlagen usw., die sich hinter den Wänden verstecken«, meint Fegerl. Das Potenzial dieser Infrastruktur will sie bewusst machen: Sie verlegt Leitungen in die Wände und überlastet sie absichtlich und kontrolliert mit Starkstrom. »Die Leitungen brennen sich dann durch die Wand, und der Kabelbrand erzeugt ein „wall drawing". So wird sichtbar, welches Potenzial, welche Macht der Strom hat.« Das Ergebnis sehe jedes Mal anders aus. »Das kann ich nur bis zu einem gewissen Grad bestimmen. Welche Farbe die Stromdrahtzeichnung bekommt, wie groß sie wird, wie und ob es raucht, ob Stichflammen aus der Wand schlagen – das alles ist immer eine große Überraschung. Und es ist auch mit einem Nervenkitzel verbunden, denn es gibt dabei schon ein gewisses Maß an Gefahr.«

Genau dieser Aspekt steht im Vordergrund der Installation *moment*. Skulpturen aus massivem Stahl werden durch einen starken Elektromagneten zusammengehalten. »Kommt es zu einem Stromausfall, bricht das Ganze auseinander«, so Fegerl. Es gibt also eine immanente Gefahr – und sobald diese den Museumsbesucher*innen klar wird, steht plötzlich nicht mehr die Kunst im Vordergrund. »Die Betrachterinnen und Betrachter rücken ins Zentrum: Sie müssen ihre eigene Position innerhalb des Gefüges, das ich gestaltet habe, finden, sie müssen entscheiden, welche Distanz sie zu der Arbeit einnehmen wollen. Da spielt plötzlich die persönliche Sicherheit eine Rolle, ins Spiel kommen Unsicherheit und Unwissen, es tauchen viele Fragen auf. Durch die zunehmende Komplexität sind wir nicht mehr in der Lage, alles zu verstehen.«

Das nächste Projekt, das Judith Fegerl am AIT umsetzen will, hat mit elementaren Kräften der Natur zu tun: Sie will im Hochspannungslabor Blitze und Lichtbögen durch ein Sandbett jagen. Dadurch schmilzt der Sand teilweise und erstarrt in gezackten Formen, sogenannten Fulguriten. »Es ist vielleicht die spontanste Emergenz, mit der ich jemals gearbeitet habe: Energie manifestiert sich als Materie.« Letztlich handle es sich um einen sehr physikalischen Versuch, den Fegerl in die Kunst hineinziehen will. »Es gab schon kleinere Tests, die sehr vielversprechend verliefen. Jetzt werden wir es in größerem Maßstab und mit längerer Dauer versuchen.« Es gebe mehrere Variable, wie zum Beispiel die Zusammensetzung des Sandes oder die gewählte Spannung, die das Aussehen der Fulgurite beeinflussen werden – in welcher Art und Weise werde sich zeigen.

Überdies will die Künstlerin den Versuch des Menschen, diese Naturgewalt zu zähmen, thematisieren: Sie hat alte Blitzableiter von Wiener Häusern gesammelt, die nun im Hochspannungslabor noch einmal durch einen künstlichen Blitzeinschlag aktiviert werden. »Ich bin schon neugierig, was da passiert.« ✖

a giant machine with cables, pipes, air conditioning, etc. hidden behind the walls," Fegerl points out. It is the potential of this infrastructure she wants to make people aware of. She lays cables in the walls and overloads them deliberately and in a controlled manner with high voltage current. "The cables burn through the wall, and the cable fire generates a 'wall drawing.' This shows the potential and power of electricity." The result is different every time. "I can only determine the outcome to a certain degree. What color the electric wire drawing assumes, how large it gets, how and whether it gives off smoke, whether flames burst out of the wall—all this is always a big surprise. And it also implies a thrill as there is a certain degree of danger after all."

Exactly this aspect is in the focus of the installation *moment*. Sculptures made of solid steel are held together by a strong electromagnet. "If there is a power failure, the whole thing breaks apart," says Fegerl. So, there is an imminent danger—and as soon as museum visitors become aware of it, art is suddenly no longer what is of importance. "The viewers move to center stage: they have to find their own position within the structure I have designed and make up their mind from what distance they want to view the work. Suddenly, personal security begins to matter, uncertainty and ignorance come into play, numerous questions arise. The increasing complexity entails that we are no longer able to understand everything."

The next project that Judith Fegerl plans to realize at the AIT will be concerned with elementary forces of nature. She wants to send flashes of lightning and arcs through a bed of sand in the high-voltage laboratory. This will make the sand partially melt and solidify into jagged shapes, so-called fulgurites. "This is perhaps the most spontaneous emergence I have ever worked with: energy manifests itself as matter." Ultimately, it is a very physical experiment that Fegerl wants to bring to art. "There have been smaller tests that showed great promise. Now we are going to try it on a larger scale and for a longer period of time." There are several variables, says Fegerl, such as the composition of the sand or the chosen voltage, which will influence the appearance of the fulgurites—we will see how.

Moreover, the artist wants to shed light on the human attempt to tame this force of nature: She has collected old lightning conductors from Viennese houses, which will be activated in the high-voltage laboratory by means of an artificial lightning strike. "I am curious to see what'll happen." ×

reservoir
2019–2020
ARTTEC, the art program
of AIT Austrian Institute
of Technology

Im Rahmen des
Artist-in-Residence-
Programms zum
Thema Energie

Zwölf Kupfer- und
zwölf Aluminiumplatten
werden in Glasbehältern
mit Salzwasser einer
elektrochemischen
Behandlung ausgesetzt.
Diese installative
Versuchsanordnung
folgt dem Funktionsprin-
zip der Batterie, die hier
Energie nicht nur freigibt,
sondern sie in den Metallplatten festschreibt.
Nach etwa zwei Monaten
werden die Platten ent-
nommen und Teil der
Ausstellung.

Part of the artist-in-
residence program on
the subject of energy

Twelve copper and
twelve aluminum
plates are subjected
to electrochemical
treatment in glass
containers with salt
water. This installative
experimental arrange-
ment follows the
functional principle
of the battery, which
in this case not only
releases energy but
also inscribes it into
the metal plates. After
about two months, the
plates are removed and
become part of the
exhibition.

© Judith Fegerl,
Courtesy Galerie
Hubert Winter, Wien
Foto / Photo: AIT Thomas
Lerch

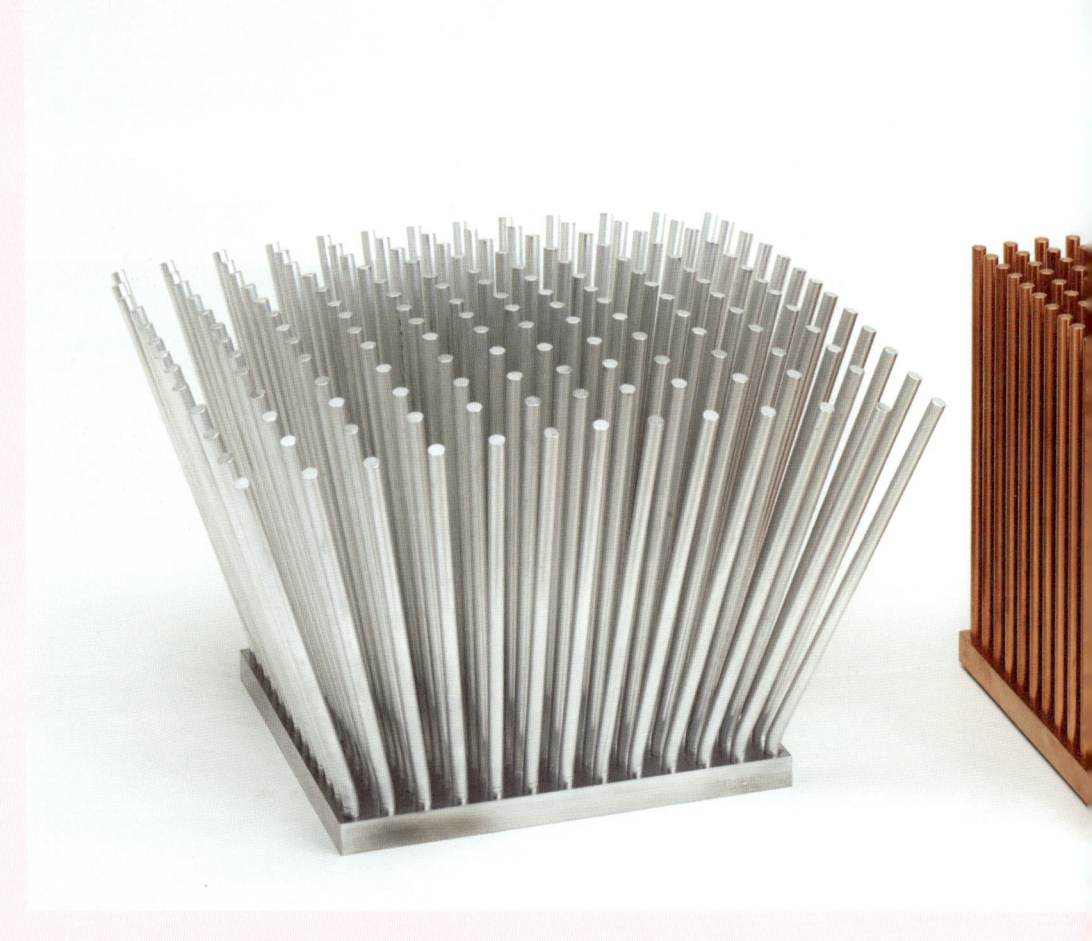

still
2019

Kühlelemente, Kupfer
und Aluminium, 169
Stäbe, je 30 × 30 × 30 cm

Judith Fegerl erstellt
kontinuierlich neue,
mit Kühlelementen aus
Metall assoziierte
Objekte, wie sie auf
Computerprozessoren
und anderen digitalen
Geräten vorkommen
(Passivelemente). Die
industrielle Ästhetik
der Objekte erinnert an
minimalistische Kunst-
werke. Die Minimal Art
der 1960er- und frühen
1970er-Jahre behandelte
die Form losgelöst von
Kontext, überflüssigen
Details und Assoziatio-
nen. Fegerls Werkgruppe
still entgegnet dieser
Haltung mit Formen,
deren Gestalt und Gestal-
tung ausschließlich auf
der Optimierung ihrer
Funktion beruhen –
Objekten, die diese Funk-
tion permanent als stille
Maschinen und als
Kunstobjekte ausführen:
Die spezifische Setzung
der Stäbe vergrößert die
Oberfläche und erzeugt
Luftwirbel; die Wärme
wird effizient abgeleitet
und dadurch neutrali-
siert. Das Form-follows-
function-Prinzip wird auf
künstlerische Objekte
angewandt, die den
Prozess des Wärmeaus-
tauschs und somit auch
die Debatte über
Technologie im Kontext
von Erderwärmung und
Klimawandel verhan-
deln.

Cooling elements,
copper and aluminum,
169 rods, 30 × 30 × 30 cm
each

Judith Fegerl continu-
ously creates new
objects associated with
metal cooling elements
as they appear on com-
puter processors and
other digital devices
(passive elements). The
objects' industrial
aesthetic echoes
minimalist works of
art. The Minimal Art
of the 1960s and early
1970s treated form
detached from context,
superfluous details,
and associations.
Fegerl's work group
still counters this
attitude with forms
whose shape and design
are based exclusively
on the optimization of
their function—objects
that permanently
perform this function
as silent machines and
as objects of art: the
specific setting of the
rods enlarges the
surface and creates air
vortices; the heat is
efficiently dissipated
and thus neutralized.
The principle of form
follows function is
applied to artistic
objects that deal with
the process of heat
exchange and thus the
debate about technolo-
gy in the context of
global warming and
climate change.

anchors
2019

Permanente Installation
Landesgalerie
Niederösterreich, Krems

Die Arbeit *anchors*
befasst sich mit der in
der spezifischen Form
eines „verdrehten"
Gebäudes gespeicherten
Spannungsenergie. Im
Erdgeschoß des Mu-
seums definiert sie drei
Druckpunkte, von denen
imaginäre Kräfte der
Drehung des Gebäudes
ausgehen. An diesen
Stellen setzt sie geome-
trische Griffe aus Beton
in Negativ- und Positiv-
formen ein. In einer
These stellt die Künst-
lerin die Form des
tatsächlichen Museums-
baus einem virtuellen
geometrischen Körper,
dem Kubus, gegenüber
und befasst sich mit den
Kräften, die nötig wären,
um eine vom Kubus
ausgehende Verformung
zur tatsächlichen Form
des Museums durchzu-
führen. Es werden
sogenannte „Ankerfor-
men" generiert, die
Information über Kraft
und Richtung der Trans-
formation in Bezug auf
die Ausgangsform
(Kubus) liefern und den
virtuellen Vorgang der
Verformung des Gebäu-
des nachvollziehbar
machen.
*(Text: Günther
Oberhollenzer)*

Permanent installation
Landesgalerie
Niederösterreich, Krems

The work *anchors* deals
with the stored tension
energy in the specific
form of a "twisted"
building. Fegerl defines
three pressure points
on the ground floor of
the museum, from
which imaginary forces
of the building's rota-
tion originate. She
furnishes these points
with geometric con-
crete handles in nega-
tive and positive forms.
In one thesis, the artist
juxtaposes the form of
the actual museum
building with a virtual
geometric body, the
cube, and explores the
forces that would be
necessary to carry out
a deformation springing
from the cube to the
museum's actual form
The generated so-called
"anchor shapes" provide
information about the
force and direction of
the transformation in
relation to the initial
shape (cube) and make
the virtual process of
deformation of the build-
ing comprehensible.
*(Text: Günther
Oberhollenzer)*

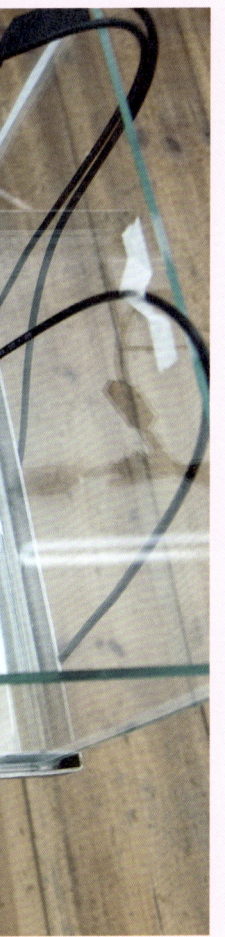

I can speak so softly because I hold so much power (incubator)
2010

Galvanisches Bad für
Vergoldung, Wiegenge-
stell, menschliches Haar,
Kabel, Strom, Elektrolyt
100 × 60 × 45 cm

In die Wanne, deren Form
an eine Wiege erinnert,
wurde eine elektrolyti-
sche Flüssigkeit einge-
lassen. Die Wanne hat
geschwungene Kufen
und soll vom Betrachter
bewegt werden, was
für den galvanischen
Prozess förderlich ist. Am
Boden der Wanne liegt
eine menschliche (wohl
weibliche) Haarsträhne.
An deren Enden sind
Elektroden befestigt.
Das Schaustück wirkt
ebenso steril wie morbid.
Entblößte Haare erin-
nern an Reliquien und
Märchen, an Kult und
Gewalt, an Verehrung
und Beschämung.
Zwiespältig sind solche
Zurschaustellungen, weil
sie in der Betrachtung
entweder Überhöhung
oder Unterwerfung
provozieren – für Judith
Fegerl ein guter Grund,
nicht nur die Rolle der
Frau, sondern auch der
Künstlerin zu thematisie-
ren. Im Titel I can speak
so softly because I hold
so much power schwingt
dieses Selbstbewusst-
sein der Künstlerin-Her-
stellerin mit, die durch
technische Kompetenz
und die Arbeit mit Tech-
nologie und Strom
die biologiebasierten
Klischees weiblicher
Reproduktion ins Ab-
seits verweist.
(Text: Thomas Trummer)

Galvanic bath for
gilding, weighing rack,
human hair, cables,
electricity, electrolyte
100 × 60 × 45 cm

The tub, whose form
evokes a cradle, holds
an electrolytic liquid.
The tub has curved
runners and is intended
to be moved by the ob-
server, which is con-
ducive to the galvanic
process. A human
strand of hair (probably
a woman's) lies at
the bottom of the tub.
Electrodes are attached
to its ends. The show-
piece appears both
sterile and morbid.
Exposed hair is reminis-
cent of relics and fairy
tales, of cult and vio-
lence, of worship and
shame. Such displays
are ambivalent because
they provoke either
exaggeration or sub-
jugation—which Judith
Fegerl considers a good
reason to address not
only the role of women
but also that of the
artist. The title *I can
speak so softly because
I hold so much power*
resonates with this
self-confidence of the
artist-producer, who,
through technical
competence and her
work with technology
and electricity, puts
the biology-based
clichés of female
reproduction offside.
(Text: Thomas Trummer)

---

cauter

2015
Kunsthaus Glarus

Zarte linienartige Wandzeichnungen entstehen durch das Verlegen elektrischer Verkabelung in Wände. Wenn Judith Fegerl die installierten Kabel unter Starkstrom setzt, werden sie kontrolliert überlastet und brennen langsam durch den Verputz. Indem die Kabel ihrem Nutzen gemäß verwendet werden (um Strom zu leiten), erzeugt Fegerl damit Spuren, die nicht nur die sonst verborgene Position und Präsenz der Kabel verraten, sondern auch deren Potenzial. Auf der Wand werden Brandlinien in unregelmäßiger Stärke und Form erzeugt. Die Enden jeder Linie sind durch blanke verdrillte Stahlkabel markiert, die aus der Wand herausstehen. Von Weitem ist die Wandzeichnung kaum sichtbar; beim Nähertreten erscheinen die feinen Linien, nach und nach erschließt sich auch deren Entstehung.

Judith Fegerls *cauter* folgt einer stringenten Reihe von Arbeiten, die sich mit der Funktion, Konstruktion und Identität von Raum und dem Menschen dienender Maschinen beschäftigen, beides betrieben und abhängig von elektrischem Strom.

Delicate linework-like wall drawings are created by laying electrical cabling in walls. When Judith Fegerl places the installed cables under high voltage current, they are overloaded in a controlled manner and slowly burn through the plaster. By using the cables according to their purpose (to conduct electricity), Fegerl creates traces that reveal not only the otherwise hidden position and presence of the cables but also their potential. Fire lines of irregular thickness and shape are created on the wall. The ends of each line are marked by bare twisted steel cables protruding from the wall. The wall drawing is barely visible from a distance; on approaching it, the fine lines appear, and, by and by, the viewer also realizes their origin.

Judith Fegerl's *cauter* follows a stringent series of works that deal with the function, construction, and identity of space and machines serving man, both powered and dependent on electric current.

tension object
2006
Porzellankugel,
menschliches Haar,
Kupferbeschichtung,
400.000 Volt

Porcelain sphere,
human hair, copper
plating, 400,000 volt

———————————

© Judith Fegerl, Courtesy
Galerie Hubert Winter,
Wien

self

2010

Judith Fegerl zeigt den Kunstraum als architektonische und Energie liefernde Hülle für Kunstobjekte – wie ihre Mensch-Maschine-Einheiten als einen Körper ohne Organe. *self* ist gedankliche Grundlage und Voraussetzung für all ihre vorangegangenen Arbeiten. Der Kunstraum ist ausgehöhlt und an vielen Stellen geöffnet. Wie Adern aus einem sezierten Körper ragen Stromkabel aus Decke, Wand und Boden, und die subkutane Struktur des Raumkörpers, das Innenleben der Maschine, wird sichtbar. Mit *self* bringt Fegerl eine Maschine zum Vorschein, die üblicherweise möglichst dezent im Hintergrund arbeitet, und lässt uns tief in diesen Körper blicken. Sie hat den Kunstraum entkleidet und lässt sein Selbst zum Vorschein kommen. Für das Publikum wird der mit ungewohnter Radikalität exponierte Raum zum Ort der Begegnung mit der Künstlerin und der Konfrontation mit den eigenen eingefleischten Sehgewohnheiten.
(Text: Verena Kaspar-Eisert)

Judith Fegerl shows the art space as an architectural and energy-supplying shell for art objects—as a body without organs like her man-machine units. *self* is the conceptual basis and prerequisite for all her previous works. The art space has been hollowed out and opened up in many places. Power cables protrude from the ceiling, wall, and floor like veins from a dissected body, and the subcutaneous structure of the spatial body, the inner life of the machine, becomes visible. Fegerl's self brings to light a machine that usually works as discreetly as possible in the background, allowing us to look deep into this body. She has stripped the art space and allows its self to emerge. For the viewers, the space, exposed with unusual radicality, becomes a place of encounter with the artist and a place of confrontation with their own ingrained habits of seeing.
(Text: Verena Kaspar-Eisert)

temporal deflector
2008

Magnetisches Feld,
elektronische Steuerung,
Kompass

Die Arbeit *temporal deflector* besteht aus einem Kompass, um den kreisförmig 60 Induktionsspulen angeordnet sind. Die sich verändernden Magnetfelder der Spulen zwingen die Kompassnadel in eine ständige Rotation, in Intervallen von jeweils einer Sekunde bzw. zu einer vollen Umdrehung pro Minute. Die technische Apparatur greift in ein von der Natur vorgegebenes Gesetz, das Zeigen einer Kompassnadel nach Norden, ein. Ein Instrument zur Bestimmung der Position im Raum wird zu einem Instrument zur Bestimmung der Zeit. In dieser Anordnung verschränken sich Zeit und Raum, wenn die empfindliche Nadel den Intervallsignalen der Magnetspulen folgt. Die Sekunde als zeitliche Einheit, die dadurch auch eine dimensionale Richtung beschreibt, treibt die Kompassnadel um ihre eigene Achse. Sie dreht sich in 60 Einzelschritten um 360 Grad pro Minute.
(Text: Moritz Stipsicz)

Magnetic field,
electronic control,
compass

The work *temporal deflector* consists of a compass with sixty induction coils arranged in a circle around it. The coils' changing magnetic fields force the compass needle to rotate continuously at intervals of one second or one full revolution per minute. The technical apparatus interferes with a law given by nature, the pointing of a compass needle to the north. An instrument for determining the position in space becomes an instrument for determining the time. In this arrangement, time and space intertwine when the sensitive needle follows the magnetic coils' interval signals. The second as a unit of time, which thus also describes a dimensional direction, drives the compass needle around its own axis. It rotates 360 degrees per minute in sixty separate steps.
(Text: Moritz Stipsicz)

**the kitchen
(was what she had given
of herself to the world)**
2019

| Magnetischer Edelstahl, Induktionstechnik Vier Elemente, je 60 × 60 × 90 cm | Magnetic stainless steel, induction technology Four elements, 60 × 60 × 90 cm each |

Quaderförmige Objekte in den standardisierten Abmessungen europäischer Küchenmodule (60 × 60 × 90 cm) aus magnetischem Edelstahl werden einer induktiven Erhitzung unterzogen, im Zuge deren sich ihre Form destabilisiert und ihre Oberfläche sich regenbogenähnlich einfärbt. Judith Fegerl nutzt die Technik dazu, einem Material eine Signatur einzuschreiben, die metaphorisch alle mit ihm verbundenen Erinnerungen und Verhaltensmuster löscht: Durch das Erhitzen verliert das Metall jede Spur seines magnetischen Gedächtnisses. Der Hightechküche führt Fegerl jene Energie zu, die letztlich einen auch ideologischen Kurzschluss erzeugt: Nicht sie – als Künstlerin – passt sich der Struktur an, sondern die Strukturen verändern sich ihren Vorgaben gemäß. *(Text: Anne Faucheret)*

Cuboid objects in the standardized dimensions of European kitchen modules (60 × 60 × 90 cm) made of magnetic stainless steel are subjected to inductive heating in the course of which their shape destabilizes and their surface takes on a rainbow-like coloration. Judith Fegerl uses technology to inscribe a signature on a material that metaphorically erases all memories and patterns of behavior associated with it: heating the metal makes it lose every trace of its magnetic memory. Fegerl supplies the high-tech kitchen with the energy that ultimately creates also an ideological short circuit: it is not she— as an artist—who adapts to the structure, but the structures change according to her specifications. *(Text: Anne Faucheret)*

Alpbacher Technologiegespräche
»Fundamentals«

27.–29.08.2020

Die Alpbacher Technologiegespräche werden vom AIT Austrian Institute of Technology, Österreichs größter Research-and-Technology-Organisation, und ORF Radio Österreich 1 veranstaltet. Das Projekt wird von Mag. Michael H. Hlava (AIT) und Dr. Martin Bernhofer (ORF Ö1) geleitet, das Projektbüro von Claudia Klement (AIT). Dem Steering Committee der Alpbacher Technologiegespräche gehören als Vorsitzender Dr. Hannes Androsch (Präsident des Aufsichtsrats des AIT, Vorsitzender des Rats für Forschung und Technologieentwicklung), Prof. Dr. Wolfgang Knoll (wissenschaftlicher Geschäftsführer des AIT) und Monika Eigensperger (Radiodirektorin ORF) an.

Wissenschaftliche Partner der Alpbacher Technologiegespräche 2020 sind die Helmholtz-Gemeinschaft Deutscher Forschungszentren, Industrial partner ist die Industriellenvereinigung (IV).

Die Veranstaltung wird vom österreichischen Bundesministerium für Klimaschutz, Umwelt, Energie, Mobilität, Innovation und Technologie (BMK), vom Bundesministerium für Digitalisierung und Wirtschaftsstandort (BMDW) sowie vom Bundesministerium für Bildung, Wissenschaft und Forschung (BMBWF) unterstützt.

Das rationale wissenschaftliche Weltbild hat in Teilen der Gesellschaft an Strahlkraft verloren. In Zeiten des rasanten technologischen und gesellschaftlichen Wandels sind aber sichere Fundamente wichtiger denn je – man denke nur an den Klimawandel, an die Digitalisierung und, nun akut, an die Coronapandemie mit ihren vielfältigen Folgen. Die Technologiegespräche machen sich auf die Suche nach neuen Antworten: Wie sehen unsere Grundlagen heute aus? Worauf ist künftig zu achten? Was bedeutet das für Technologien der Zukunft? Welchen Herausforderungen muss sich die Industrie stellen, um wettbewerbsfähig zu bleiben? Diskutiert werden dabei u. a. neue Sichtweisen auf Gesellschaft und Wirtschaft, wie sie etwa die Komplexitätsforschung eröffnet, und neue europäische Perspektiven zur Bewältigung der Klima- und Umweltprobleme. Wertvolle Beiträge zum Umgang mit den Zukunftsfragen können überdies die Künste bieten, denen breiter Raum eingeräumt wird. ✕

Alpbach Technology Symposium "Fundamentals"

August 27—29, 2020

The Alpbach Technology Symposium is organized by AIT Austrian Institute of Technology, Austria's largest research and technology organization, and ORF Radio Österreich 1. The project is managed by Mag. Michael H. Hlava (AIT) and Dr. Martin Bernhofer (ORF Ö1); Claudia Klement (AIT) is head of the project office. The Alpbach Technology Symposium's Steering Committee includes Dr. Hannes Androsch (head of the supervisory board of AIT, chairman of the Austrian Council for Research and Technology Development), Prof. Dr. Wolfgang Knoll (scientific managing director of AIT), and Monika Eigensperger (radio director ORF).

Scientific partner of the Alpbach Technology Symposium 2020 is the Helmholtz Association of German Research Centres; its industrial partner is the Federation of Austrian Industries (IV).

The Symposium is supported by the Austrian Federal Ministry for Climate Action, Environment, Energy, Mobility, Innovation and Technology (BMK), the Austrian Federal Ministry of Digital and Economic Affairs (BMDW), and the Austrian Federal Ministry of Education, Science and Research (BMBWF).

The rational scientific worldview has lost its radiance in parts of society. In times of rapid technological and social change, however, foundations are more important than ever before—one only has to think of climate change, digitization, and the pressing coronavirus pandemic with all its consequences. The Alpbach Technology Symposium is looking for new answers: What are our fundamentals today? What should be paid attention to? What does that mean for technologies of the future? What are the challenges for industry to remain competitive? The discussions include new perspectives on society and economy, such as those of complexity research, and new European perspectives for coming to terms with climate and environmental problems. As art can offer valuable contributions to handle the important questions about the future, it is given ample space. ×

Wir bedanken uns herzlich bei all unseren
Partnern, die auch heuer – trotz der außer-
gewöhnlichen Umstände – die Alpbacher
Technologiegespräche möglich gemacht haben:

We would like to thank all of our partners
who, despite the extraordinary circumstances, have made the Alpbach Technology Symposium possible this year:

Organisatoren Organizers:
AIT Austrian Institute of Technology GmbH
ORF Radio Ö1 Austrian Broadcasting Corporation – Programme Radio 1

In Kooperation und mit Unterstützung von
in cooperation with and sponsored by
Bundesministerium für Klimaschutz, Umwelt, Energie, Mobilität, Innovation
und Technologie (BMK) Austrian Federal Ministry for Climate Action,
Environment, Energy, Mobility, Innovation and Technology
Bundesministerium für Digitalisierung und Wirtschaftsstandort (BMDW)
Austrian Federal Ministry for Digital and Economic Affairs
Bundesministerium für Bildung, Wissenschaft und Forschung (BMBWF)
Austrian Federal Ministry of Education, Science and Research

Industriepartner Industrial partner:
Industriellenvereinigung Federation of Austrian Industries

Wissenschaftlicher Partner Scientific partner:
Helmholtz-Gemeinschaft Deutscher Forschungszentren

Die Veranstaltung wird von folgenden Organisationen unterstützt
The event is being supported by the following institutions:
Bundesministerium für Landesverteidigung (BMLV)
Austrian Federal Ministry of Defence
Klima- und Energiefonds Climate and Energy Fund
Falling Walls Foundation gGmbH
Forschung Austria
ITG Innovations- und Technologietransfer Salzburg GmbH
Joanneum Research Forschungsgesellschaft mbH
ecoplus / Land Niederösterreich ecoplus / The Province of Lower Austria
TU Austria Austrian Universities of Technology
Verein zur Förderung von Forschung und Innovation (VFFI)
Virtual Vehicle Research GmbH
Patentamt Austrian Patent Office

Medienpartner Media partner: Die Presse
IT-Partner Information Technology partner: APA Austrian Press Agency

(Stand: 7.7.2020)

Jahrbuch anlässlich der Alpbacher
Technologiegespräche 2020
Yearbook on the occasion of the
Alpbach Technology Symposium 2020

TEC

Alpbach Technology Symposium
Alpbacher Technologiegespräche

Idee und Konzept Idea and concept
Hannes Androsch, Michael H. Hlava, Martin Kugler
Alpbacher Technologiegespräche

Sarah Hellwagner, Clemens Kopetzky
art:phalanx, Kultur & Urbanität

Medieninhaber Media owners
art:phalanx, Kultur und Urbanität

Herausgeber Publishers
Hannes Androsch, Wolfgang Knoll, Anton Plimon
und art:phalanx Kommunikationsagentur GmbH,
Wien

Projektmanagement Project management
Selina Kainz, Sarah Hellwagner
art:phalanx, Kultur & Urbanität

Redaktion Editor
Martin Kugler

**Lektorat und Übersetzung
Copy-editing and translation**
Wolfgang Astelbauer, Roman Stoiber,
Brigitte Willinger

Grafische Gestaltung Visual design
The Graphic Society

Druck Printed by
Medienfabrik Graz GmbH

Lithografie Lithography
Pixelstorm, Wien

Papier Paper
Pergraphica smooth

Schriften Fonts
Vista Sans, Vista Slab (Xavier Dupré)

Verlag Publishing house
Verlag Holzhausen GmbH

© 2020 art:phalanx, Kultur & Urbanität
Kommunikationsagentur GmbH, Wien

Bildnachweis Photo credits
S./p. 4: © AIC, Peter M. Mayr; S./p. 44: © Heimo Aga;
S./p. 62: © Christine Knoll-Ramach;
S./p. 134: © MIT Connection Science;
S./p. 158: © Corn; S./p. 180: © Klaus Fritsch;
S./p. 191, 192, 195, 196, 198, 201: © Judith Fegerl

1. Auflage 2020 First Edition 2020
ISBN 978-3-903207-37-0

Printed in Austria, EU
Alle Rechte vorbehalten
All rights reserved

**Bibliografische Informationen der Österreichi-
schen Nationalbibliothek und der Deutschen
Nationalbibliothek**
Die ÖNB und die DNB verzeichnen diese Publikation
in den Nationalbibliografien; detaillierte bibliografische Daten sind im Internet abrufbar. Für die
Österreichische Bibliothek: http://onb.ac.at, für
die Deutsche Bibliothek: http://dnb.ddb.de.

**Bibliographic information published by the
Österreichische Nationalbibliothek and the
Deutsche Nationalbibliothek**
The ÖNB and the DNB are listing these publications in in their national bibliographies;
detailed bibliographic data are available on the
Internet. For the Österreichische Nationalbibliothek: http://onb.ac.at; for the Deutsche Nationalbibliothek: http://dnb.ddb.de.

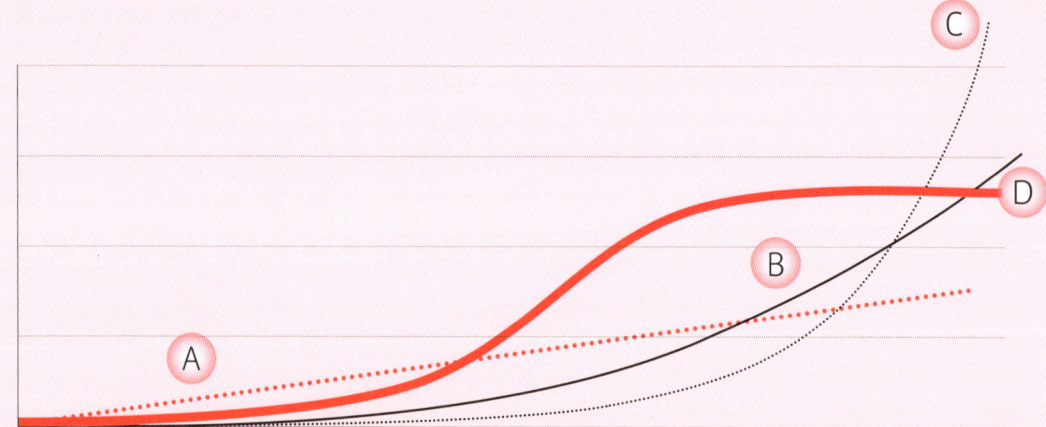

Lineares Wachstum weist eine konstante Änderungs-rate (Steigung) in der Zeit auf. Das bedeutet, dass in gleichen Zeiträumen die gleiche Menge dazu kommt. Ein Beispiel: Ein Tropfstein wächst jedes Jahr um einen Millimeter.

A

Linear growth has a constant rate of change (slope) over time. This means that the same amount is added in the same time periods. An example: A stalactite grows by one millimeter every year.

Bei Wachstum nach Potenzgesetzen (z. B. quadrati-sches oder kubisches Wachstum) verändert sich die Steigung proportional zur Zeit (z. B. zurückgelegte Wegstrecke bei gleichmäßiger Beschleunigung).

B

With growth according to power laws (e.g., quadratic or cubic growth) the slope changes proportionally to the time (e.g. distance traveled with steady acceleration).

Beim exponentiellen Wachstum vervielfacht sich die Bestandsgröße pro Zeiteinheit immer um denselben Faktor (Verdopplungszeit ist konstant). Typisch für die Anfangszeit einer Epidemie – bis Gegenmaßnah-men greifen oder eine hohe Durchseuchung erreicht wird.

C

With exponential growth the stock size per unit of time always multiplies by the same factor (doubling time is constant). Typical for the beginning of an epidemic—until countermeasures take effect or a high level of infection is reached.

Beim logistischen Wachstum wächst die Bestands-größe anfangs exponentiell, flacht sich aber später durch eine Kapazitätsgrenze oder einen Sättigungs-effekt ab. Typisch für Bakterienwachstum oder die langfristige Ausbreitung einer Epidemie.

D

With logistical growth the stock size initially grows exponentially but later flattens out due to a capacity limit or a saturation effect. Typical of bacterial growth or the long-term spread of an epidemic.

Wir leben in einer VUCA-Welt

VUCA ist ein Akronym und steht für:

- **Volatility:** Die Welt ist unbestän-dig geworden, sie verändert sich stark und rasch.
- **Uncertainty:** Vieles ist heute ungewiss und unsicher.
- **Complexity:** Probleme sind oft komplex und nicht einfach zu lösen. Es treten viele Interdepen-denzen auf.
- **Ambiguity:** Wir müssen Zwei-deutigkeiten und Widersprüche aushalten und akzeptieren.

Der Begriff wurde erstmals 1987 verwendet (gestützt auf Führungstheorien von Warren Bennis und Burt Nanus) und etablierte sich in den 1990er-Jahren am United States Army War College (USAWC). VUCA war eine Antwort auf den Zusammenbruch der UDSSR: Anfang der 1990er-Jahre diente der Begriff zunächst dazu, die multilaterale Welt nach dem Ende des Kalten Krieges zu beschreiben. Später breite-te sich der Begriff in andere Bereiche strate-gischer Führung aus und wurde schließlich in den 2000er-Jahren in breiten Schichten populär.